About the Author

Jo Doezema holds a PhD from the Institute of Development Studies at the University of Sussex. She is a member of the Paulo Longo Research Initiative, which works shaping new directions in sex work research and policy, and has been involved in advocacy and research on sex worker rights for two decades. Her research interests include sex work and human rights, feminism, masculinities and trafficking. In developing her research, Jo has worked closely with sex worker rights organizations around the world. She is the co-editor of *Global Sex Workers: Rights, Resistance and Redefinition.*

SEX SLAVES AND DISCOURSE MASTERS

The Construction of Trafficking

Jo Doezema

Zed Books
LONDON & NEW YORK

Sex Slaves and Discourse Masters: The Construction of Trafficking was first published in 2010 by Zed Books Ltd, 7 Cynthia Street, London N1 9JF, UK and Room 400, 175 Fifth Avenue, New York, NY 10010, USA

www.zedbooks.co.uk

Designed and typeset in Dante by Kate Kirkwood
Index by John Barker
Cover designed by www.alice-marwick.co.uk
Printed and bound in Great Britain by CPI Antony Rowe,
Chippenham and Eastbourne

Distributed in the USA exclusively by Palgrave Macmillan, a division of St Martin's Press, LLC, 175 Fifth Avenue, New York, NY 10010, USA

A catalogue record for this book is available from the British Library
Library of Congress Cataloging in Publication Data available

ISBN 978 1 84813 413 3 hb
ISBN 978 1 84813 414 0 pb
ISBN 978 1 84813 415 7 eb

Contents

Acknowledgements

This book was inspired by the work of the wonderful sex workers and sex worker rights activists that I have worked with throughout the years, and especially my former colleagues at the Network of Sex Work Projects. I would also like to thank the members of the Human Rights Caucus, with whom I shared an intense and exciting political experience.

Andrea Cornwall and Anne-Marie Goetz were a constant source of support throughout the process of writing this book. They challenged me and inspired me, encouraging me continually to push myself and my analysis. They continued to believe in me, even when I doubted myself.

My research would not have been possible without the financial support of the ESCR. In particular, I would like to thank Chris Read for his understanding and support.

I would also like to thank Matt Gaw for his excellent editing of the book.

At the Institute of Development Studies, Naomi Hussain provided loads of laughter and insightful comments on my writing. Marc Fiedrich, from our first shared coffee through to the final paragraph, has been a constant source of help and inspiration. Kath Pasteur provided a much-needed refuge. Dom Furlong, Charlie Severs, Jen Leavy and Susie Jolly kept reminding me that there was life outside the book.

Also at the Institute of Development Studies, Sue Ong, Julia Brown and Angela Dowman helped me unfailingly and always with a smile to sort out the often bewildering administrative matters. Chris Stevens gave excellent support as the Director of Graduate Programmes.

Ruth Mackenzie showed enormous patience throughout, and her encouragement never flagged. I could not have completed the book without the deep love and support of my parents, David and Carolynn Doezema, who believed in me when times were the hardest.

Finally, I give my deepest thanks to my partner Peter Spencer, who saw me through the wilderness years.

Acronyms

AIDS	Acquired Immune Deficiency Syndrome
AMBAR	Asociacion de Mujeres para el Bienestar y Ayuda Reciproca (Association of Women for Welfare and Mutual Help), Venezuela
APNSW	Asia-Pacific Network of Sex Workers
AWHRC	Asian Women's Human Rights Council
CATW	Coalition Against Trafficking in Women
CD Acts	Contagious Diseases Acts
CEDAW	Convention on the Elimination of All Forms of Discrimination Against Women
CEE	Central and Eastern Europe
CHANGE	Center for Health and Gender Equity
COIN	Centro de Orientacion e Investigacion Integral
COYOTE	Call Off Your Old Tired Ethics
DMSC	Durnar Mahila Samanwaya Committee
ECOSOC	United Nations Economic and Social Council
GAATW	Global Alliance Against Trafficking in Women
GSN	Global Survival Network
HRC	Human Rights Caucus
HRLG	Human Rights Law Group
ICPR	International Charter for Prostitute's Rights
IJM	International Justice Mission
ILO	International Labour Organization
IGO	inter-governmental organization
IHRLG	International Human Rights Law Group
IOM	International Organization for Migration
IUSW	International Union of Sex Workers
NGO	non-governmental organization
NIS	Newly Independent States
NSWP	The Network of Sex Work Projects
NVA	National Vigilance Association

OSCE	Organization for Security and Co-operation in Europe
PATH	Programme for Appropriate Technologies in Health
PEPFAR	US President's Emergency Plan for AIDS Relief
SAARC	South Asian Association for Regional Cooperation
SANGRAM	Sampeda Maheen Mahila Sanstha
STD	sexually transmitted disease
STV	Stichting Tegen Vrouwenhandel
TAMPEP	Transnational IDS/STD Prevention Among Migrant Prostitutes in Europe
TVPA	Trafficking Victims Protection Act, US
UN	United Nations
UNESCO	United Nations Educational, Scientific and Cultural Organization
UNHCHR	United Nations High Commissioner for Human Rights
UNICEF	United Nations Children's Fund
UK NSWP	United Kingdom Network of Sex Work Projects
WHISPER	Women Hurt in Systems of Prostitution Engaged in Revolt

Introduction: Positioning trafficking in women

What is trafficking in women? After reading personal narratives of trafficking victims as reported in newspapers (see Boxes 1, 2 and 3 below) the answer to the question may seem obvious.[1] While the average newspaper reader is unlikely to be familiar with the sources of the quoted statistics and the politics of the groups that produce the reports, the picture painted by such stories (which are only three examples out of thousands produced over the past decade) seems fairly clear: trafficking in women means young women and girls being transported and forced into prostitution. Accounts such as these, with their graphic accounts of violence, heart-rending first-person testimonies, and ominous warnings of the increasing nature of the problem, paint a picture that disturbs and distresses readers and creates a sense of urgency that 'something must be done' to solve what is taken as a global problem of alarming dimensions. I borrow my tone from the accounts themselves, which rely on idiomatic, emotive language to engage the reader.

In such reports, an image of the 'typical' trafficking victim becomes evident. Even in these few examples, we can see an emphasis on certain words and phrases: 'young', 'naïve', beauty', 'better life', 'lured, deceived and forced into prostitution'. These words show us the youth and beauty of the victims, their desperate economic plight, their lack of knowledge of the fate that awaits them, and their transformation from hopeful to hopeless, from 'naïve' to 'hardened', as the 'life on the streets' takes its toll. The image of the traffickers also emerges: shadowy syndicates, mysterious ladies who glide and tempt, brutal eastern Europeans and rapacious Africans – all lying in wait to prey upon the naïve and innocent young girl. If my tone sounds melodramatic, it is deliberately so. The above accounts, as is explored in Chapters 2 and 3, borrow their structure from melodramatic narrative. They tell a familiar tale of the loss of female virtue, the essence of nineteenth-

Box 1 • 'Italy's sex slaves'

Young women from Africa and Eastern Europe are lured to Italy with the promise of good jobs and a new life. But when they get there they are beaten, raped and forced into prostitution ... Most of the girls we talk to – a group of Libyans, a dark-haired Romanian with a scarred face, a young mother from the Ukraine – didn't come here to be prostitutes. They thought they were coming to Italy to make money working in a hair salon, a bar or as an au pair. But the people who made those promises and smuggled them into the country took away their passports and forced them to work the streets instead. The immigrants, most who barely speak Italian, usually work 12-hour shifts, engaging in quick sexual encounters in clients' cars or behind bushes by the road. Most have pimps who monitor their every move by cell phone. Some are brought to their places on the streets blindfolded, so they won't know the route home in case they try to escape. They're locked up during the day, beaten if they don't work hard enough, and rarely see any of the money they earn ...

At one desolate corner, we stop and let a Nigerian, Marika, into the van ... She's wearing a miniskirt that barely covers her bottom, gold eyeshadow, a ratty pair of high-heeled black boots, long fake black braids, and a top that reveals most of her breasts. Marika complains that there isn't much work this evening, because there are too many police in the area (while prostitution on the streets is legal in Italy, the girls get hassled anyway). She's worried because she still owes $15,000 to the people who brought her here, even though she's already paid them $40,000 – at about $5 per five-minute trick. 'Two more years,' she tells me wearily, 'and I can do some other kind of work.' It may be longer, though, if her recent luck holds up – she was robbed a few days before at gunpoint by a client who took all her money.

'When I came here,' she says, 'I thought I was getting a job at a supermarket.' She rolls her eyes at her childish naïveté – she was 19 then, and now she's a much older, harder 21. But at least, she tells me, she doesn't have the problems the Albanian women on the street have. 'The Albanian women are raped by their pimps, but not the Africans,' she tells me in her broken Italian. 'The Albanians hit them. All I have to do is pay back my debt.' (*Salon*, August 2003)[2] century penny-dreadful seduction stories (Haag 1999; Walkowitz 1992) recast for a contemporary audience. A young girl falls into the hands of malevolent men or tainted women, consequently losing her (sexual) innocence. Like their nineteenth-century counterparts, these popular accounts combine salaciousness with moral righteousness – causing in the reader a discomfiting but also pleasurable mix of outrage and titillation.

Present-day concerns with prostitution and trafficking in women find a historical precedent in the campaigns against 'white slavery' that occurred at

---

Box 2 • 'Human trafficking: charming girls and greedy merchants!'

Trafficking in girls and women has easily become the modern parallel to the Atlantic slave trade. ... Pretty Osaro was in the 200 level class in a prominent university when she lost her father in a car accident in 1999. Thereafter things became so difficult that she had to leave the university and take up a job as a cashier in a supermarket in Benin City to help with the upkeep of the family. One fateful afternoon, precisely 2 March 2000, an expensively dressed lady of Osaro's age glided into the supermarket clutching a mobile phone. She turned out to be Ogechi, Osaro's childhood friend, with whom she had lost contact for years, and who now claimed to work as a model in Italy. She promised to link Osaro with a friend who would facilitate her movement to Italy where she would work and earn big money.

Ogechi kept her promise and a week later Osaro's passport and visa were ready. In Italy her travelling papers were seized, and she was thereafter sold like a chattel to a 'madam' who forced her to sleep with different men. She was however caught one day while on her way from the hospital where she had gone for treatment by the Italian Police, and she was repatriated back to the country along with some [other] Nigerian girls.

Like Osaro, thousands of women and girls are being lured and coerced from the developing countries and also eastern Europe, to Italy, Spain, Paris, Zurich etc. every year, to engage in prostitution. Conservative estimates put the number of women and girls smuggled each year into the sex trade in Europe at over a million worldwide. This is twice the International Organization for Migration's (IOM) estimated 500,000 for 1995. (*The Daily Trust*, Abuja, January 2002)

Box 3 • 'Filipinas end up as fun girls in South Korea'

They are called 'juicy girls', a back-handed compliment to their youth and beauty. But the local slang for Filipino 'entertainers' in Songjan City barely masks the harsh fates of the young, hopeful women who end up captives of a white slavery syndicate. Their plight has sparked tensions among Korean bar owners in Songjan, and Filipino-American servicemen, who are suspected of having helped in the escape of some sex slaves ... Maxi works in an area reminiscent of Fields Avenue, once the red-light district of Angeles City, when American troops were still stationed in Clark Air Base.

Living hell
Maxi and colleagues dance naked for customers and provide sexual favors. For $200, they will perform all imaginable sex acts for clients. They only get 30 percent of the fee, what their Hajuma or Mama San calls their 'commission.' ... Philippine and Korean officials say there is little they can do in the absence of a law against human trafficking ... Korean officials curtly deny the existence of white slavery despite charges raised by Seoul-based religious and civic groups. (*Manila Times*, January 2002)

---

the turn of the twentieth century. 'White slavery' refers to the supposed traffic in women and girls for the purposes of prostitution, primarily between the mid-nineteenth and the mid-twentieth centuries. Prominent feminists, including Josephine Butler and Catherine MacKinnon, have played a central role in both past and present campaigns (Walkowitz 1980; Doezema 2000). Typical white slavery narratives involved the abduction of European women for prostitution in South America, Africa or 'the Orient' by 'foreigners'. In the campaigns that started in the early 1980s, the focus was originally on the 'traffic' from Latin America and Asia to western Europe. Thus, the geographical direction of the 'traffic' has changed. Yet the rhetoric accompanying today's campaigns against trafficking in women is strikingly similar to that used by the anti-white-slavery activists. Then as now, the paradigmatic image is that of a young and naïve innocent (assumed to be female) lured or deceived by evil traffickers (assumed to be usually male) into a life of horrifying sexual degradation from which escape is virtually impossible.

Defining trafficking in women

Trafficking is not a discursively neutral terrain, unwritten and unblemished, upon which facts and responses can simply be attached. Even a recognition that disputes over the meaning of trafficking involve politics and ideology does not go far enough: it still leaves intact the idea that trafficking can be defined satisfactorily if political will, clear thinking and practicality prevail. The 'white slave'/'victim of trafficking' is immediately recognizable in her role as subject of melodramatic narrative. However, as I argue in this book, she proves more elusive when, wrested from her narrative context, she becomes the subject of social scientific enquiry. The phenomenon of trafficking, like the trafficking victim herself, somehow resists or deflects definition and quantification. For, despite widespread agreement among both NGOs and governments regarding the prevalence and severity of 'trafficking', problems of definition and quantification have continually hampered anti-trafficking efforts.

How then are we to define trafficking in women? Definitions abound. Often, they are accompanied by calls for better definitions that appeal to the 'real' situation – the need for a definition that will more accurately reflect what is *really* going on.[3] When activism around the topic of trafficking began in the late 1980s, very little research on the subject existed. Trafficking was mainly the preserve of feminist non-governmental organizations (NGOs), which were focused on front-line care and on lobbying governments. As their lobbying efforts became more successful in eliciting public concern (and funding), opportunities for research grew. The concern with trafficking has led to a large amount of new research, much of it encouraged by governments worried about not only their international reputation, but also their restive native populations grousing about the floods of illegals washing on to national shores.

Despite the increase in research, it is still difficult to quantify trafficking. A report by the International Organization for Migration (IOM) examines the problems around the lack of statistical evidence, stating, 'It is almost axiomatic for papers reviewing trafficking to lament the huge lack of statistics and to call for research to fill the many *lacunae*' (IOM 2000: 30). Indeed, the lack of statistical evidence is mentioned in nearly all of the reports, papers and statements I have reviewed. This does not, however, lead to the degree of caution that might be expected. While acknowledging the difficulty of putting hard and fast numbers to trafficking, most reports go on to quote large numbers without any indication of what they are actually referring to:

'The lack of hard data, combined with the fact that many commentators on trafficking repeat estimates derived from interviews with officials, means that many of the statistics quoted are in (often large) round numbers, are uncheckable and are frequently reiterated' (IOM 2000: 31).

While making this valuable point, the IOM itself provides a telling example of the carelessness with which statistics on trafficking are treated.

'500,000 in Western Europe alone'

CEE [Central and Eastern Europe] and the NIS [Newly Independent States] now constitute the fastest growing source for trafficked women and girls for the sex industry. A US Government source has conservatively estimated that more than 175,000 women and girls are trafficked from CEE and the NIS each year. In 1995, IOM estimated the number at 500,000 annually to Western Europe alone. (OSCE 1999: 7)

How are we to interpret the number 500,000 that is cited in this quotation? In the context in which it is presented, it would seem to have to be a misprint, as 500,000 is much larger than the total of 175,000 trafficked women mentioned earlier in the paragraph. The number itself is not directly referenced, but a list of resources at the end of the Organization for Security and Co-operation in Europe (OSCE) report mentions a 1995 IOM report (IOM 1995). The number 500,000 does not appear anywhere in this report. Given that it seems so obviously a misprint, it would be tempting to dismiss it. However, this number is mentioned repeatedly when trafficking in Europe is being discussed. The number 500,000 has gone on to live a life of its own in newspaper reports, for example: 'It is estimated that around 500,000 women have been beaten or drugged into submission by pimps working in Europe's biggest organized crime gang' (*Daily Mirror*, Dublin, 4 July 2000).

I checked all possible sources to track down the basis for the figure of '500,000', reviewing IOM publications and writing and phoning the IOM in Geneva and in Brussels. I was unable to find any material indicating how the IOM arrived at this number. One official in Geneva suggested that the number had been cited in a presentation by an IOM official at a meeting of the European Parliament, and had been picked up by journalists there. I was unable to confirm this.

Most reports on trafficking tend to assume that estimates of trafficking are too low, rather than too high: 'Despite the lack of concrete statistical data, experts in the field agree that it is a growing (and evolving) phenomenon' (OSCE 1999: 5). One of the reasons most often given for the lack of evidence on trafficking is that it is a 'hidden' phenomenon, taking place in the 'underworld', and that victims of trafficking are too afraid of reprisals to report to the police. Another reason given is the lack of specific legislation relating to trafficking, so that figures for complaints, arrests and convictions are very difficult to obtain. While this may be the case, the lack of reliable evidence of trafficking has done little to diminish anxieties around the issue.

Weitzer's (2007) review of trafficking statistics found that 'there are no reliable statistics on the magnitude of trafficking' (p. 455) and quotes the Bangkok office of the United Nations Educational, Scientific and Cultural Organization (UNESCO) as suggesting that most statistics in circulation were 'false' or 'spurious' (p. 455). One problem in attempting to glean anything meaningful from trafficking statistics is that it is rarely clear exactly what is being measured. As the newspaper reports cited in Boxes 1–3 show, the term 'trafficking' is anything but unambiguous, and can refer to a number of different situations. The IOM report is one of many that notes that trafficking is often confused with 'smuggling' or with illegal migration (IOM 2000).[4] This is confirmed in a highly influential report on international trafficking by the Global Alliance Against Trafficking in Women (GAATW).[5] The authors note that 'when statistics are available, they usually refer to the number of migrant or domestic sex workers, rather than cases of trafficking' (Wijers and Lin 1997: 15).

As Guy (1991) records, statistics on 'white slavery' to Buenos Aires a century ago were based on the numbers and nationalities of registered prostitutes. In a striking parallel, a Global Survival Network (GSN) report of 1997 uses the rise in numbers of Russian and eastern European women in the sex industry in western Europe and the USA as evidence of trafficking. But even figures on the number of sex workers are not to be trusted: Kempadoo notes the extreme variations in estimates of numbers of prostitutes in Asia – estimates for the city of Bombay alone range from 100,000 to 600,000. As she remarks: 'To any conscientious social scientist, such discrepancies should be cause for extreme suspicion of the reliability of the research, yet when it comes to sex work and prostitution, few eyebrows are raised and the figures are easily bandied about without question' (1998a: 15).

The problem of collapsing trafficking into 'illegal migration' or 'migrant prostitution' is compounded by the fact that when official statistics on trafficking exist, they are most often compiled by police and ministries of justice. Some countries have no laws on trafficking; others, such as Austria, include *any* transportation of a woman across a border under trafficking (IOM 2000). What does appear to be clear is that the number of migrant sex workers is increasing throughout the world (Mak 1996; TAMPEP 1999; Brussa 1999, Agustín 2008, Kempadoo 2005). In Europe, sex workers are on the move from eastern to western Europe and from one country to another within these areas. Sex workers from Europe, Asia and Latin America hope to better their earnings in the US, the Middle East, and affluent Asian countries. It is very tempting in this situation to see trafficking where the only certain element is migration.[6]

Even when authors are admirably clear about what they consider trafficking to be, numbers are used that may not conform to their chosen definition. A 1999 OSCE report contains a very clear definition of trafficking, that stresses the elements of coercion and forced labour (OSCE 1999). It states that trafficking involves men as well as women and children, and that it can occur for purposes other than forced prostitution. However, when numbers are counted again, this is done in a manner that gives the impression that most of the women are trafficked for prostitution:

> Every year, millions of men, women and children are trafficked worldwide into conditions amounting to slavery. Among these, many thousands are young women and girls lured, abducted, or sold into forced prostitution and other forms of sexual servitude ... In 1997, an estimated 175,000 women and girls were trafficked from Central and Eastern Europe and the Newly Independent States alone. (OSCE 1999: 3)

The placing of the second sentence in the quoted paragraph gives the impression that these 175,000 women 'trafficked' have all been trafficked for prostitution. Moreover, it is impossible to tell how this number was arrived at, and on what sort of evidence it is based.

Significantly, there are emerging indications that it is sex workers, rather than 'coerced innocents' that form the majority of this 'traffic'. GAATW, whose report is based for a large part on responses of organizations that work directly with 'trafficking victims', found that the majority of trafficking cases involve women who know they are going to work in the sex industry, but are lied to about the conditions they will work under, such as the amount of money they will receive, or the amount of debt they will have to repay (Wijers and Lin 1997: 99). The report's authors also conclude that abduction for purposes of trafficking into the sex industry is rare (p. 99). GSN (1997) relates the testimonies of a number of women who had been sex workers before their migration and who were lied to about working conditions, rather than the nature of the work. Research by the Foundation for Women in Thailand concluded that the largest group of Thai migrants working in the sex industry in Japan had previously worked in the sex industry in Bangkok (Skrobanek 1997). Watenabe (Watenabe 1998), who worked as a bar girl herself in Japan in the course of her research into Thai women migrating to the Japanese sex industry, found that the majority of Thai sex workers she interviewed were aware of the nature of the work on offer before they came to Japan. Other research, such as that by Brockett and Murray (1994) in Australia, Anarfi (1998) in Ghana, Kempadoo (1998b) in the Caribbean, Centro de Orientacion e Investigacion Integral (COIN 1994) in the Dominican Republic, TAMPEP in Europe (Brussa 1999), Gülçür and Ilkkaracan (2002) in Turkey, Blanchet (2002) in Saudi Arabia, India, Nepal and Bangladesh, Pearson (2002) in England, Italy, Thailand and the USA, Agustín (2005, 2006, 2008) in Europe and Mai (2009) in the UK, indicates that women seeking to migrate are not so easily 'duped' or 'deceived', and are often aware that most jobs on offer are in the sex industry.

Myth and consent

In this book, I argue that a turn (and return) to the unfashionable conceptual apparatus of 'myth' and 'ideology' provides the most satisfactory explanation of these evidential problems. Taking my inspiration from historians of white slavery, I fit myth to the maiden. I bring the mythical subject of trafficking in women into focus through applying a 'genealogical' lens, one that considers the historical circumstances of the trafficked women's production (Haag 1999). This involves delving into historical accounts of 'white slavery', critically examining the figure of the 'white slave' as she existed in popular and political imagination in the first half of the twentieth century. It involves incorporating the insights of this examination into the consideration of the contemporary subject of 'trafficking in women'. This excavation takes place in the analytical territory of 'myth'. The process of 'unearthing' the 'trafficked woman' through exhuming the buried images of the white slave is central to this book.

This book is structured around two key concepts: myth and consent. I will not, thus, be looking at the image of the 'white slave' or her modern-day counterpart, the 'trafficking victim', and contrasting it with the 'reality' of prostitutes' lives, as though this image were simply a matter of ill-informed representation. Nor will I be attempting to 'uncover the meaning' of myths of 'white slavery' or 'trafficking' as a metaphorical or allegorical correspondence. Instead, I approach the arena of debates around white slavery and trafficking as the effects of *discourse*. In approaching 'trafficking in women' as a discourse, I am concerned with how certain definitions of the problem become dominant, with whose knowledge is accepted and whose sidelined, and with the social practices involved in constructing and legitimating knowledge: in short, I am concerned with the relationship between power and knowledge. This research uses the concepts of myth and ideology to interrogate the knowledges (truth claims) – both empirical and theoretical – about 'trafficking in women' through a genealogical examination of the historical circumstances of their production. The research is concerned with, in Hajer's words, 'the ways in which certain problems are represented, differences are played out, and social coalitions on specific meanings somehow emerge' (Hajer 1995: 44).

Hajer notes that, 'It has become almost a platitude to characterize public problems as socially constructed' (1995: 42). Nonetheless, most research into trafficking eschews a social constructionist approach in favour of a positivist approach. By far the majority of research on trafficking in women is concerned with documenting and explaining the 'phenomenonon' of trafficking itself: it attempts to establish who is being trafficked, who is doing the trafficking, how it is happening, why it is happening, and what can be done. This research can be helpful in correcting assumptions and misunderstandings about 'trafficking in women', and can serve as a basis for creating policy that will better protect the human rights of migrant (sex) workers.

However, an approach that seeks to establish the 'facts' about trafficking, valuable as it may be, leaves unanswered the questions of how these 'facts' will be interpreted and which interpretations will come to be accepted as legitimate knowledge. To answer this, we need to look at the effect of power on knowledge: the way in which social power is exercised in knowledge creation, and the ways in which representations of people and problems are used to legitimate knowledge. Foucault (1975 [1991]) suggests that we abandon the idea that knowledge can exist where power is absent:

> We should admit, rather, that power produces knowledge (and not simply by encouraging it because it serves power or by applying it because it is useful); that power and knowledge directly imply one another; that there is no power relation without the correlative constitution of a field of knowledge, *nor any knowledge that does not presuppose and constitute at the same time power relations* ... In short, it is not the activity of the subject of knowledge that produces a corpus of knowledge, useful or resistant to power, but power-knowledge, the processes and struggles that traverse it and of which it is made up, that determines the forms and possible domains of knowledge. (pp. 27–8, emphasis added)

Even social constructionist research that focuses more directly on power, such as feminist research, tends to look at power relations only in so far as they are seen to cause the 'real practices' of 'trafficking in women'. Thus trafficking is characterized as the result of women's sexual subordination (Barry 1979; 1995) and/or women's economic subordination as well as the result of inequitable development and 'globalization' (e.g. Sassen 2002; Outshoorn 1998; Wijers and Lin 1997; Lazaridis 2001). Of course, power relations – gendered, economic, class-based – do impact on migration for the sex industry, and are worthy of investigation. However, what is missing in these accounts is a critical examination of the power involved in producing knowledge about 'trafficking in women' and the ways in which dominant constructions of the issue emerge and are incorporated into policy. What remains to be investigated are the relationships among those who shape meanings of 'trafficking in women' and between these 'discourse masters' and the object of their concern: the 'sex slaves'.

METHODOLOGY, MYTH AND MEANING

When I first came across the notion of white slavery as a myth, when researching my MA thesis, it seemed to me to be the perfect concept through which to explore the productions of meaning around trafficking.[7] The notion of trafficking in women as myth seemed to apply so aptly to the dissonances between my own experiences, the experiences I knew from other sex worker rights activists, and the way that sex work was being portrayed in 'trafficking in women' discourses. Its immediate appeal lay in the idea that what was being said was a distortion of what was 'really happening'. In my MA thesis, I argued that 'trafficking in women' was a contemporary manifestation of what historians characterized as the myth of 'white slavery'. Accounts of trafficking, I argued, consistently coupled their arguments for protection of innocent women with narrative elements that undermined women's agency and amplified the threat of migration. I am not the first to note the similarities between campaigns and narratives of 'white slavery' and 'trafficking' (see Chapkis 1997 and Murray 1998); indeed my own research direction was heavily influenced by discussion with sex worker rights advocates. Our concern with these similarities was mainly activist, rather than academic. Much more so than anti-trafficking activists, sex worker advocates were aware of the political legacy of white slavery and its long-reaching effects on the lives of sex workers today.

My interpretation of trafficking in this MA research relied on a concept of myth that consisted of two elements: first, that of myth as a distortion of the truth (trafficking 'hid' what was really occurring in terms of migration of sex workers) and, second, that of myth as a metaphor, a way of explaining a complicated and threatening reality (trafficking narratives as stories that encoded, for example, fear of women's sexuality). While this dualistic interpretation of myth allowed me to explore trafficking discourses in a way that involved questioning otherwise accepted meanings, it was unsatisfactory for a number of reasons, which I have sought to resolve in this book. In summary, my key discomfort with this interpretation of myth is that it depends on a static, reified and a historical notion of 'consent' in attempting to 'disprove' the myth of white slavery/trafficking.

This insight was facilitated through my discovery of the work of historian Pamela Haag (1999). In her fascinating study of sexual consent and its relationship to American liberalism, Haag devotes a section to white slavery. She explores it as a 'dominant idiom' of sexual violence. Haag offers a corrective to the ahistorical approach to myth, as she explains:

> My approach here is not to question, as other historians have done, whether white slavery was 'true' or functionally a myth, an expression of the notorious sexual queasiness and inability on the part of the middle class to envision women as agents or to see how women might have exercised 'choice'. *Such a question assumes that coercion or 'sexual slavery' has a fixed meaning – that if women were not literally taken or physically restrained then white slavery was a distortion of situations that were not 'really' coercive as we understand that term. Yet white slavery was as real or as true as other definitions of coercion or consent, given that these terms acquire substantive meanings in historical context.* (p. 64, emphasis added)

Haag's observation points to the ways in which the 'truth' of white slavery was related to the concepts of consent that informed it. At the Trafficking Protocol negotiations in Vienna that led to the signing in 2000 of the UN Protocol to Suppress, Prevent and Punish Trafficking in Persons, Especially Women and Children (hereafter, the Trafficking Protocol), as explained below, the definition of trafficking became completely dependent on interpretations of the idea of women's consent in relation to prostitution. These debates, like those around white slavery, were entered into by different social groups whose ideological struggle was articulated through 'consent', as displayed in discourses of trafficking.

The perspectives of another theorist, Ernesto Laclau (1990; 1997), helped me give needed depth to the idea of myth as a metaphor. Two parts of Laclau's analysis of myth and ideology proved particularly illuminating: first, his concept of myth as the metaphor for an ideal society and, second, his concept of myth as a necessary part of any society. Throughout this book, I have sought to braid Haag's insights about the construction of 'consent' with Laclau's insights regarding myth as a inevitable part of social struggle. In contrast to a reading of myth which sees it as powerful because it can provide a singular, simple explanation of reality, this combined theoretical perspective suggests that white slavery/trafficking is a powerful myth, not because it unifies or crystallizes different perceptions of consent, but precisely because it can, and does, accommodate and provide a powerful vehicle for the advancement of varied and even opposing ideologies, including opposing feminist ideologies.

Chapter 1 takes the ideas of myth and ideology as its central focus. It sets out the theoretical context for my exploration of 'trafficking in women' as myth, through bringing together the work of 'white slavery' historians and putting these in critical conversation with theorists of myth and ideology. Theories of political myth are reviewed, through which the notion of ideology emerges as a key concept for an understanding of myth. The chapter draws on Laclau and Eagleton to illustrate how 'ideology' can help in understanding the power and persistence of the myth of white slavery/trafficking. The chapter uses the exploration of political myth and ideology to interrogate the basis of the truth claims of white slavery and trafficking narratives, setting out the limitations of a purely empirical approach to the subject of 'trafficking in women'.

Chapters 2 and 3 focus on a historical exploration of the myth of white slavery, analysing it in the context of myth as set out in Chapter 1. These chapters lay the groundwork for an examination of the parallels in the narratives of white slavery and trafficking. They are close readings of historical accounts of white slavery. As this Introduction began by showing present-day narratives of trafficking, so the analysis of these two chapters is based on popular narratives of white slavery. At the same time, the analysis continues to put the various historians of white slavery in conversation with each other, and subjects them to the developing theoretical framework of myth and ideology. The aim of the analysis is to set out a framework for exploring trafficking in women as a myth, historicizing current debates.

Chapter 2 explores the myth of white slavery as it appeared in Britain. Looking at the works of the feminist Josephine Butler and the journalist William T. Stead, the chapter examines the function of narrative in the context of myth. It demonstrates the ways in which narrative contributes to the 'real seemingness' of myth, making it appear as a description of reality. It explores the way in which the figure of the white slave was constructed as an innocent victim, in opposition to the willing whore, complicit in her own downfall. The notion of consent runs through these conceptions of the victim/whore, marking the dividing line between those deserving of rescue and those deserving condemnation. The chapter explores how discourses of white slavery, and the ideas of consent they contained, also worked within larger discourses of class and empire. Throughout the analysis, parallels are signposted between the manoeuvrings of consent in white slavery discourses and in contemporary discourses of trafficking.

Chapter 3 moves to examination of the myth of white slavery in the United States, setting the concept of 'metaphor' as central. The chapter critically investigates the idea, used by many historians, of white slavery as a 'metaphor' for social anxieties caused by rapid processes of social change. It suggests that a more satisfactory concept of metaphor is achieved through taking account of Laclau's ideas of myth as the model of an ideal society. Drawing on a variety of narratives of white slavery, the chapter investigates how differing notions of consent were articulated through differing interpretations of what white slavery 'really' was. Discourses of race and nation and their relationship to the myth of trafficking are explored, and implications for current discourses of trafficking are indicated.

The second half of this book takes the concepts and analysis presented in the discussion of the myth of white slavery as a theoretical template through which to view discourses of trafficking in women. Myth, metaphor, ideology and narrative are employed to address the knotty questions of how NGOs and states have tried to define trafficking. My experiences as a lobbyist in Vienna during the Trafficking Protocol negotiations form the basis of the analysis in this section.

Chapter 4 begins with an examination of early twentieth-century international agreements on white slavery, tracking the ways in which the notion of consent was used in these early agreements. The lexical threads of consent are pulled through to the Vienna negotiations, showing how the distinction between the 'victim' and the 'willing whore' shaped NGO and state responses in Vienna. In particular, the chapter examines the ways in which the 'suffering body' of the prostitute informed the neo-abolitionist lobby headed by the Coalition Against Trafficking in Women (CATW) in Vienna. I argue that CATW's abolitionist feminist arguments about the nature of prostitution were refracted by those of states that sought to close borders and limit human rights protections for 'trafficking victims'.

Chapter 5 combines a close analysis of the relationships between sex workers and anti-trafficking activists in the Human Rights Caucus with an examination of the development of the definition of trafficking in persons at the Vienna negotiations. It returns in depth to the questions set out in the early part of this Introduction around the complicated relationships between feminism, sex worker rights, and the need to define trafficking in women at the Trafficking Protocol. It shows the ways in which the discourse of trafficking, even when used by feminists sympathetic to sex worker rights, can in effect make the subject of the sex worker 'disappear'.

If it becomes increasingly difficult to pin down exactly what 'trafficking' might be and who the victims are, one thing the 'evidence' does point to is how emotionally potent the images used in trafficking narratives are. This is not the first time that such images have been used to evoke a more generalized sense of moral panic, or the first time that feminists and other political actors have employed these images in calls for intervention.

THE RESURRECTION OF A MODERN MYTH?

From the time they were produced to the present time, the narratives of the 'white slave trade' have been accepted as literal truth by many, including feminist anti-trafficking activists. However, a number of today's historians question the extent of the 'white slave trade'. Their research suggests that the actual number of cases of white slavery was very low (Bristow 1977; 1982; Connelly 1980; Corbin 1990; Fisher 1997; M. Gibson 1986; Grittner 1990; Guy 1991; Haveman 1998; Rosen 1982; Walkowitz 1980; 1992). The lack of hard empirical evidence about the scope of the phenomenon has led to analyses that have sought to locate discourses of white slavery on a broader ideological terrain, looking at both their discursive and their material consequences.

In attempting to ascertain the extent of white slavery, these historians attempt to verify the trade through using its own terms, 'projecting themselves into the past'. That is, they take the dominant meaning of white slavery and look for evidence to support or debunk it in a variety of empirical sources, including arrest records from police files and prostitutes' testimonies to immigration officials. Thus, they look for empirical evidence of innocent young girls being kidnapped, deceived, drugged or otherwise coercively obtained and forced to be prostitutes. But their efforts unearth scant evidence of this sort. Corbin (1990), who examines the French campaign, consulted judicial and police records and government reports. Typical of the reported statistics was the finding that after the adoption in 1903 and 1906 of a new law against white slavery, 754 'pimps' were arrested. However, only eight were charged with white slavery. An analysis of these and other statistics of the time leads Corbin to observe that:

> the virgin abducted against her will or the woman raped and transported either by force or by deception to a far-off brothel was a rare exception. Of course, the commission of inquiry and the abolitionist societies proved the existence of such incidents, but the trafficking in women, whether on a large or small scale,

15

concerned almost exclusively girls and women who were well aware of what was expected of them and who, without compulsion, were willing to be sent abroad. (p. 285)

He concludes that 'the statistics undermine the myth of an international white slave trade involving violence against innocent virgins' (p. 296). Gibson, in her study of white slavery campaigns in France, uses police statistics to back up her claim that 'proof of widespread trafficking in women against their will is lacking ... the reality of white slavery never approached its notoriety' (1986: 83). Even Rosen (1982), who of all historians I studied is most concerned with proving the existence of a white slave trade, concludes that white slavery accounted for no more than 10 per cent of all prostitution. In general, historians concur that while white slavery did exist, its incidence was greatly exaggerated.

If the data show so little white slavery, where did the huge numbers quoted by the campaigners against it come from? Sometimes these numbers were purposefully misrepresented by campaigners eager to show the importance of their cause. Guy (1991) discovered that statistics relating to the numbers of foreign prostitutes in Buenos Aires were taken to prove the existence of large-scale international white slavery. Connelly (1990) traces the ways in which statistics and findings of the Chicago Vice Commission report of 1911 were used by all subsequently published white slavery narratives in the US in a way that was 'provocative, lurid, emotionally overwrought, and misleading' (Connelly 1980: 119).[8]

Even a cursory comparison of the white slavery era with today throws up a number of similarities. Then as now, feminists were heavily involved in the campaigns, often in coalition with those who would otherwise be antithetical to feminist goals. The wide extent of the panic is similar, as are the sheer numbers of people involved, the resources dedicated to eradication of white slavery/trafficking, the extensive coverage in the media and national and international legal changes (see Chapkis 1997). And there are also similarities in the way the 'story' of trafficking is told. Yet very few present-day accounts of trafficking make mention of white slavery, or do so more than in passing. If they mention it, they do so generally with a sense that trafficking actually occurred in history, though it was called white slavery. Thus the comparison is to presumed actual events. Some accounts, such as Chapkis (1997) and Berman (2003), go further, recognizing the parallels between representations of prostitutes in white slavery accounts and in writings on trafficking.

16

Today's stereotypical 'trafficking victim' bears as little resemblance to women migrating for work in the sex industry as did her historical counterpart, the white slave. The increase in female migration, including migration for sex work, since the year 2000 is in part the result of women seeking increased autonomy and economic independence (Wijers and Lin 1997, Kempadoo 1998a, 2005; Watenabe 1998, Agustín 2008). For some third world or 'non-Western' women, temporary work in the sex industry in another country is one of a number of livelihood strategies (Kempadoo 1998a, Agustín 2008). The majority of 'trafficking victims' are aware that the jobs offered them are in the sex industry, but are misled about the conditions under which they will work (Wijers and Lin 1997). Yet policies to eradicate trafficking and reintegrate victims into society continue to be based on the notion of the 'innocent', unwilling victim. They often combine efforts designed to protect 'innocent' women with efforts designed to punish 'bad' women: i.e. prostitutes (Doezema 1998).

If the issue of women being trafficked into prostitution has thus resurfaced as a matter of international concern after remaining dormant for nearly eighty years, what can be learned from tracing debates back over time? What light could be shed on contemporary debates around trafficking if we look at the ways in which positions on prostitution have been developed and articulated over time? In such a process, parallels between discourses on 'white slavery' and 'trafficking in women' become even more evident.

ABOLITIONISM AND REGULATIONISM

As in the current 'crisis' of trafficking, people of widely disparate occupations, values and political convictions found in white slavery a cause that brought them together in unlikely coalitions. In a similar fashion to today, ideological differences between the different groups engaged in attempts to combat white slavery concerned consent. Many campaigners against the white slave trade saw all prostitutes as victims in need of rescue; others argued the importance of distinguishing the willing prostitute from the victimized white slave. The distinction between white slavery and prostitution was maintained by campaigners of differing ideological bent.

One group were the so-called purity campaigners, who aimed to rid society of 'vice', focusing in particular on youthful sexuality. For example, the US District Attorney Edwin W. Sims wrote in the preface to the influential 1910 tract, *Fighting the Traffic in Young Girls or War on the White Slave Trade*,

The characteristic which distinguishes the white slave traffic from immorality [prostitution] in general is that the women who are the victims of the traffic are forced unwillingly to live an immoral life. The term 'white slave' includes only those women and girls who are actually slaves. (Sims 1910a: 14)

Purity reformers' relationship with the prostitute herself was ambiguous: while professing sympathy for the lost innocents sacrificed by white slavers, they were severe in their judgement of girls and women whose immodest behaviour led them into a life of shame. Most purity reformers espoused an approach to prostitution that has been termed 'prohibitionist'. Prohibitionist systems of regulating prostitution make the act of prostitution itself illegal, with prostitutes and procurers alike subject to arrest. As Gibson remarks of the Catholic Church-influenced prohibitionist campaign in Italy: 'Thus a number of prohibitionists joined the white slave campaign to advance their own final aim, ridding the world of prostitution, by punishing the malicious procurers and redeeming the sinning women' (1986: 72).

Another approach was advocated by regulationists, who believed that the necessary evil of prostitution should be controlled by stringent state regulations. Dr Parent-Duchatelet, whose 1836 study of French prostitutes was a model for regulationists, wrote: 'Prostitutes are as inevitable in a great conurbation as sewers, cesspits and refuse dumps. The conduct of the authorities should be the same with regard to each' (quoted in N. Roberts 1992: 223). Harnessing rational scientific arguments to moral disapproval, regulationists argued that state regulation was the only way to control what was then termed venereal disease. Innocent women and girls needed protection from immorality; however, once fallen, it was society that needed protection from the immoral woman. The best way to protect society, argued regulationists, was to register and medically control prostitutes.[9]

Other campaigners, particularly proto-feminist activists, made little distinction between white slavery and prostitution. These early feminist attempts to break down the distinction between innocent victims and immoral prostitutes started with Josephine Butler's campaign against the regulation of prostitution through the Contagious Diseases Acts in England and Wales.[10] Under these Acts, any woman who was suspected of prostitution could be detained by the police and forced to undergo an internal examination. Butler and other abolitionists argued that men were responsible for prostitution, placing the blame for prostitution squarely on the shoulders of unbridled male lust. No women could be said to truly consent to prostitution: if a woman appeared willing, this was merely the result of the power that men held over her. By turning all prostitutes into victims, Butlerite feminists undercut the rationale for regulationist systems.

When the Contagious Diseases Acts were repealed in 1886, Butler and her followers turned their attention to the fight against white slavery. In the abolitionist vision, prostitution and white slavery would come to an end if laws targeted those who made money from prostitutes, rather than the prostitute herself. No woman would enter prostitution of her own accord, they reasoned, with no one to lure or deceive her; woman's innate moral superiority would ensure her purity. In this, feminist abolitionists shared a view of women's sexuality that was common to all the various campaigners against white slavery. Women were considered sexually passive, which made them more 'virtuous' than men, but, paradoxically, once that virtue was 'lost' through illicit sexual behaviour, women's sexual nature became dangerous. Consequently, calls for the need to protect women's purity alternated with attempts to reform and discipline prostitutes. Abolitionist feminism spread to Continental Europe and the United States: 'The image of the victim of white slavery being that of a young and innocent girl, women of all ideologies could agree that she deserved defense, both from the trafficker and from her own unnatural desires' (Gibson 1986: 74).

LIBERALISM, FEMINISM, SEX

Just as feminists in early twentieth-century Europe and the United States articulated dissatisfaction with their position under liberalism through the trope of prostitution (Chapkis 1997; Doezema 2001; Haag 1999), second-wave Western feminists too grappled over the issues of prostitution and pornography. Yet while feminists in the United States and Europe were staging 'reclaim the night' marches through red-light districts, sex workers began forming their own organizations, demanding that prostitution and related types of activity – exotic dancing, porn acting and 'glamour' modelling – be recognized as work. Accounts of the Western sex worker rights movement cite the formation of COYOTE (Call Off Your Old Tired Ethics) in 1973 in California and the sex workers' strike and occupation of a church in Lyon in 1975 as key moments in the start of the sex worker rights movement. These groups and activities were followed by many similar ones throughout the 1970s and 1980s, with the formation of groups such as the Prostitutes Collective of Victoria in Australia, and de Rode Draad (the Red Thread) in the Netherlands. Nor was this organizing limited to Europe and the United States; as Kempadoo and Doezema (1998) document, sex worker organizing throughout the Third World has a long history and an active present, though it is often ignored by Western accounts of 'the sex worker rights movement'.

Feminism in the West has tended to see women's oppression through the lens of liberalism, in which 'violence' – in particular sexual violence – comes to be seen as '"the core" of women's oppression ... by denying women "ownership" of their bodies' (Haag 1999: xiii). In liberal terms, 'liberation' for women means asserting women's status as individuals and as owners of their own bodies. In the tradition of feminists such as Carole Pateman (1988) (whom Haag explicitly follows), Haag sets out to question the legacy of liberalism for feminism, in particular liberalism's relationship to sexuality. Pateman famously put the liberal legacy in question by identifying the 'contract' – liberalism's political centre – as the source of women's oppression, rather than the site of their potential freedom. Pateman argues that liberalism works to hide the operations of sexual power. For Pateman, the notion of prostitution as a 'consensual' relationship is an example of how women's subordination is constructed as 'freedom' under the liberal contract.

Haag chooses as her focal point 'a historical analysis of the ideas of consent and coercion, a "presuppositional opposition" by which rights and sexual personality are governed in American culture' (1999: xiii). While Haag's concern is with the US genealogy of consent, the language of choice and rights reaches far beyond American shores. Liberalism's legacy for feminism is global: as the notion of human rights has expanded and become a legitimate and powerful arena to argue for liberatory ideals around gender, sexuality and a host of other concerns, global feminism has been largely constructed in liberal arguments, as these fit into a human rights framework. This has not gone uncontested, with powerful critiques of Western liberal feminism emerging from post-colonial feminists (e.g. Spivak 1988; Mohanty 1988). Yet in the international policy arena, human rights remains the most prevalent discourse for articulating struggles around oppression and freedom. Feminists have relied on liberal precepts to argue their cases in the international sphere, with 'choice' and 'coercion' framing questions about reproductive rights and health.

Contextualizing consent: the forced/voluntary dichotomy

The history of sex worker rights organizing did not develop in opposition to feminism. A number of sex worker organizations, such as the Red Thread in the Netherlands, receive active support from feminist organizations. Many sex worker activists have been schooled in the feminist tradition (Alexander and Delacoste 1987; Nagle 1997). A glance through the 'canon' (Kempadoo 1998a) of the sex worker rights movement in the West shows the embeddedness, both in terms of 'thought' and of persons, of sex worker rights in feminism. These texts, such as the *World Charter for Prostitutes' Rights* (ICPR 1985), Pheterson's *The Whore Stigma* (1986), Alexander and Delacoste's *Sex Work* (1987) and Nagle's *Whores and Other Feminists* (1997) seek to analyse and defend sex work in feminist terms, in conversation with prominent anti-prostitution feminists such Sheila Jeffries (1997; 2008), Catherine MacKinnon (1987; 1989) and Kathleen Barry (1995).[11]

Central to this often bitter conversation between sex worker rights advocates and anti-prostitution feminists has been the notion of consent. Haag writes:

> Because the stakes are so high for women in their daily lives, feminists for decades have tried to nail down and specify what violence is. The strategy has been to position a definition of violence beyond the vagaries of interpretation, where historically women's injuries and accounts of sexual violation often have been derided and systematically represented as indications of the woman's own sexual licentiousness. In such an environment it is only logical that feminism seeks after essences, unconditional properties, of 'consent', or of violence, so that these cannot be misinterpreted or talked out of view. (1999: xv)

Abolitionist feminism remains a potent force in the campaign against trafficking in women. Like their foremothers, today's 'neo-abolitionist' feminists deny that prostitution can be considered a true choice or legitimate enaction of the will (e.g. Barry 1995; Hughes 2002; O'Conner and Healy 2006; Raymond 1999; 2004). Because all prostitution is inherently violence against women, they argue, no true consent is possible. Regulationist arguments are also very much alive today – indeed, with AIDS, regulationism has regained the ground that it had lost to prohibitionist and abolitionist arguments. Sex workers have argued that what is needed is a fourth type of state policy approach to prostitution; distinct from abolition, prohibition and regulation. The approach advocated is 'decriminalization' – that is, that all aspects of the sex industry be taken out of the criminal code – including not only laws supposedly designed to protect sex workers by criminalizing 'pimps and procurers' but also those intended to control prostitutes, such as mandatory health checks.[12] This position, articulated in the 1986 World Charter for Prostitutes' Rights (ICPR 1985), entwines its views on labour with those on consent to sex and consent to work.[13] The charter declares:

> Decriminalize all aspects of adult prostitution resulting from individual decision.
> Decriminalize prostitution and regulate third parties according to standard business

codes … Prostitutes should have the freedom to choose their place of work and residence.

In this view of prostitution, adults are capable of consenting to sex and thus to sex work, children cannot. The Charter thus declares that:

Employment, counselling, legal, and housing services for runaway children should be funded in order to prevent child prostitution and to promote child well-being and opportunity. (ICPR 1985)

While the charter is now nearly twenty years old, and repeated calls have been voiced to update it, its principles are still widely accepted by sex worker rights supporters and organizations (Nagle 1997; Kempadoo and Doezema 1998). For example, the DMSC Calcutta, one of the world's largest sex worker rights organizations, wrote in a recent position paper,

DMSC sees sex work as a contractual service, negotiated between consenting adults. In such a service contract there ought to be no coercion or deception. As a sex workers' rights organisation, DMSC is against any force exercised against sex workers, be it by the client, brothel keepers, room owners, pimps, police, or traffickers. (Jana et al. 2002: 75)

Many sex worker rights groups call for recognition as unions, such as AMBAR in Venezuela. Others have been successful in gaining local union recognition of sex work as labour, including the UK-based International Union of Sex Workers (www.iusw.org), and the Exotic Dancers Alliance in the US (Kempadoo and Doezema 1998).

This adoption of the 'forced versus voluntary' framework shows the close links between sex worker rights politics/activism and feminism, for this distinction was an attempt to keep true to the feminist strategy of taking up 'violence against women' as a way of furthering a feminist agenda. 'Voluntary versus forced prostitution' was not a rejection of the feminist conception of prostitution but a refinement of it. As a conceptual framework for understanding sex work, the voluntary/forced model, with 'consent' operating as the hinge between coercion and choice, had (has) a number of distinct advantages. As 'consent' had become the standard by which heterosexual sexual behaviour had come to be determined as harmful or not, as illustrated by the 'brilliant literalism' of the feminist slogan 'no means no' (Haag 1999), sex worker rights activists and theorists were taking familiar concepts and applying them in unfamiliar territory. Combined with the 'pro-choice' abortion rhetoric familiar to a generation of feminists, the voluntary/forced model enabled sex workers and their feminist supporters to carve out a space in which certain sex workers could convincingly argue, using acceptable liberal feminist terms, for recognition of their liberal rights – as well as create a space for the 'forced' prostitute, denied her liberal right to 'free choice' of sexual contact *and* labour.

However, the implicit distinction between forced and voluntary prostitution, based on consent, raises a number of disturbing questions. Briefly outlined, these are, first, the problem of calling any choice truly free when practical constraints on choice always exist; second, the problem of measuring choice; third, recognition that using 'choice' as a standard implicitly legitimizes the 'choices' of Western women living in liberal societies organized around choice at the expense of others; and, fourth, that a woman's choice to do sex work is rightly, as the abolitionist argument runs, irrelevant if sex work is defined as necessarily and intrinsically harmful.

Abolitionism and regulationism reconfigured

Neo-abolitionist feminists, such as CATW, reject the distinction between forced and voluntary prostitution. Not only do they deny that it is possible to 'choose' prostitution, they argue that the distinction between forced and voluntary prostitution means that prostitution policy reinforces traditional distinctions between 'innocent' women and 'guilty' prostitutes (Barry 1992). As both historical and recent accounts have demonstrated, abolitionist laws – those which ostensibly protect the prostitute by criminalizing only those who profit from her or force her – the 'pimps' procurers', 'traffickers' and, now, even clients – are used instead against sex workers and their families (Bindman and Doezema 1997).[14] Despite these repressive effects, neo-abolitionist feminists continue to argue for these policies. In the face of the overwhelming evidence of the use of these laws against sex workers, it is difficult to take the neo-abolitionist claim to want to help prostitutes as transparent.[15] As with their abolitionist foremothers, the desire to help the unwilling and abused is mixed with a maternalist desire to discipline the naughty girls who refuse to acknowledge their victimhood (Doezema 2001).[16]

Yet sex worker rights movements and supporters – including myself – can perhaps be accused of the same wilful blindness when it comes to the policy implications of our position. When policies are adopted – by states, NGOs or international bodies – that recognize the difference between forced and voluntary prostitution, their implementation, if not their intent, has been to lend support to regulationist effects. While the contemporary wave of worldwide sex worker activism, which began in the mid-1970s (Kempadoo and Doezema 1998), was influenced by feminism, the advent of AIDS and gay activism meant that, in the words of Cheryl Overs, founder of the Network of Sex Work Projects (NSWP) sex worker rights 'found a new political family' (Overs 1998). And 'the AIDS world', dominated as it is by medical discourses – the home of regulationism – has proved itself a more nurturing environment for sex worker rights movements, in terms both of resources and of political support, than the feminist/women's human rights world. However, this support has been by no means consistent or whole-hearted.

While paying lip service to the need to empower sex workers for effective HIV prevention, AIDS organizations are too often guilty of keeping sex workers out of decisions made on their behalf, and of implementing or supporting government programmes that are actually regulationism by the back door (Overs, Doezema and Shivdas 2002). A notorious example of regulation and repression in the name of 'empowerment' are the so-called '100% Condom Programmes' first instituted in Thailand in the late 1990s. These programmes give the police increased powers over sex workers, and often involve forcible testing of sex workers for sexually transmitted diseases (STDs), and public identification of sex workers found to be infected. The World Health Organization (WHO) has recommended that these programmes be adopted throughout Asia, despite the vociferous objections of regional sex worker organizations. The NSWP is running an international campaign documenting and denouncing abuses connected to these programmes.[17]

CONSENSUAL DILEMMAS

The conundrum of the free/forced dichotomy – of consent as envisioned in relation to prostitution – is one of the most compelling and persistent problems in a study of sex work. The 'choice' question in writings and debates about prostitution just will not go away.[18] It is very common to hear sex workers asked by journalists or seminar attendees, 'But did you really *choose* to be a prostitute?' Or, the question is phrased so that it addresses sex workers perceived to be different than the interviewee: 'But can you say that Third World [or poor, or underage] women also *choose* to be prostitutes?'[19] In my own earlier work, I still was looking for answers in a more nuanced vision of 'choice'. I articulated this in an interview with Wendy Chapkis: 'The idea that there are two distinct poles of "forced" and "free" is a false dichotomy. I mean who really freely chooses to work at any kind of job? I want to get the whole choice argument off the prostitutes' political agenda.

24

We'll never win it and it's useless as a political strategy' (quoted in Chapkis 1997: 52). Chapkis herself follows with an expression of the most familiar strategy used by sex worker rights supporters when faced, yet again, with the 'choice' question: 'Very few women's lives are models of "free choice". Most women's "choices" are severely limited by their disadvantaged position within hierarchical structures of sex, race, and class.'[20]

This argument, which can be called the 'modified choice' argument, is not wholly satisfactory. In order effectively to combat the neo-abolitionist position that choosing sex work is impossible, the argument moves sex worker politics to neo-abolitionist ground. What does this mean? The problem of choice is an epistemological one. For neo-abolitionists, sex work is *per se* a human rights abuse, and thus choice is negated, irrelevant. In the context of this framework, to argue that prostitution is a legitimate profession because some women and men choose it is completely useless. It in no way challenges the foundations of the neo-abolitionist position – it is like using a vacuum cleaner to mow the lawn.

Radical feminist analysis locates the source of the illegitimacy of 'consent' in the construction of sexual relations of power: prostitution is seen as 'sexual exploitation'. Kathleen Barry, founder of the neo-abolitionist Coalition Against Trafficking in Women, sees women's subordination as the result of sex. Sex is defined as 'the condition of subordination of women that is both bodied in femaleness and enacted in sexual experience' (Barry 1995: 278). Women's subordination is seen as analogous to class subordination, that is, women's 'class position' is one of sexual subordination to the dominant 'class' of men. The 'injury' of sex is thus that which constitutes the 'class' of women. For Barry, as well as other feminists such as Sheila Jeffries (1997; 2008), and Catherine MacKinnon (1987; 1989), sex is power: male power over women. Barry sees prostitution as the ultimate expression of male dominance.

> My study of sex as power ... inevitably, continually, unrelentingly returns me to prostitution ... [O]ne cannot mobilize against a class condition of oppression unless one knows its fullest dimensions. Thus my work has been to study and expose sexual power in its most severe, global, institutionalized, and crystallized forms ... Prostitution – the cornerstone of all sexual exploitation. (1995: 9)

Other feminist approaches broaden the scope beyond sexual power relationships, and incorporate analyses of the effects of economic, racial and military aspects of power relations, as well as sexuality, on prostitution and its organization in diverse settings (Troung 1990; Kempadoo 1999; Lim 1998;

Sturdevant and Stoltzfus 1992; Enloe 1989; Moon 1997). These approaches take in the wider realm of globalized power relations, but for most feminist research, as West and Austrin (2002) point out, the problematic locus of power remains the prostitute–client relationship. O'Connell Davidson (1998) argues that the radical feminist conception of consent is dangerous because it implies that prostitution is the same as rape. Nonetheless, though supportive of sex worker calls for decriminalization, O'Connell Davidson concludes that while prostitution is different from rape, consent in prostitution will always only be a 'sheen' of consent. For O'Connell Davidson, this remains the case even though prostitutes themselves may subjectively experience the relationship as consensual. True consent, she argues, is impossible, given the relative positions that the sex worker and client occupy in the intimate encounter – positions structured by economic, gendered, sexualized and radicalized power dynamics.

Sullivan (2000) argues that O'Connell Davidson relies on a liberal notion of consent, in which the only 'real' consent is seen to exist in the absence of power relations. While I believe O'Connell Davidson's argument takes a more sophisticated and contextualized approach to consent than this suggests, I agree with Sullivan that O'Connell Davidson's analysis is implicitly contingent on an abstract standard of consent in the absence of power differences, against which standard actually occurring sexual relationships are measured. Sullivan argues that because sex always takes place in existing power relationships, feminists' attention should go towards finding ways to help sex workers maximize their power, particularly by improving their working conditions. The analysis of West and Austrin (2002) locates sex work, as 'mainstream' work, on a broader canvas, and their analysis moves away from the more restricted vision of those who focus only on the intimate sphere to explore how prostitution is 'produced as work'. They contend that an analysis of sex work *as work* 'requires replacing the emphasis on worker–client encounters with analysis of the ways in which variable network ties and specific discourses of sexuality are mobilized in and constitute particular settings' (2002: 499). Their discussion of O'Connell Davidson's work articulates the shortcomings of the narrow focus on sex worker–client interactions, in which the power of third parties such as the police and the state is barely interrogated. This is an essential argument: one of the key differences between most feminist analysis and that of sex worker organizations concerns precisely this. Sex worker activists place most emphasis on their struggles against the police and the state, rather than against clients. This is one of the major reasons that sex worker activists are reluctant to join feminists' effort to 'stop trafficking', as this is seen to entail increasing the power of the state over the sex industry. This is explored in detail in Chapters 5 and 6.

Despite these more nuanced approaches to prostitution as work and the role of consent in the construction of prostitution, the political debate on prostitution and trafficking is largely polarized between the absolute impossibility of choice and the distinction between 'forced' and 'voluntary' prostitution. This was shown in the debates on the 2000 Trafficking Protocol in Vienna, where states and feminists placed themselves on either side of this divide.

The Vienna negotiations concerning the 2000 UN Trafficking Protocol

In December, 2000, over eighty countries signed the Trafficking Protocol in Palermo, Italy. This event was the culmination of over two years of negotiations at the UN Centre for International Crime Prevention in Vienna (also known as the Crimes Commission). The Trafficking Protocol was the subject of intense lobbying by transnational networks of feminist anti-trafficking NGOs. What is particularly interesting about the Vienna process is that the transnational networks of feminist anti-trafficking NGOs were bitterly divided in their approach to trafficking in women. In effect, the lobby was split into two camps: both framing their approaches to trafficking in feminist terms, in agreement about the size and scope of the problem, and univocal in demanding an international response. Both groups were made up of feminists and human rights activists from the developing world and the developed world. Yet, these similarities proved meaningless in the face of the deep ideological divide that split the lobby groups. The essence of this ideological divide concerned the relationship between 'trafficking in women' and 'consent'.

One of the lobby groups was spearheaded by CATW, an international NGO with strong local affiliates throughout the world. This lobby group referred to itself as the 'International Human Rights Network'. CATW is an 'abolitionist' organization: its members argue that prostitution is a form of sexual violence which can never be consented to or chosen as a profession. CATW co-director Dorchen Leidthold writes:

> The sexual exploitation of women and children by local and global sex industries violates the human rights of all women and children whose bodies are reduced to sexual commodities in this brutal and dehumanising marketplace. While

experienced as pleasure by the prostitution consumers and as lucrative sources of income by sex industry entrepreneurs, prostitution, sex trafficking, and related practices are, in fact, forms of sexual violence that leave women and children physically and psychologically devastated. (Leidthold 2000: 1)

In keeping with this view, CATW advocates for measures to make prostitution illegal and to punish clients as well as brothel owners and other 'third parties'. If all prostitution is violence, it follows that anyone involved in helping a woman move from one place to another to engage in sex work is a trafficker.

The other lobby group was headed by the International Human Rights Law Group (IHRLG) with the Global Alliance Against Trafficking in Women (GAATW) and the Asian Women's Human Rights Council (AWHRC). This configuration of transnational lobby groups called itself the Human Rights Caucus (HRC). Like CATW, IHRLG and GAATW are international NGOs with strong local affiliates throughout the world. Yet their vision on trafficking and consent could not be more different: inspired by the global sex worker rights movement, GAATW sees prostitution as labour. Accordingly, for GAATW, trafficking is characterized by the use of force during the migration process and/or the consequent labour or services. Traffic in persons and forced prostitution are manifestations of violence against women and the rejection of these practices, which are a violation of the right to self-determination, must hold within itself the respect for the self-determination of adult persons who are voluntarily engaged in prostitution (Wijers and Lin 1997).

Consent was the most highly contested term during the Protocol negotiations. The differences between the lobby groups became most apparent in the most controversial part of the Protocol negotiations: deciding just how 'trafficking in persons' should be defined. CATW's lobby group argued that a woman should be considered a victim of trafficking regardless of any force or deception. Simply by virtue of having a third party involved in her movement, she was to be considered a victim of trafficking. The Human Rights Caucus argued that force or deception was a necessary condition in the definition of trafficking, and that 'trafficking' and 'prostitution' should not be linked in the Protocol, as men, women and children are trafficked for a large variety of services, including sweatshop labour and agriculture.

The Protocol serves as a 'discourse event' through which to track traces of narratives on trafficking, and in which to locate some of the contested threads of debate – from the forced/voluntary distinction, to neo-abolitionist and neo-regulationist perspectives on appropriate inter-national policy. More than anything, it serves – in a way that mere documentary analysis and interviews never could – as a rich site for ethnographic analysis, juxtaposing my engagement as a participant observer against the backdrop of internet activism which I had privileged access to as an activist. It allowed comparison with behind-the-scenes interactions and the play of discourse and power in the negotiations themselves. As activists engaged in lobbying on the Protocol, members of the Human Rights Caucus used email discussions to work out positions regarding the questions around prostitution, choice and the need to define trafficking. Email discussions also took place on the NSWP list, which gave all NSWP members the chance to comment on these questions and the stance of the HRC in regard to them.

As an event with significant international visibility, the Protocol negotiations were refracted in accounts in the media, as well as in documents of various kinds. These range from proposals and positions of NGOs to national government policy proposals. The Protocol can be seen as the codification of consent in an international agreement. This rich and complex field of meanings, stalked by the spectre of 'white slavery' debates and paralleled not just by framings and arguments but also by the kind of actors who were part of them, sheds important light on the questions with which this book engages.

1 White slavery and trafficking as political myth

I don't know anything about the so-called white slave trade, for the simple reason that no such thing exists ... it was left for the enlightened twentieth century to create the Great American Myth. 'White slavery is abroad in our land! Our daughters are being trapped and violated and held prisoners and sold for fabulous sums (a flattering unction, this) and no woman is safe ... the belief in this myth has become a fixed delusion in the minds of many otherwise sane persons. – Madeleine, an early twentieth-century prostitute and madam (quoted in Connelly 1980: 132)

The parallels between the manipulation and misrepresentation of statistics in the campaigns against white slavery and in today's anti-trafficking campaigns are easy to draw. However, to see all white slavery campaigners, and, by analogy, all anti-trafficking campaigners, as deliberately exaggerating to achieve political goals is to impute an undeserved cynicism. With the exception of newspapers eager to increase circulation through sensationalism, or perhaps politicians ready to hop on a bandwagon for political gain, we cannot assume that most of these dedicated campaigners, then and now, were/are deliberately spreading falsehoods. While exaggeration may at times be a political strategy, the depth of commitment among today's campaigners and their historical counterparts attests to their belief in the existence of trafficking/white slavery on a vast scale. Why did so many people believe in white slavery? And if records of the time show so little evidence, how are we to account for white slavery's political potency?

Similar questions might be asked of today's trafficking narratives. In this chapter, I draw on some of the theoretical resources that may be useful to make sense of the phenomena of white slavery and trafficking. Drawing on the work of historians of the white slavery era, and particularly that of Grittner (1990), I suggest that the concept of myth offers a useful starting point for an analysis of trafficking. It can move us beyond an empirical focus to an examination of why and how certain groups in society, including feminists, are so invested in the myth. If, as Grittner argues, white slavery was a cultural myth with repressive consequences for women, especially prostitutes, and subaltern men, what are the implications of this for the current campaign against 'trafficking in women'? This chapter argues that an understanding of the ways in which myth is informed by ideology can help us understand not only the reasons for the appearance of the white slave in history, but also the reappearance of her mythical successor, the trafficking victim.

Myth and ideology

Current accounts of 'trafficking in women' vie with 'white slavery' stories in their use of sensational descriptions and emotive language, though the 'victims' are no longer white, western European or American women, but women from the Third World or the former Eastern bloc.

> *Trafficking Cinderella* features gut wrenching testimonies of broken dreams, withered illusions, rape and humiliation from six Eastern European girls sold as prostitutes throughout the world. This film was made on behalf of all these lost girls; confused by the crumbling post-communist reality they became an easy prey for pimps, procurers and sex-traffickers.[1]

> Think of it. You're a young girl brought from Burma, you have been kidnapped or bought. You're terrified ... if you haven't already been raped along the way (or sometimes even if you have) you're immediately brought to the 'Room of the Unveiling of the Virgin'. There you are raped continuously – until you can no longer pass for a virgin. Then you are put to work. (Mirkenson 1994: 1)

It is possible to see in these stories the reworking of several of the motifs identified in the Introduction: innocence; youth and virginity; deception and violence. Looking at Grittner's use of the notion of 'cultural myth' can begin to provide some first clues towards an explanation for the similarity in white slavery and trafficking narratives. According to Grittner, a myth does not simply imply something that is 'false'; rather, it is a collective belief that simplifies reality. Grittner explains his conception of myth as follows:

> As an uncritically accepted collective belief, a myth can help explain the world and justify social institutions and actions ... When it is repeated in similar form from generation to generation, a myth discloses a moral content, carrying its own meaning, secreting its own values. The power of myth lies in the totality of explanation. Rough edges of experience can be rounded off. Looked at

structurally, a cultural myth is a discourse, 'a set of narrative formulas that acquire through specifiable historical action a significant ideological charge'. (Grittner 1990: 7, quoting Slotkin 1985)

In this conception, myth is seen as more than a simple distortion or misrepresentation of facts. Slotkin's (1985) definition points to the ways in which myth is connected to ideology. This broad notion of myth – as a narrative or story which carries ideological overtones – moves us beyond a search for the simple factuality of white slavery and trafficking narratives. Flood's 1996 study of political myth argues that an understanding of ideology is essential to understanding how myth functions in the political process.[2] Flood defines political myth as 'an ideologically marked narrative which purports to give a true account of a set of past, present, or predicted political events and which is accepted as valid in its essentials by a social group' (1996: 44). Flood's comprehensive review of theorists of political myth demonstrates the ways in which different conceptions of ideology in turn influence how theorists conceptualize myth. One of the most famous examples of this is Sorel's idea of the syndicalist general strike as a utopian social myth which embodies in its totality the idea of socialism:

> The question whether the general strike is a partial reality, or only a product of popular imagination, is of little importance. All that it is necessary to know is, whether the general strike contains everything that the Socialist doctrine expects of the revolutionary proletariat ... general strike ... is ... the myth in which Socialism is wholly comprised, i.e. *a body of images capable of evoking instinctively all the sentiments which correspond to the different manifestations of the war undertaken by Socialism against modern society.* (Sorel 1908 [1999]: 5, emphasis added)

Contemporary theorists of myth, as examined below, have retained these ideas of political myth as images or stories that are able to promote a collective response, the notion of myth as a reflection of how society should be. These theorists view myth as the expression of ideology. However, to define myth in terms of its relationship to ideology begs the question of what exactly 'ideology' is.

DO WE NEED IDEOLOGY?

The notion of ideology is anything but uncontested: Eagleton (1991) lists sixteen ways in which 'ideology' might be approached. Thus it comes as no surprise that distinctions between myth and ideology often blur in studies of political myth. For example, Tom Brass's (2000) study of the 'agrarian myth' of peasant societies both equates myth with ideology – 'the agrarian myth is an essentialist ideology' (p. 11) – and argues that the agrarian myth 'by itself' is powerless: only 'deployed as part of wider ideological struggle is it capable of exercising a political impact' (p. 313). Eagleton states that the relationship between myth and ideology is not clear, and indeed, he himself is not clear, arguing both that the concept of myth is more and that it is less inclusive than ideology. For the purposes of this study, I wish to avoid an overly schematic and ahistorical search for 'ideal types'. The concept of ideology is important for the study of the myth of white slavery/trafficking for the light it can shed on important questions relating to the origin, validity, function and power of the myth, rather than as an abstract theoretical construct. I will thus leave fluid the boundaries between myth and ideology, as well as definitions of them. As Eagleton says:

> the term 'ideology' has a whole range of useful meanings ... to try to compress this wealth of meaning into a single comprehensive definition would thus be unhelpful even if it were possible. The word 'ideology', one might say, is a text, woven of a whole tissue of different conceptual strands ... it is probably more important to access what is valuable or can be discarded ... than to merge them forcibly into some Grand Global Theory. (1991: 1)

Nevertheless, it is helpful to review some of the most prevalent conceptions of ideology in order to determine just what is 'valuable' and what can be 'discarded' for the purposes of this study.

Though the term 'ideology' is still very much in use in everyday speech, it has gone rather out of fashion in academia, replaced by the more capacious 'discourse'. Ideology's traditional concern with 'truth' and distortion seems decidedly old-fashioned when faced with the body blow dealt to notions of ahistorical, transcendental 'truth' by post-modernism. And if ideology is out of fashion, myth is the academic equivalent of love-beads and peace-sign necklaces. Myth was a central concept in the work of the standard-bearers of high structuralism, theorists such as Barthes and Lévi-Strauss, but like 'ideology' was outshone by the 'discourse' and 'deconstruction' of the hot young designers of post-structuralist haute couture.

Terry Eagleton, in his 1991 book *Ideology: An Introduction*, argues that the academic and progressive-left abandonment of 'ideology' for 'discourse' ended up throwing out the baby with the bathwater. For Eagleton, the diffuseness of power as diagnosed by Foucault's (1975 [1991])'disciplinary mechanisms' leaves us with no centre to fix our analysis upon. This centre can be found, he suggests, in the notion of 'ideology'. This view is linked to his condemnation of what he views as the relativism of post-modernism.

For Eagleton (2003), the notion of a superior, or even an 'absolute' truth is not an anathema but the cornerstone of ethical political and cultural life. Eagleton argues that focusing on 'ideology' can help bring questions of truth to the forefront, banishing the spectre of the post-modern scenario of a bunch of commensurate truths.

Ernesto Laclau (1997) looks for the 'resurrection' of ideology in a different area. Rather than arguing against the post-modern attack on truth, Laclau pushes the post-modern case against ideology to the point that it collapses under its own inherent contradictions.[3] At this point of collapse, ideology emerges transfigured (if marked by the resurrection). Thus we see that the lack of a centre identified by Eagleton as a reason to reclaim ideology from the morass of post-modern relativism is for Laclau the cornerstone upon which ideology is resurrected, 'a starting point for a possible re-emergence of a notion of ideology which is not marred by the stumbling blocks of an essentialist theorisation' (p. 300). Rather than distort an original truth, the function of ideology, according to Laclau, is in giving the illusion that this truth ever existed. Ideological distortion exists even in the absence of an original truth to distort.

Laclau achieves his resurrection with Althusser playing Lazarus. Dead and staying dead are Althusser's notions of the strict separation between science and ideology. Alive again and rolling away the stone from the tomb are Althusser's ideas about the indispensability of ideology, ideology as a 'necessary illusion', and in particular the idea of interpellation – of a necessary misrecognition in the constitution of the individual subject. Althusser, in his essay 'Ideology and Ideological State Apparatuses' (1971 [2001]), stated that: 'Ideology represents the imaginary relationship of individuals to their real conditions of existence' (p. 109). This misrecognition takes place through 'interpellation', in which individuals are turned into ideological subjects.[4] Laclau retains Althusser's idea of ideology as a necessary illusion, but moves the grounds of illusion from the individual to the very idea of society itself. If for Althusser it is the subject that is interpellated through ideology, for Laclau it is society – the community as a whole.

Laclau turns Eagleton's argument on its head: it is *because* there is no centre, no ultimate truth, that ideology is necessary. Ideology is thus also, of course, impossible, for no distortion can occur without something that is undistorted to begin with. This impossible 'constituent distortion' of ideology is a necessary condition of society, making society the 'impossible and necessary object'. The dialectics between the antimonies of impossibility and necessity is the process of ideology.

Laclau gives the following example of how ideology works:

> Let us suppose that at some point, in a Third World country, nationalisation of the basic industries is proposed as an economic panacea. Now this just a technical way of running the economy and if it remains so it will never become an ideology. How does the transformation into the latter take place? Only if the particularity of the economic measure starts incarnating something more and different from itself: for instance, the emancipation from foreign domination, the elimination of capitalist waste, the possibility of social justice for excluded population, etc. In sum: the possibility of constituting the community as a coherent whole. That impossible object – the fullness of the community – appears here as depending on a particular set of transformations at the economic level. This is the ideological effect *strictu sensu*: the belief that there is a particular social arrangement which can bring about the closure and transparency of the community. (1997: 303)

Ideology and trafficking

The value of Eagleton's arguments for this study lies first of all in the refocusing on truth, on questions of epistemology. In the study of white slavery as myth, we return time and time again to the question of truth. The word 'myth' connotes falsehood, and this is how the myth of white slavery has largely been understood by historians. To deal with the questions regarding the falsehood of myth means that we also need to deal with its postulated opposite. As reviewed below, attempts to distinguish the truth about white slavery from the myth preoccupy historians. Similarly, research on trafficking today is dominated by empirical studies. The questions policy makers and NGOs want answered is how many women are being trafficked? From where? I hope to show that these questions cannot be answered by a straightforward review of empirical evidence; that the problem is not one of inadequate definitions or statistical shortcomings (as has most often been argued), but a matter of differing ideologies.

Second, ideology as theorized by Laclau inspires a focus on community and conflict. Ideology effectively captures the idea of political struggle, of winners and losers, of strategies and compromise, of power given and taken: it foregrounds conflict in a way that the rather bloodless 'discourse' does not.[5] This is important for trafficking, as meanings about what trafficking is have been the site of major political conflicts between feminists, sex workers and states. Chapters 4 and 5 concentrate on this political struggle, showing how different groups have wielded their ideologies in the international policy arena in the discussions around the 2000 Trafficking Protocol. Combined with Laclau's (1990) own earlier theorizations about the role of myth in society, examined in Chapter 3, analysis of these discussions enables us to begin to answer the question of why the myth of trafficking is powerful again at this point in history.

Ideology, truth and power

These aspects of ideology – epistemology and political struggle – which are most helpful in relation to a study of white slavery/trafficking are loosely reflected in what Eagleton (1991) and McLellan (1995) have distinguished as the two main strands of thought around ideology.[6] One of these is primarily concerned with ideology as epistemology and a distortion of truth. The second leaves aside epistemological questions, looking instead at how ideology functions in society. The influence of both these approaches on histories of white slavery is examined in the following section. The purpose of this review is to find out whether the approaches historians apply to the ideological narratives of the white slavery myth are suitable for examining contemporary ideological narratives of trafficking in women. Through an examination of their work, a new understanding of how to apply theories of ideology to an understanding of trafficking can emerge: a synthesis of contemporary approaches to ideology.

IDEOLOGY AND MYTH AS DISTORTED REALITY

Historians' search for the empirical truth of white slavery fits in with what Eagleton terms the 'rationalist' approach to ideology, in which ideology is seen as 'a collection of distorting representations of reality and empirically false statements' (Eagleton 1991: 18). The purpose of this distortion, according to this view of ideology, is political: it is concerned with the getting or keeping of power by particular social groups. This is a very common way of viewing ideology. John B. Thompson's (1984) definition of ideology as 'the ways in which meaning (or signification) serves to sustain relations of domination' (p. 45) is, according to Eagleton, 'the single most widely accepted definition of ideology' (1991: 5). According to Thompson (1990), a dominant power uses a number of ideological strategies to legitimize itself: this 'mystification' involves distorting or obscuring that social realities in ways to suppress conflict. Political myth in this conception of ideology is a weapon of the powerful, a falsehood through which the dominant power can legitimize and consolidate its position. For example,

Bank (1999) uses Thompson's framework in his genealogy of the Afrikaner 'Great Trek' myth, central to the ideology of apartheid. He writes: 'the stories embodied in myths should be interpreted as universal features of ideo-logical structures. As such, they need to be located within these wider ideological structures and analyzed in terms of the mobilization of meaning in the context of unequal relations of power' (p. 462).

To what extent has this approach been used in histories of white slavery? Guy (1991) argues that white slavery was primarily a vehicle for patriarchal and racist ideologies. Other historians, such as Hobson (1987), Nead (1988) and Walkowitz (1980; 1992) detail how groups that might be considered 'dominant' used white slavery to promote their agenda. However, while historians have shown white slavery's links to dominant ideologies, they also document how oppositional groupings, such as those concerned with women's suffrage, harnessed the myth of white slavery to their political chariot. The perception of political myth as a falsehood which helps to sustain a dominant ideology runs into a number of problems when applied to white slavery. It cannot satisfactorily explain why so many people appeared genuinely to believe in the existence of white slavery, nor can it account for the wide appeal of the myth to both dominant and oppositional political groupings.

WHITE SLAVERY AS A MAP OF REALITY

In recognition of these problems, a number of historians have taken a more neutral approach to myth and ideology in order to explore white slavery's impact. This approach is less concerned with the truth or falsehood of myth than with its function in society. As discussed above, many historians of white slavery have argued on the basis of historical evidence that the campaign around white slavery distorted reality. Finding little evidence of actual white slavery, the bulk of their work is then concerned with determining what 'lay behind' the concern with white slavery. Also discovering through historical research that the myth of white slavery did not conform to the facts, they look for reasons for myth's believability in its function. This approach is summarized by Henry Tudor as: 'Myth is believed not because it accords with the facts, but because it makes sense of people's experience' (1972: 24). This process is evident in the following observation by historian Donna Guy: 'Rather than reflecting a completely verifiable reality, white slavery was the construction of a set of discourses about family reform, the role of women's work in modernizing societies, and the gendered construction of politics' (1991: 35). Irwin leaves aside altogether the question of white slavery's empirical truth: 'Whether or not white slavery actually existed or represented a significant factor in prostitution will not be argued here. Many Victorians were convinced that white slavery existed, while many others were just as certain that it did not; what is of concern is the dialogue itself' (1996: 1).

Of the white slavery historians, Grittner (1990) is most explicit in his use of the terms 'myth' and 'ideology' to analyse the response to white slavery. His use of the analytical category of myth is linked in his work to a notion of ideology derived from the anthropologist Geertz (1969 [1973]). For Geertz, ideology is less a matter of truth or falsehood than a sort of 'map' that helps people make sense of complicated reality. Ideologies are 'maps of problematic social reality and matrices for the creation of collective conscience' (p. 220). According to Geertz, people need ideologies when certain ways of viewing the world no longer make sense: ideologies arise in times of social and cultural stress. Drawing on literary theory, Geertz examines how ideology functions as a 'metaphor' for problematic social reality.

In his analysis of the metaphorical aspects of white slavery, Grittner also draws on the work of Connelly (1980). Connelly takes as his subject the campaign against prostitution in the US at the end of the nineteenth and beginning of the twentieth century, which he calls 'antiprostitution'. According to Connelly, campaigns against white slavery were a part of the general antiprostitution movement. Connelly argues that antiprostitution was about more than prostitution itself: 'antiprostitution had at least as much to do with the anxieties produced by the transformation of American society ... as with the actual existence of red-light districts ... Prostitution became a master symbol, a code word, for a wide range of anxieties' (1980: 6). Other historians also use this 'map of reality' framework, emphasizing different aspects of reality that the metaphor of white slavery corresponds to. Irwin (1996) writes:

> In following this evolution, it becomes evident that the white slavery metaphor comprises an intriguing cluster of ideas concerning men and women, sex and society, rich and poor, villains and victims, corruption and exploitation. These themes and the rhetoric of white slavery are connected to the conditions and cultures of Victorian society. (p. 1)

Hobson writes: 'White slavery was a highly charged metaphor in the Progressive Era: not only did it capture a belief that all women were potential victims of sexual enslavement; it had as its protagonists an underworld of European immigrants operating an international traffic in women's bodies' (1987: 142).[7]

A NEUTRAL APPROACH TO THE MYTH OF TRAFFICKING?

What are the implications of the above discussion for a study of trafficking in women as myth? In order to argue that trafficking is a political myth, is it also necessary to show that it is empirically false? Given the confusing and contradictory nature of the evidence on trafficking, it is a tempting possibility to argue that trafficking in women is a myth from a neutral standpoint, that is, to leave aside questions of its empirical truth or falsity. This is entirely in keeping with what Eagleton terms the discrediting of epistemology in the social sciences. If political myth (and ideology) is seen in a neutral sense – as a narrative that helps explain the world, arising in times of crisis – then an analysis of trafficking as myth could proceed without an examination of its status as 'true' or 'false', limiting the analysis to the content of trafficking narratives and their political/ideological function. It is entirely possible to decry sexist, racist and nationalistic elements in trafficking debates without questioning the legitimacy of evidence of trafficking or even the 'reality' of trafficking itself. This is the route taken by a number of perceptive studies of trafficking discourses, such as those by Pike (1999), Lyons (1999), Gibson (2003), Stenvoll (2002) and Chapkis (2003).

There are other pressing reasons to abandon the 'myth as falsehood' approach when discussing trafficking in women. The word 'myth' used in conjunction with stories of trafficking in women can seem insensitive at best, and at worst to be an exercise in revisionism of the most reprehensible sort. Added to the evidential and ethical problems involved with judging the myth of trafficking as a falsehood are conceptual/theoretical ones. These have been alluded to in the discussion of historians' approach to white slavery. A number of theorists of political myth argue that approaching myth as straightforward falsehood is too limiting (Flood 1996). They argue that what is important in myth is not its truth, but rather the way it operates in social and political contexts. The arguments for a neutral approach to myth mirror arguments that have been made against the notion of ideology as 'false consciousness'.

Like many other concepts which started life with a particular, specific, meaning, the concept of 'false consciousness' is as misunderstood as it is familiar. Once a popular feminist epithet hurled at ideological opponents, it is now nearly as vilified a term as 'political correctness'.[8] I do not intend to reclaim it: merely to note its importance for the study of myth. Among Marxist theorists, two broad positions regarding 'false consciousness' can be distinguished (Eagleton 1991). One strand is represented by Barthes, whose structuralist *Mythologies* (1973) sees myth as a linguistic distortion linked to bourgeois dominance. The other strand is represented by Althusser, who like Gramsci (1971), rejects the notion of ideology as false consciousness (McLellan 1995).

As we have already seen, one argument against the 'false consciousness' interpretation of myth is that it seems arbitrary to call only beliefs of powerful groups ideological. Another is that the notion of myth as 'false' (corresponding to ideology as 'delusion') emphasizes either the deliberate, propagandist spreading of myth or attributes myth to collective irrationality or delusion (Flood 1996). This, as Eagleton (1991) notes, seems to imply that the 'truth' is accessible only to a scientific elite. Also, as Flood (1996) notes, 'we can't know the intentions of those who tell myths or judge the state of mind of those who appear to believe them, except insofar as plausible inferences can be drawn from contemporary evidence of what these tellers and believers say or do' (p. 7). The correspondence between empirical fact and political myth is not straightforward: there can be disagreement not only about whether the events in question actually occurred, but also about the way in which certain information is chosen for inclusion, and other information is left out (Flood 1996). Certain myths will be regarded as true by certain social groups and as untrue by others: and the reason for these differences is a matter not of 'getting the facts right' but of differing ideological positions (Flood 1996). Thus Flood argues the need for 'close attention to the social contexts in which political myths are circulated' (pp. 7, 8).[9]

Is the implication of the above that we should adopt a neutral stance to the myth of trafficking? That is, that we should examine its form and function, rather than attempting to demonstrate its empirical falseness? The answer is a qualified 'yes'. Qualified, for while the neutral approach avoids the pitfalls outlined above, it runs into some problems of its own, as we shall see.

True myths?

If political myth is not to be identified primarily because of its falsehood, what criteria are left for judging whether a statement is a political myth? Theorists who opt for a 'neutral' approach to ideology move from a concern with the truth of certain ideological statements to a concern with their purpose and their form: in other words, the approach changes from an epistemological to a sociological one. There are two possible ways of seeing the relationship of myth to truth in this approach. The first approach could be considered Althusserian. In this approach, questions of truth and falsehood would be seen as largely irrelevant to ideology or political myth, because ideology and myth are considered to be above all expressions of lived experience.[10] As Eagleton explains: 'Ideology for Althusser does indeed represent – but what it represents is the way I "live" my relations to society as a whole, which cannot be said to be a question of truth or falsehood' (1991: 18). Against 'ideology' Althusser opposes 'science', which is seen as the only 'true' (cognitive) knowledge, open to judgements of truth.

Taken in the Althusserian sense, a neutral approach means that questions of truth or falsehood would not apply to the concept of political myth. Yet it is also possible to argue that one should not immediately condemn all myths as false, but should still be able to judge individual myths according to their truth or falsehood. This is the argument of a second group of theorists, including Tudor (1972) and Thompson (1984), who state that individual myths may be true or false (in terms of their adherence to fact), but that this does not affect their status as myth: what makes myth/ideology mythical is its function and its form (Flood 1996). Thus where Althusser posits an 'epistemological break' between ideology and science (Eagleton 1991), the second group smoothes over that break, allowing that myth may be objectively, scientifically, judged true or false, but that the outcome of this judgement is either irrelevant to its function as myth (Tudor 1972) or may be seen simply as one criterion by which myth should be measured (Thompson 1984). However, this approach does not resolve the problems of the 'myth as falsehood' approach simply by allowing that some myths may be true.

HAVING IT BOTH WAYS: THE FALLACY OF TRUTH

If we accept that a neutral approach to the myth of trafficking offers a more satisfactory analytical framework than one that sees myth as falsehood, does it matter which approach we take: that of myth as possibly either true or false or one that argues that judgements of truth cannot be applied to myth? After all, what concerns us in this approach is the form and function of myth, not its objective truth. Yet there is a problem with the first approach, a problem involving a contradiction of method. If myth/ideology is seen as a sociological *process* that enables people to make sense of their world, 'what are the criteria for identifying an objectively true [or false] myth?' (Flood 1996: 46). As Flood recognizes, when political myth is judged according to its narrative form and social function, 'the functions ascribed to myths are incompatible with a straightforward judgment of truth or falsehood'(p. 46). These arguments are akin to those made by Turner (1983) in his discussion of the falseness of ideology. If ideology is a matter of 'lived belief' – of ideas that people adopt in order to make meaningful action in the world possible – how can it be said to be false? As Eagleton (1991) interprets Turner's work: 'if our lived beliefs are in some sense internal to our social practices, and if they are thus constitutive of those practices, they can hardly be said to "correspond" (or not correspond) to them' (p. 24).

An illustration of the contradiction between attempting to assess myth's truth while at the same time treating it as 'lived belief' is to be found in some of the work of white slavery historians. As seen above, a number of historians such as Connelly (1980), Hobson (1987), Grittner (1990) and Corbin (1990) attempt both to assess the empirical extent of white slavery and to examine its form (such as film, newspaper accounts) and its function (as symbol or metaphor). We can take Grittner (1990) as an example. Grittner's approach to myth, as shown above, is in the Althusserian mode and thus incompatible with judgements about the factual truth of a statement. He explains white slavery's hold on the public imagination in terms of a Geertzean 'map of problematic reality'. On the one hand, he interprets white slavery as a symbolic, metaphoric response to the social strains of early twentieth-century America such as fears around urbaniza-tion, around immigration, and around women's growing independence. On the other, he also makes pronouncements, based on historical records, about the factual truth of white slavery. He writes: 'White slavery did exist, especially within the immigrant communities of large cities, but it was not the main cause of prostitution' (p. 64). Thus, in Grittner's work, white slavery is seen as both a false description of reality and as an expression of lived reality, as a statement to which the criteria of truth and falsehood do not apply. This contradiction is more than a methodological inconsistency. It carries profound political consequences, examined below.

To avoid this contradiction, we can follow the Althusserian path, and view ideology purely as an expression of lived reality, which cannot be considered true or false. Althusser has been widely criticized for his strict separation between science and ideology. However, one need not follow an Althusserian elevation of science as value-free knowledge, whose truth is independent of history, to use his points about the nature of representation in ideology/myth. To argue that in trafficking and white slavery, myth is incorrectly mistaken for fact is not to adhere to a positivist or rationalist view of myth/ideology. These views would see a strict separation between fact and value: in a positivist approach, myth does not belong to the realm of scientific investigation; in a rationalist approach, myth is error as opposed to the truth of science.

Returning again to Sorel allows us another way out of the contradiction. Sorel's impassioned defence of the necessity of the myth of the general strike, marred by a romanticization of violence, wrenches apart 'myth' and 'reality'. In the passage quoted above he summarily dismisses the central theoretical concern of myth studies: that is, the relationship of myth to reality or 'truth', the ways in which it reflects or transforms reality, its status as falsehood, distortion or fanciful tale. For Sorel, the epistemological status of myth is of no significance: myth's essence and its essentialness are found in its power to move – a power evoked by a body of images. Sorel shows us myth as an active, indeed cataclysmic, social force. For Sorel (unlike traditional anthropological considerations), myth is not a static and timeless story of explication or glorification, to be arranged in neat categories according to archetype or origin, but an entity or event capable of not only encompassing the entirety of socialist ideology, but also of instigating the revolution itself.

Sorel's belief in the power of myth as social force and its ability to 'instinctively invoke' socialist sentiments prefigures, in certain significant ways, Althusser's insights into the nature of ideology. If, as argued above, myth has a necessary relationship to ideology (both expressing and activating it), we can apply Eagleton's (1991) appraisal of contemporary interpretations of Althusser:

> Ideology, Althusser claims, 'expresses a will, a hope or a nostalgia, rather than describing a reality'; it is fundamentally a matter of fearing and denouncing, reverencing and reviling, all of which then sometimes gets coded into a discourse which looks as though it is describing the way things actually are. It is thus, in the terms of the philosopher J. L. Austin (1962), 'performative' rather than 'constative' language: it belongs to the class of speech acts which get something done ... rather than to the discourse of description. (p. 19)

Or, as Michael Sprinker (1987) interprets Althusser: 'Ideology is a performative; as such, it is not regulated according to a regime of truth and falsehood, but by its sheer power to move' (p. 36). This conception of ideology thus, though arrived at through a much longer and later theoretical trajectory, harks back to Sorel: 'myths are not descriptions of things, but expressions of a determination to act ... A myth cannot be refuted, since it is, at bottom, identical with the conviction of a group' (Sorel 1908 [1999]: 132, 53).

When I first found Eagleton's description of ideology as performative, it was familiar to me from studying the areas of gender and sexuality. The idea of particular types of speech as 'performative' was enormously influential in the 'high theory' 1980s and 1990s, for example in 'queer theory', with Butler's *Gender Trouble* (1990) introducing the ideas of gender and sexuality as performative. However, as with all explanations that seem to provide the answers, reflection shows that the preceding argument does not provide them all. One problem is that the distinction between 'performative' and 'descriptive' language isn't as readily apparent as it might seem. A second problem is that, as used in the description above, there still exists a sense of a reality that can be misrepresented underlying the notion of a realm of 'constative' language. While this solves the problem of the concept of ideology growing too large to be useful (Žižek 1994) by bracketing off an area of language and experience that is untouched by it, the dichotomy between performative and constative language leaves a realm of language uncontaminated by ideology. A third problem with the above description, though not necessarily related to the notion of ideology as performative speech, is that it shows ideology purely in a negative light: 'fearing and denouncing, reverencing and reviling' (Eageleton 1991: 19). But if ideology also 'expresses a will, a hope, or nostalgia' (Eagleton 1991: 19), then surely it must also be possible for ideology to be positive, even joyful.

This does not mean that the notion of ideology as performative isn't useful, however. It is through the view of the performativity of the language of ideology that we can reconcile the epistemological and sociological approaches to ideology, as well as synthesize Eagleton's and Laclau's arguments about the desirability of retaining 'ideology' as an analytical construct. Laclau begins his 'resurrection' of ideology through a re-examination of Althusser. As we have seen, in Laclau's reading, it is not the individual that is called into being (interpellated) through ideology and its narrative expression in political myth, but society itself.

If we recognize that political myth is performative, that its function/existence is due to the creation of (impossible) society, it then becomes possible to recognize the manner in which historians like Grittner fall into the contradiction described above. While recognizing on the one hand the symbolic and metaphorical function of myth, they nonetheless at the same time also reify its symbolic content. That is, they have attempted to find out how many innocent young white women were kidnapped or lured by foreigners to be prostitutes. In so doing they have taken the symbolic and metaphorical figures of myth – 'the innocent virgin', the 'evil foreigner' – and attempted to turn them into real, existing, flesh-and-blood people whose numbers can be counted. It is only after the move is made from symbolic to literal truth, from descriptive to emotive or conative language,

44

from constative to performative language, that myth can be seen as the sort of statement deserving of empirical enquiry. There is thus already a mechanism of legitimation, of naturalization, at work: a mechanism that conceals its own workings in the process. This process is a key to myth's believability and hence its power. It is, as Barthes (1973) famously argued, through naturalization that myth maintains its hold. Or, as Frank Kermode observes, 'myths have mistaken their symbolic worlds for literal ones and so come to naturalize their own status' (Kermode 1969 [2000], quoted in Eagleton 1991: 91).

DEALING WITH MYTH

It is precisely this mythical trap that I set out to avoid in researching for this book. This is why I have not chosen to 'expose' the myth of trafficking through research that would 'prove' that the claims of anti-trafficking advocates are exaggerated or distorted. First, because to do so would mean making precisely the same error as the white slavery historians. It would mean, on the one hand, attempting to investigate myth, and, on the other, allowing the myth to dictate the terms of my research. Second, because this is not simply a question of methodological consistency, I believe that to search for 'hard' numbers about trafficked women without a deep under-standing of the source and power of the political myths that inspired current concerns will have devastating real-life consequences for sex workers and migrants. Third, there is the issue of 'taking symbolic worlds for literal ones', as Kermode writes (above). To research the 'facts' in order to separate the myth from the truth would mean being seduced by the slippery power of the myth, to be fooled by its appearance as a description of reality. The ironic power of the myth of trafficking is that in attempting to lift the mask through exposure of the 'facts', it only settles firmer. The face appears to be the true face but, as Laclau demonstrates, there is no 'true face', only the impossible but necessary space enacted by ideology and sutured by myth. The myth of trafficking persuades us that we are on the right course: we investigate the facts, denounce the distortions and triumphantly claim that the myth of trafficking is no more – exposed to the harsh light of truth. Yet, our every step has been at the behest of myth. We imagine ourselves free from trafficking at the moment we are most captured by it.

In the age of statistics, as Connelly notes, old myths are given new validity through use of statistics to prove them. Those who believe in the myth attempt to lend it scientific validity (necessary in this scientific age), but so do those who attempt to disprove it scientifically. They thus accept the validity of the epistemological pretensions of the proponents, even while they may dispute their findings. Connelly (1980) remarks that it is not the statistics on white slavery themselves that are so interesting, but rather the question of why it was thought they were necessary. The same question goes for those historians (and for us today) who attempt to win a war on the terrain of myth, metaphor and morality with the inappropriate weaponry of positivist science. It reflects a lurking belief in the ability of science – statistics – to illuminate 'reality' and dispel the darkness of unscientific, irrational, beliefs. As Žižek explains Michel Pecheux's interpretation of Althusser: one of the fundamental stratagems of ideology is the reference to self-evidence – 'Look, you can see for yourself how things are! … 'Let the facts speak for themselves' is perhaps the arch-statement of ideology – the point being, precisely, that facts *never* speak for themselves but are always *made to speak* by a network of discursive devises' (Žižek 1994: 11, emphasis in original).[11]

The task I have set myself is to identify the mechanisms through which the myth of trafficking purports to be a description of reality. I argue that it is not possible to make an ultimate, sure, incontestable pronouncement on the 'truth' or 'falsity' of any trafficking story, analysis or statistic. One can only explain how they came about, what they are based on, and their link to ideology; examine the political and social context in which they occur and finally examine their links to political power struggles. The way to do this is not through a comparison with the 'facts', but from a careful analysis of the mythical narrative itself, and within its social and political context, most importantly its connections to power.

I argue that narratives of trafficking in women, like those of white slavery, appear to be descriptions of reality, but are actually mythical narratives closely bound up with ideologies concerning sexuality, race and the state. If this is so, it follows that questions such as 'Did white slavery exist?', 'Does trafficking in women exist?' and 'How much trafficking is there?' are not questions that can simply be answered through empirical investigation. What is required is an examination of the context in which statements about trafficking are made; investigation into the 'slipperiness' of the debate on trafficking that masks profoundly normative views with the neutral language of fact, description and statistics; and an excursion into the historical shapings of the meaning of trafficking in women.

Myth and its political effects

If myth is not to be judged on the basis of its truth or falsehood, then how are we to evaluate myth? There is a problem with jettisoning critical appraisal because of a reluctance to pronounce on 'truth'. The neutral or sociological approach does not seem to allow for criteria for judging myth – if all myth is 'lived belief', and if, in any case, all forms of thought are 'socially conditioned', who is to say whether any given myth is right or wrong, bad or good? Does a non-evaluative concept of myth lead inevitably to relativism?[12]

To solve this dilemma, Eagleton advocates a position of 'moral realism'. He reviews the arguments that state that judgements of truth cannot be made of ideology, and accepts many of them, but his unease with 'post-modern relativism' and the 'reformist' politics he claims this entails, means he seeks unassailable grounds of 'truth' from which to condemn certain ideologies. Rather than seeking to resolve Mannheim's paradox by twisting and turning over the relative epistemic values of 'science' and 'ideology', a moral realist position maintains that 'value judgements' as well as 'scientific statements' can be judged 'true' or 'false': 'There are "moral facts" as well as physical ones' (Eagleton 1991: 17).[13] However, Eagleton offers no guide other than 'those values which can be held to be definitive of what it is for human beings in a particular situation to live well' (p. 21) to judge the 'truth' of a moral statement. This offers no answer to relativism, it is simply a restatement of the notion of values based on eternal truth that relativist/post-modernist arguments opposed in the first place. More serious than this, though, is the question it raises of why it is necessary to justify our condemnation of something we find politically and morally *wrong* or *unjust* by calling it *untrue*.

This question is particularly relevant for a study of the myth of trafficking, with feminist claims to be telling the 'real' story about trafficking backed with statistics and real-life stories. Wendy Brown (1995), in *States of Injury*, casts a critical eye on feminist attempts to present feminist arguments based on 'women's experience' as truth. According to Brown, certain types of feminism prefer

> Truth (unchanging, uncontestable) over politics (flux, contest, instability) ... This particular modernist reaction to postmodernism makes sense if we recall that the promise of the Enlightenment was a revision of the old Platonic promise to put an end to politics by supplanting it with Truth ... Modernity could not make good on this promise, of course, but modernists do not surrender the dream it instilled of a world governed by reason divested of power. Feminist modernists are no exception. (1995: 44)

The dangers, as Brown sees it, of the 'Platonic strategy for legitimizing "our truth through its relation to worldly powerlessness, and discrediting "theirs" through its connection to power' (p. 46) is that feminism becomes invested in powerlessness. This leads to a politics that seeks protection from the state rather than power for itself. As Brown (and others) have pointed out, state 'protection' for women often comes at the cost of limitations on freedom.

As Laclau reminds us, ideology and hence myth are not only unavoidable, they are necessary. Rather than arguing that 'myths' of trafficking need to be replaced with the truth about 'what is really happening', I suggest that it may be necessary to replace old myths with new ones. The concluding chapter of this book begins to sketch out what a new myth might look like. In the following two chapters, I set the context for an examination of 'trafficking in women' as myth through exploring the ways in which ideological suppositions concerning class, race, empire and sexuality informed the myth of white slavery.

2 The construction of innocence and the spectre of chaos

In the Introduction, we saw some examples of the ways in which contemporary accounts of trafficking tell their tales. A key theme is the loss of innocence – innocence being an initial state which needs to be narratively established in order for its subsequent loss to have dramatic impact on the reader.[1] A variety of rhetorical devices are used to signify innocence: the repetition of key phrases such as 'naïve' and 'innocent', the invocation of iconic indicators of youth such as dolls and teddy bears, the lingering descriptions of fresh youthful beauty, and the pitiful descriptions of poverty. These devices serve a moral as well as a dramatic function, marking the line between good and bad women – for the assumption of the innocence of prostitutes is anything but a given. As a delegate to a conference in Budapest exclaimed: 'How can I distinguish an innocent victim from a sex worker?' (quoted in Wijers 1998: 11).[2]

In historians' accounts of white slavery, the white slave as the 'beautiful victim' (Haag 1999: 65) has been well illuminated. Connelly (1980), for example, focuses his analysis on the image of the white slave as a victim, representing in her ruined innocence the real and imagined loss of American rural innocence. Many of the devices used today to establish innocence in accounts of trafficking (written, spoken, drawn and filmed) are echoes of those used to create the *dramatis personae* of the white slave. This chapter examines these narrative devices, focusing on the work of two key figures in the fight against white slavery: William T. Stead and Josephine Butler.[3] Recalling the trafficking stories in the Introduction, though, we note that the linguistic creation of innocence isn't the only narrative sleight-of-hand at work. In the story from Nigeria, for example, the innocent girl is changed into the threatening harlot. This telling, too, is genealogically linked to white slavery narratives. If innocence was a constantly reoccurring theme in narratives about white slavery, this was complicated by the presence of the image of the prostitute as ruiner, herself the destroyer of innocence.[4] It is no surprise that the magic word that performs the transformation is 'consent'.

An investigation into these two mythical figures – the white slave and the 'destructive whore' – forms the heart of this chapter's analysis. That said, I'd like to take a brief methodological pause. The moral urge to distinguish between good and bad women on the basis of sexual virtue – the madonna/ whore dualism – is now such a familiar idea that it has achieved the status of a truism: to invoke it as the basis of an analysis can run the risk of banality, of taking the argument down well-trodden paths – a comfortable walk, but with no surprises along the way.[5] Yet it is impossible to ignore the familiar dichotomy when researching white slavery and trafficking, for it jumps off the pages. The challenge for the researcher is to find a way to make the whore/madonna dichotomy fresh, to sharpen the analytical edge dulled by overfamiliarity.

One way to do this is to apply Haag's (1999) insights about the socially situated nature of consent in order to investigate how the categories of madonna and whore were constructed. This means not taking the notion of consent as a given, through either anachronistically projecting our ideas of consent into the past or even through a more historically conscious effort to discover what consent 'meant' to the late Victorians. Rather, it means investigating the ways in which consent came to mean what it did. Thus, in this case, not only how the representation and political/legal persona of the white slave were established through consent, but also how narratives of white slavery themselves modified other social relations, such as those of class and those implicated in empire.

The two caricatures of melodrama were the result of the particular historical social/political moment, of the way heterosexual consent was being constructed and understood. Social/political movements such as nineteenth-century feminism and socialism, the political realities of empire, and new medical/scientific learning shaped the discursive landscape in which consent was constructed. In all of this, the prostitute took a central place as the public symbol (public woman) of the price to pay for getting consent wrong. This is enormously important for a study of trafficking, given that the innocent victim and the destructive whore are the central figures in both popular perceptions of trafficking and in policy response. Contemporary discourses of trafficking have performed a macabre 'zombie magic', rousing the corpses of the Victorian imagination from their well-deserved rest. Genealogy as necromancy – the myth of white slavery has been exhumed to clumsily stalk the living.

Narrative and truth

Before I examine the constructions of consent in white slavery in Britain, I will look in more detail at a term which I have, until now, used without definition or elaboration: narrative.[6] 'Narrative' as a focal point of investigation has been immensely influential across a wide range of disciplines as part of the linguistic turn in post-modernism. The influence of linguistics on modern myth study cannot be overstated. From Lévi-Strauss's (1978; 1968) semiotic structuralism through Barthes's (1973) both playful and highly formalized Saussurian (1959 [1974]) schema of myth to contemporary theorists of political myth such as Flood (1996), the study of myth has been the study of the way myth is told: myth *is* its narrative. An examination of the construction of 'myths of sexuality' (Nead 1988) through narrative allows us to revisit and re-evaluate the connections between myth and ideology that were introduced in the preceding chapter, as well as a way to put a perspective on the political consequences of the myth of white slavery / trafficking.

The study of myth and the study of narrative, as indicated above, are historically and theoretically connected. The study of the narrative structure of myth was introduced by Propp in his highly influential study of Russian folktales *Morphology of the Folktale* (1928 [1968]). Barthes's *Mythologies* (1973) famously follows in the same vein. In this work, the analysis of linguistic structure is applied to everyday cultural production, including advertising, stripping and wrestling. Using a Saussurian structuralist analysis, Barthes wrested the notion of myth away from its traditional connection with 'primitive' or ancient cultures to show how myths operate in sustaining relations of domination through the regulation and production of meaning in modern political cultures. Barthes argues that myths support bourgeois hegemony by naturalizing what is contingent and historically produced into that which is timeless. Nead (1988) uses a Barthian perspective to argue that 'the image of the prostitute as helpless victim' was a 'dominant myth' in mid-Victorian Britain, 'implicated in the preservation of middle-class hegemony. The myth, conveyed through the narrative of the "temptation–fall–decline" of the prostitute, made this sequence seem natural, inevitable, and true' (p. 141).

Following historians Walkowitz and Nead, we can argue that the narrative aspect of the myth of white slavery appears, not simply as convenient or contingent, but as an essential element of its meaning-making: 'Narrative, then, was fundamental to the effectiveness of the myth of the life and death of the prostitute ... Its sequence was seen as the unveiling of reality, the revolution of truth' (Nead 1988: 141). Walkowitz explicitly concentrates on the narrative form of prostitution myths, while Nead's work is concerned primarily with visual images of the prostitute. However, though 'narrative' is *the* concept which explains for Nead the persistence and power of the myth of the prostitute's decline and fall, she does not explain how narrative is related to or expressed in other, non-literary forms. This brings us to the question of whether narrative is necessarily an element of myth.

The question of political myth's relationship to narrative is a central question in myth scholarship. Scholars of myth do not agree on the question; for those such as Sauvy, 'it is the beliefs themselves, abstracted from their discursive expression, which constitute the myths' (Flood 1996: 101). I align myself with those such as Tudor (1972) and Flood (1996) who argue that narrative is essential to myth. If myth is to retain any significance as an analytical concept, it must express something that other concepts can and do not. As Flood (1996) argues, 'without reference to discursive form [narrative], the myth becomes little more than a synonym for ideological belief' (p. 102).[7] Myth is able to pack an analytical punch precisely because it expresses the powerful synthesis of deeply held beliefs with the specific form which the articulation of those beliefs assumes. Thus an understanding of narrative is key to the understanding of the political effects of myth. Narrative is not synonymous with ideology, yet it has a necessary relationship to it, examined below.

What about words or phrases and visual images? Can these be myths as well? Flood (1996) argues that myth can also be condensed into a sentence or a phrase as well as embodied in visual images. While an image or phrase may not be in itself a myth, it may have 'the capacity to evoke a myth ... a photograph, a painting, a piece of sculpture, a carving , a cartoon, a poster, a mosaic, a collage, among other things, can all represent an established political myth or a set of myths by a form of synecdoche – part for the whole' (pp. 166, 167). I interpret this to mean that something can be *mythical* without necessarily appearing in the traditional narrative form of a written or spoken story with a beginning, middle and end. This 'broad' interpretation of narrative is not far from that set out by Barthes in his later work: 'Contemporary myth is discontinuous. It is no longer expressed in long fixed narratives but only in "discourse"; at most it is a phraseology, a corpus of phrases (or stereotypes); myth disappears, but leaving – so much the more insidious – the *mythical*' (Barthes 1980 [1975] in Flood 1996: 167, emphasis in original). (It should be clear, however, that Flood [and I] do not agree with

52

Barthes that the narrative form of myth has been wholly supplanted.) The whole thrust of Barthes's method – which was part of the great project of structuralism – was that structural analysis did not have to be limited to the study of language (Torfing 1999). Therefore, for Barthes, myth did not have to take the form of language. Insofar as a mythical object/instance conveyed mythical meaning it could be *considered as speech*: 'a photograph will be a kind of speech for us in the same way as a newspaper article, *even objects will become speech*, if they mean something' (Barthes 1973: 111, emphasis added).[8]

Including visual and truncated narrative forms is essential for the study of white slavery and trafficking as myth. White slavery, as is shown primarily by Nead (1988), but also by other historians such as Grittner (1990) and Connelly (1980), was narrated not only in a great variety of written forms – plays, fiction, government reports, memoirs, newspaper reports – but also in non-written forms – paintings, photographs, cartoons and sculpture. Synecdoche was at work when the statue of *The White Slave* (reproduced in Grittner 1990) – a nearly nude woman in chains – was understood by the vast numbers who viewed her to represent the entire sequence of the fall of innocence. Today's manifestations of the myth are equally varied. Some of the most potent synecdochal effects are achieved by the posters made to accompany information campaigns about trafficking. A particularly notorious example is a poster produced by IOM Lithuania in 2002 (at www.iom.org).[9] It is a digitally manipulated photograph, showing an attractive young woman with barbed hooks imbedded deep in her naked flesh. These hooks are attached to strings which are manipulated by a giant hand at the top of the poster. This poster powerfully narrates the myth in a single static image.

What can we now initially postulate about the relationship between narrative, myth and ideology in white slavery and trafficking? The myth of white slavery/trafficking, the story of innocence lured, innocence betrayed and innocence destroyed, is implied and evoked in a variety of linguistic and non-linguistic forms, including law, paintings, film and sculpture. Through narrative, the myth of white slavery/trafficking takes on the appearance of reality: 'narrative is, as it were, the transformation of representation into "Reality", the demonstrating of its truth, the discovery of its meaning ... The effect of narrative is exactly that of tightening, action is moulded in a *destiny*, an inevitable coherence of the real' (Heath 1982, cited in Nead 1998: 140). Narratives are stories: in their straightforward representation of a series of events, they work to give coherence to contradictory reality, to give *closure*. As the extract from Heath indicates, not only did the narrative make the fate of the white slave appear *believable*, it made it seem *inevitable*. Narrative achieves closure by 'leaving the audience with an implicit or explicit assurance that what was to be shown has indeed been shown' (Flood 1996: 115). The mythical operation identified by Barthes consists of naturalization of the historically contingent: 'myth has been one of the means by which the bourgeoisie has sought to convey the illusion ... that the interests of their class are identical with the interests of all and the values of their class are self-evidently right for all' (Flood 1996: 164). This naturalization is the ideological move – 'the "naturalisation" of the symbolic order – that is, the perception that reifies the results of discursive procedures into properties of the "thing itself"' (Žižek 1994: 85).

In Chapter 1, I argued that ideology was able to achieve its political effects because it *appeared to be a description* of reality – a representation of the real. Barthes argues that myth 'works' because it appears denotive while being actually connotive. Narrative instigates the *performativity* of ideology as it is played through myth: it makes it seem real.

The white slave (appearances and apparitions)

The campaign against white slavery in the UK formed part of a wave of what historian Connelly (1990) terms an 'anti-prostitution' sentiment throughout the then 'Western' world during the mid- to late nineteenth century. While concern with prostitution was certainly not new to this period, there was a distinct break with the way that prostitution was conceived previously. Foucault (1976 [1981]) famously argued that sexuality for the Victorians, far from being repressed, was being constantly produced, and that the production of sexualities was a privileged site for the production of selves.[10] On to the stage already set with the frenzied production and dissemination of images of the 'deviant' sexuality of the prostitute appeared the iconic image of the white slave. Her appearance at the end of the nineteenth century was heralded by the unprecedented migration of women (working-class) from the country to the city, from colonial powers to colonized countries, and from southern Europe and Asia to the US (Guy 1991; Bristow 1977). The increase in female migration was accompanied by other changes that historians have pointed to as indicative of a 'crisis' in Euro-American society in the decades bounding the turn of the century. These changes (including urbanization and the increased politicization of the working class) were initiated by the industrial revolution, but gained pace rapidly as the century drew to a close.

Connelly argues that in the US, anti-prostitution was intricately connected with fears and anxieties produced by Progressive-era social changes such as the demise of the small-town rural way of life and increased immigration:

> As a form of illicit sexual behaviour, prostitution has always provoked highly charged emotions. During the progressive years, however, its inherent capacity to provoke fear and alarm was greatly expanded. Prostitution became a master symbol, a code word, for a wide range of anxieties engendered by the great social and cultural changes that give the progressive era its coherence as a distinct historical period. (1980: 6)

Connelly's conception of the prostitute as symbolic of social disorder is also seen by Nead in mid-Victorian Britain: 'the prostitute as a figure of contagion, disease and death; a sign of social disorder and ruin to be feared and controlled' (Connelly 1980: 106). Nead argues that this image of the prostitute coexisted with another, radically different image, that of the prostitute as 'passive victim', who 'displaced these connotations of power and destruction and defined the prostitute as a tragic and suffering figure' (1988: 106).[11]

ANALYSING MYTH

In the following section, I trace the myth of white slavery as it appeared in Britain. In the process, I will make use of the interpretations of the myth by historians of white slavery. Historians such as Connelly and Grittner who do close readings of the mythical narratives of white slavery tend to locate 'the' myth of white slavery both synchronically and diachronically. A synchronic approach is used when a *single* text or image of white slavery is the subject of analysis. A diachronic approach is used in the comparison of *various* texts and images with each other in order to elucidate the core elements of the myth of white slavery. In Connelly's case, this latter method leads to the following characterization of the common elements of the myth:

> Typically, a chaste and comely native American country girl would forsake her idyllic country home and family for the promise of the city. On the way, or shortly after arrival, she would fall victim to one of the swarm of panderers lying in wait for just such an innocent and unprotected sojourner. Using one of his vast variety of tricks – a promise of marriage, an offer to assist in securing lodging, or if these were to no avail, the chloroformed cloth, the hypodermic needle, or the drugged drink – the insidious white slaver would brutally seduce the girl and install her in a brothel, where she became an enslaved prostitute. Within five years she would end up in potter's field, unless she had the good fortune to be 'rescued' by a member of one of the dedicated groups fighting white slavery. (1980: 116)

Elements of this story – and its form as narrative – were not only, as Connelly indicates, uniform throughout America, but strikingly similar as well in Britain and on the Continent.[12] The 'simple melodramatic formula' of white slavery is an old and easily recounted tale of innocence destroyed. The 'bare bones' of the story are so universal, and the archetypes of the innocent victim and the evil villain so prevalent, that in themselves they have no meaning. Attempts to find the meaning of white slavery in a reductionist search for these figures are misguided. These cardboard cutouts do not have any meaning *in themselves*: it is exactly because of their emptiness that they can carry meaning. It is through their inscription that meaning is made, and this inscription should be the focus of study. This position is derived from Laclau, whose 'main theoretical result' as summarized by Žižek (1994) is 'that meaning does not inhere in elements of an ideology as such – these elements, rather, function as "free-floating signifiers" whose meaning is fixed by the mode of their hegemonic articulation (p. 12).[13]

My discussion of the narratives of white slavery, drawing as it does on the work of these historians, will proceed diachronically, bringing together the work of white slavery historians with different emphases and historical foci.[14] The method is thus diachronic, with the following caveats: my attempt should not be taken as a Straussian attempt to find 'deep structures' within the myth, common elements in which the true meaning of the myth is to be found. The difference with a Straussian analysis is that I do not see variations and absences as accidental and irrelevant, but as precisely where the search for meaning should start.[15] Similarly, while Barthes's analysis of myth is useful and provocative, it is limited by his structuralism; in moving the linguistic analysis up to the 'second-order signs' of myth, he maintains the link, the necessary relationship, between the signifier and the signified. This link, in structuralist thinking, provides the meaning of the sign. Myth is itself closure for Barthes, its meaning complete and contained in its structure. In the insights of later deconstructionists, in particular Derrida (1967 [1977]), this closure itself is recognized as an impossibility (Laclau 1997). Thompson (1984), discussing Barthes's method, comments that while an analysis of 'structural features and systemic elements' is useful, it is also limited: 'meaning is never *exhausted by* these features and elements' (p. 143). The meaning of the myth of white slavery also has to be looked for in terms of its 'constitutive outside' (Derrida 1967 [1977]). Closure is also exactly that which ideology attempts, but is never able to achieve (Laclau 1997).

If myth can be seen as an attempt to fix the meaning of white slavery, with the narrative form providing closure, the proper method of analysis is one that exposes the attempts at closure rather than one that takes its meaning at face value. This approach attempts to show that the meaning of white slavery, in its varying socio-political settings, was a matter of what was left out: it analyses the ways in which the presence of the chaos bringer prevented a final, stable, meaning of white slavery. This deconstructive approach has been described by Catherine Belsey as efforts to:

> seek not the unity of the work, but the multiplicity and diversity of its possible meanings, its incompleteness, the omissions which it displays but cannot describe, and above all its contradictions. In its absences, and in the collisions between its divergent meanings, the text implicitly criticizes its own ideology; it contains within itself the critique of its own values. (Belsey in Doty 2000: 441)

I employ this approach to the myths of white slavery and trafficking. I focus my attention to the ways in which cultural and political productions of white slavery and of trafficking are always partial and contested. A recognition that the myth of white slavery / trafficking never 'exhausts' the meanings of prostitution, that the narratives contain, include, depend on the spectre of chaos (rather than simply supplanting it, banishing it to the margins) leads us to investigate the manner in which the absences that constructed the meaning of the white slave / trafficking victim image shaped the politics of white slavery and contemporary anti-trafficking politics.

I begin my analysis in Britain because this is where the 'moral panic' of white slavery began. The start of the campaign against white slavery, and the appearance of the first white slavery narratives, was in Britain in the 1880s. Reports of British girls working in brothels in Belgium aroused concern in religious, official and feminist circles.[16] It took the publication of one extremely sensationalist narrative, however, to spark a full-blown moral panic: Stead's 'The Maiden Tribute of Modern Babylon' (1885). I follow the emergence of the campaign against white slavery in Britain to examine the construction of the white slave through the attempted exclusion of her ever-present evil twin.

The campaign against white slavery in Britain evolved against a background of intense societal concern about prostitution (Nead 1988). Feminists, religious groups, medical professionals, journalists, policy and law makers all weighed in with their contributions as to how prostitution should be defined, what caused it, what its effects were, and what should be done about it (Bland 1992; Walkowitz 1980; Nead 1988).

THE CONSTRUCTION OF DEVIANCE AND THE PUSH FOR REGULATION

Feminist historians of Victorian prostitution such as Linda Nead, Judith Walkowitz, Lucy Bland and Antoinette Burton use a Foucaultian perspective to show the ways in which the category 'prostitute' was a flexible one, able to accommodate shifting notions of sexuality as well as of class, gender and race. Nead's (1988) analysis of artistic representations of prostitution in Victorian Britain argues that the construction of sexuality through discourses of prostitution was an essential element of middle-class hegemony:

> 'prostitute' is an historical construction which works to define and categorize a particular group of women in terms of sex and class. *The term should not be seen as an objective description of an already-determined group; rather, it actively constitutes a group which is both socially and economically specific.* In the nineteenth century this process of categorization was produced through various social practices, through legal and medical discourses, religious and cultural forms. (p. 94, emphasis added)

The mid-nineteenth-century high point of this process of categorization was the Contagious Diseases Acts, a legal codification of the prostitute that owed much to the newly acquired prestige of medical discourse (Foucault 1976 [1981], Walkowitz 1980, Nead 1988). The Acts represented a moment in which one particular image of prostitution was 'fixed' in the law; a momentary victory of the construction of the prostitute as bringer of chaos, as a conduit which transmitted disease and death to society. The Acts acted as a catalyst for the organization of a feminist-led campaign which sought to replace this image with that of the prostitute-victim (Walkowitz 1992). The fallout from the campaign against the Acts shaped the political and discursive framework for the emergence of white slavery (Irwin 1996).

Under the Contagious Diseases Acts, prostitutes found infected with a 'social disease' could be detained by the police and forced to undergo an internal medical examination. If found to be infected, they were interned in so-called 'lock hospitals': 'pseudo-medical prisons for whores' (Roberts 1992: 248). Of the many arguments used to garner support for the Acts, one of the most successful was that of the need to protect British troops from the syphilis spread (it was assumed) by working-class prostitutes (Walkowitz 1980). As such, the Acts did not in any way attempt to regulate prostitution that occurred out of the public eye, and identified the sexually active bodies of working-class women as the threat that state-power-backed medical science needed to contain (Walkowitz 1980, Bland 1992).

THE RESURRECTION OF FEMALE INNOCENCE AND THE REPEAL CAMPAIGN

The Acts aroused intense opposition, the fiercest of which was led by Josephine Butler. These feminist 'abolitionists' opposed the regulationist views of the prostitute as sexually deviant and of prostitution as a necessary evil.[17] They located the causes of prostitution not in the pathology of the individual prostitute, but in the twin evils of working-class female poverty and male lust. Abolitionism, though condemned by today's sex worker rights advocates (including myself in earlier work, for example Doezema 1998) for denying women's 'agency', was a movement whose political vision (if not its effects) cannot be simply dismissed as repressive. As Burton (1994) notes, abolitionism, like much of second-wave feminism (Burton 1994; Smith-Rosenberg 1985), sought emancipation for women through freedom from male sexual double standards. However, this freedom went hand in hand with the impulse to control women who did not live up to the high moral standards set by their sisters. This impulse informs much of today's feminist reaction to prostitution, as Chapter 4 demonstrates.

In the abolitionist version of the plight of the prostitute, it is the victim image that comes to the fore.[18] First, the prostitute was portrayed as victimized because of her sex. The sexual binary that informed Butlerite feminism did not differ substantially from that underlying regulationist arguments: the sexually active male on one side and the sexually passive female on the other. The emancipatory difference was present in their interrogation of the arguments used to justify regulation and in their linking of the control of prostitutes to the condition of all women (Walkowitz 1980). They argued that a regulationist system created a class of women who were to be used by men, who then justified this use by blaming the women: first as sinful, then as deviant. Prostitutes, argued Butler, were created and maintained by men: the prostitute herself bore no responsibility for her condition (Irwin 1996). The abolitionist vision was of a world in which prostitution was completely ended, where men and women alike clove to a single standard of chastity (except in marriage). Feminists in Butler's repeal movement saw the Contagious Diseases Acts as official state recognition of the 'double standard' of sexual behaviour for men and women (Walkowitz 1980).

Second, the prostitute was seen as victimized because of her class (Walkowitz 1980). This aspect of the argument, too, had its emancipatory as well as anti-emancipatory aspects. On the one hand, the focus on working-class female poverty as a cause of prostitution was a surprisingly revolutionary attempt to locate prostitution within societal structures. On the other, middle-class Butlerite feminists shared regulationist assumptions about the class location of prostitution, focusing their attention on the plight of prostitutes from the 'poorer classes' (Walkowitz 1992). While this led them to protest against the way the Contagious Diseases Acts gave the state additional powers to police and control the lives of working-class women, Walkowitz (1992) notes the ambiguous nature of their reaction: 'As members of the propertied classes, feminists felt obliged to redress the sexual wrongs done to poor girls by privileged men, and they often register the same repugnance and ambivalence toward "incorrigible" girls as they had towards unrepentant prostitutes' (p. 132).

The feminist abolitionist campaigners were able to construct a broad coalition of social groups, including working men's organizations and religious organizations. They were also joined by the burgeoning 'social purity' movement, whose notions of sexual chastity were more repressive and wider than the original Butlerite agenda (Walkowitz 1980). Prominent purity campaigner William Coote set up the National Vigilance Association (NVA), which espoused a repressive moral agenda with a focus on the sexual behaviour of young people (Coote 1910). The debauchery of innocent children would also form a flashpoint for the British panic around white slavery, as the NVA took up the cause. This aspect of the campaign against white slavery will strike a familiar chord with observers today, as the anti-trafficking movement is increasingly being linked to the panic around paedophilia and child prostitution.

As Grittner remarks, social purity reformers 'soon discovered the rhetorical power that "white slavery" had on their middle-class audience' (Grittner 1990: 41). After the campaign to repeal the Contagious Diseases Acts achieved its goal in 1886, Butlerite feminists continued to support the social purist campaign against white slavery, as they believed that the system of licensed brothels abroad furthered the traffic in women (Walkowitz 1980, Gibson 1986). They also supported the social purists' agenda of a single standard of chastity for both sexes and shared their concern with youthful sexuality (Bristow 1977; Walkowitz 1980). Eventually, the abolitionist campaign was eclipsed by the campaign for social purity, as the emotive issue of white slavery succeeded in whipping up public concern to a fever pitch. In other European countries and the US as well, feminists initiated, or became involved in, the drive to abolish prostitution and white slavery. And, as in England, these campaigns were increasingly dominated by repressive moralists, as alliances were forged with religious and social purity organizations (Gibson 1986; Grittner 1990; Haveman 1998).[19]

WRITING AND SPEAKING THE WHITE SLAVE

At a rally in Hyde Park in 1885, thousands of people converged to decry the white slave trade and demand that the age of consent be raised to sixteen. 'Wagonloads of young virgins in white' waved banners reading 'The Innocents, Will They Be Slaughtered?' (Bristow 1977: 113). Feminist campaigners, working men's associations, socialists, social purity activists and clergy joined together to demand that Parliament end the sacrifice of pure virgins in Britain's 'capital of shame'. The hero and instigator of this demonstration was William T. Stead, a journalist and editor whose weekly, the *Pall Mall Gazette*, was running a Stead-penned account of the debauching of young girls by depraved aristocrats in seedy London dens: 'The Maiden Tribute of Modern Babylon' (1885). Especially prominent among the demonstrators were abolitionist feminists active in the NVA. However, by this stage of the campaign against white slavery, their own leader and inspiration, Josephine Butler, had distanced herself from the more repressive aspects of the anti-prostitution movement: aspects which both Stead's and Butler's work ironically enhanced.

This enhancement was ironic because the two things that the two titans of Victorian virtue had most in common was their flair for rhetoric (often sensationalist) and their distrust of the state in its dealing with prostitutes. Butler wrote widely on prostitution and was renowned as a passionate and persuasive speaker. Stead was a pioneer of crusading undercover journalism, and his remarkable exposé employs both the sensationalist (tabloid) language of the then-popular 'true-crime' pamphlets (Walkowitz 1992) and the sober (broadsheet) language of social analysis. Stead's campaign took as its subject the London 'trade' in underage girls (that is, girls under the age of consent, sixteen years) for prostitution. Stead's account consists of four parts, in which he records interviews with prostitutes, police, politicians and rescue workers. He also recounts his adventures as a would-be slaver, as he attempts to buy five virgins from a 'firm of procuresses'.[20] Stead's diatribes against the police, in particular the last instalment of 'The Maiden Tribute of Modern Babylon', could serve as a model for sex worker activists today.[21] For example, he writes: 'To increase by one jot or one tittle the power of the man in uniform over the women who are left unfriended even by their own sex is a crime against liberty and justice, which no impatience at markets of vice, or holy horror at the sight of girls on the streets, ought to be allowed to excuse' (1885, Part 4: 1).

Walkowitz (1992) contrasts Stead's reading of the story of white slavery with Josephine Butler's accounts of her work among prostitutes. Butler's analysis of prostitution seems, in the first instance, to have banished altogether the 'sexually destructive female' aspect of the prostitute symbol.[22] In Butler's writings, the criteria by which a prostitute is judged guilty or innocent of sexual wrongdoing are reduced to her femaleness: simply by virtue of her gender, the female prostitute was a victim. According to Walkowitz: 'Feminist propaganda was severely constrained by a melodramatic vocabulary of female victimization, which demanded that registered women be innocent victims falsely entrapped into a life of vice – involuntary actors in their own history, without sexual passion' (Walkowitz 1992: 92).

Walkowitz writes that Butler, like Stead, cast her narratives in the melodramatic convention – one that was adopted by her followers in the feminist anti-prostitution and anti-white slavery movement. However, Butler's accounts were a 'feminized' version of melodrama, deriving their form from mid-eighteenth-century women's melodramas (Walkowitz 1992). These 'women's stories' allowed women to be heroines as well as, or even instead of, victims. Walkowitz argues that, like Stead, Butler cast herself in the role of the heroine: the 'saving mother' of female melodrama, rather than the courageous hero that Stead as a crusading journalist and protector of the weak attempted to be.

Prostitutes were cast in the entirely passive supporting role of grateful daughters.[23] Walkowitz concludes that in Butler's version of female sexuality, prostitutes were not made of a different sexual stuff than respectable women. Yet this claimed unity was threatened by the spectre of unruly female sexuality which for Butlerite feminists was moderated through keenly felt and observed class distinctions. The figure that interrupted the closure of Butler's feminist melodrama had a distinctly class character: 'They [Butler's narratives] assert a unified identity for women ... yet they nonetheless reveal a complicated identification with the fallen woman as both a version of the self and residual Other' (Walkowitz 1992: 89).

THE MELODRAMATIC NARRATIVE

We do not have to look far to find a connection between myth and melodrama in this instance: the title 'Maiden Tribute of Modern Babylon' itself refers to the Greek myth of the Minotaur, which Stead used to structure his introduction to the series:

> This very night in London, and every night, year in and year out, not seven maidens only, but many times seven, selected almost as much by chance as those who in the Athenian market-place drew lots as to which should be flung into the Cretan labyrinth, will be offered up as the Maiden Tribute of Modern Babylon.

> Maidens they were when this morning dawned, but to-night their ruin will be accomplished, and to-morrow they will find themselves within the portals of the maze of London brotheldom. (1885, Part 1: 1)[24]

The narrative penned by Stead took the form of a classic melodramatic tale, with elements from other, 'older' cultural forms such as 'the literature of urban exploration' and 'newer' forms such as late-Victorian pornography and fantasy, the Gothic fairy tale and detective stories (Walkowitz 1992: 84). My own reading of Stead found many of the Gothic trimmings that decorate Victorian fiction.[25] Stead spent a few weeks investigating 'undercover' and introduces his sojourns in a manner reminiscent of Poe's story 'The Fall of the House of Usher' (1839 [1984]):

> It seemed a strange, inverted world, that in which I lived those terrible weeks ... For days and nights it is as if I had suffered the penalties inflicted upon the lost souls in the Moslem hell, for I seemed to have to drink of the purulent matter that flows from the bodies of the damned. (1885, Part 1: 2)

Continuing with the trope of inversion, of things the wrong way round, Stead refers to the 'underground chambers' and the 'dread regions of subterranean vice', setting the sphere for the tale of a young girl's ruin:

> From the midwife's the innocent girl was taken to a house of ill fame, No.—, P— street, Regent-street, where, notwithstanding her extreme youth, she was admitted without question. She was taken up stairs, undressed, and put to bed, the woman who brought her putting her to sleep. She was rather restless, but under the influence of chloroform she soon went over. Then the woman withdrew. All was quiet and still. A few moments later the door opened, and the purchaser entered the bedroom. He closed and locked the door. There was a brief silence. And then there rose a wild and piteous cry – not a loud shriek, but a helpless, startled scream like the bleat of a frightened lamb. And the child's voice was heard crying, in accents of terror, 'There's a man in the room! Take me home; oh, take me home!'. (1885, Part 1: 8)[26]

Stead's narratives are produced out of his own experience as an investigative journalist and include 'true life stories' told directly to him, as he claimed, by girls of the street. The incorporation of these first-person tales gave Stead's account the ring of truth, a veracity enhanced by the familiarity of the melodramatic tale (Walkowitz 1992).[27] In this, 'true-life' accounts share their real-seemingness with the conventions of realistic fiction: 'Realism is plausible not because it reflects the world, but because it is constructed out of what is (discursively) familiar' (Belsey, quoted in Doty 2000: 440). Unlike others who have studied Stead's work, Walkowitz's probing of the 'truth' of Stead's account is self-consciously not concerned with its factual status. Rather, she locates its believability, its 'true-seeming-ness', in its narrative structure as melodrama. Passive female sexuality, predatory male sexuality, youth and sexual unknowingness, the venality of poor women, and all the conventions of melodrama were 'discursively familiar' to Stead's audience. This familiarity gave the tales not only their veracity, but also their resonance, their ability to speak to, to be 'meaningful' (literally to have meaning) for different constituencies:

> Narratives of the 'real', such as history and news reporting [and I would add academic research writings and NGO reports], impose a formal coherence on events: they 'narrativize' data into a coherent 'well-made' tale, converting 'chaotic experience into meaningful moral drama'. (Micahel White in Walkowitz 1992: 83)

TODAY'S TRUE STORIES

Narrative – the telling of a tale – thus contributes to its believability. This sheds light on the staging of trafficking melodramas in today's news-papers. To leave Stead in his 'Moslem hell' for the time being, I will move to a contemporary description of an investigation into the 'underworld' that in melodramatic structure shares much with 'The Maiden Tribute of Modern Babylon'. This account, too, is discursively familiar to its audience, with still-relevant notions of female passivity and venality coupled with images of chaos and corruption in the aftermath of the Balkan wars. Following (unknowingly?) in Stead's footsteps, the investigators from the Institute for War and Peace Reporting, UK, undertake an undercover investigation of trafficking in Romania, posing as customers to try to 'buy' a girl.

Their report begins with a first-person account that with its shameless portrayal of a terrified innocent could have been written by Stead himself:

> 'Can I be sure you're not giving me back to them?' Diana whispered from the backseat of the car. 'I'm scared.' The trembling figure, huddled in a blanket against a cold Bucharest night, had only minutes earlier been just one of the legion of girls for sale in Romania's human-trafficking market. Driven by fear, her words tumbled out, "They hit me. He stabbed me with a knife. You want to see the wound? I'm hungry. Do you like me? You want sex with me? Can I have your kids afterwards? I'll be a good wife. Do you want to marry me? You know, they starved me. Do you want me to take off my blouse? I need to eat something! Promise I will never be starved ever again? I want to smoke, too. And don't forget to buy me chocolate.' (Radu 2003)

64

These 'wild and piteous cries' (Stead 1885 Part 1: 1) 'told in her own words' enact the coherence and believability of the account. As in Stead's tale, the crusading male journalist is also the hero (Walkowitz 1992). He sets off to buy underage girls – and, like Stead, is increasingly frustrated by his lack of success. At every turn, taxi drivers and doormen are willing to introduce him to prostitutes (and as a good journalist he films them all) but all refuse to bring him (to) children. Stead, from his inability to buy children (under thirteen) concluded – in what seems a sensible outcome of investigative journalism – that if the investigation failed to turn up children on the streets, they probably weren't there. However, our modern-day hero is undeterred. With the easy shift in register that is characteristic of trafficking reports, the narrative moves from children to prostitutes to victims of trafficking without a hitch.

The prose has a decidedly Victorian flavour (this is common: not only the narrative form of the myth but certain stylistic flourishes are repeated through the decades, as Irwin [1996] also remarks). Despite the professed desire to throw light on the trade through showing 'a victim's point of view', the text is mainly concerned with the journalist's scary adventures in Bucharest's seedy underworld, peopled with such Victorianesque characters as 'the Dwarf'. After much effort and reported danger to his own person (and, unlike Stead, with no effort to record the stories of any of the prostitutes he encounters) the journalist finally succeeds in 'buying' a nineteen-year-old 'mentally retarded' woman from a man and woman, and as her saviour, delivers her to an NGO. The description of the NGO is telling: the supposed 'victims' saved and taken to the shelter also seem to posses the ability to return willingly to prostitution. The measure of their consent is the measure of the programme's success: 'The programme has been a success story, as only five girls have since returned to prostitution' (Radu 2003: 5). He follows this with the statement: 'One is now a psychology student at university.' The university for today's 'white slaves' fulfils the narrative function of a marriage in the Victorian melodrama, underscoring the dramatic difference between hopelessness and hope, saved and fallen.

'SACRIFICES WILLING AND UNWILLING'

Sold initially for their virginity, Stead's maidens are unable to escape their inevitable, mythical, fate:

> The maw of the London Minotaur is insatiable, and none that go into the secret recesses of his lair return again. After some years' dolorous wandering in this

palace of despair – for 'hope of rest to solace there is none, nor e'en of milder pang', save the poisonous anodyne of drink – most of those ensnared to-night will perish, some of them in horrible torture. (1885, Part 1: 1)

Though Stead's text itself revels as much as supposedly did the 'silk-hatted, kid-gloved Minotaur' (Irwin 1996: 2) in the destruction of maidenly innocence, Stead was unable to exorcize completely from his narrative the spectre of an active, destructive, female sexuality. Indeed, he actively invokes it when apportioning blame. Stead did not fit all prostitutes into melodrama's victim role – not all were worth saving from the Minotaur. While Butler's attitude towards streetwalkers who resisted her saving grace was ambiguous in its mixture of pity and contempt, Stead is completely clear about who deserves to be saved:

London's lust annually uses up many thousands of women, who are literally killed and made away with – living sacrifices slain in the service of vice. That may be inevitable, and with that I have nothing to do. *But I do ask that those doomed to the house of evil fame shall not be trapped into it unwillingly*, and that none shall be beguiled into the chamber of death before they are of an age to read the inscription above the portal – 'All hope abandon ye who enter here' ... if we must cast maidens ... nightly into the jaws of vice, *let us at least see to it that they assent to their own immolation*, and are not unwilling sacrifices procured by force and fraud. (1885, Part 1: 2, emphasis added)

Female sexuality received its own reward. While ignorant of the mechanics of sex, the girls he attempts to buy are willing to be 'seduced' for money, despite Stead's exhortations to upright behaviour. What is most regrettable, to Stead, is the loss of virginity, the 'most valuable thing a woman possesses' (1885, Part 1: 2). Far from decrying the commodification of sexuality (as is today's feminist argument), Stead explicitly uses the language of the market:

I do not ask for any police interference with the liberty of vice. I ask only for the repression of crime. Sexual immorality, however evil it may be in itself or in its consequences, must be dealt with not by the policeman but by the teacher, so long as the persons contracting are of full age, are perfectly free agents, and in their sin are guilty of no outrage on public morals. Let us by all means apply the sacred principles of free trade to trade in vice, and regulate the relations of the sexes by the higgling of the market and the liberty of private contract. (1885, Part 4: 3)

Stead's 'maidens', as Walkowitz notes, 'speak the undramatic language of sexual barter' – even signing contracts agreeing to their seduction for a certain sum. As reproduced by Stead, one such contract reads:

Agreement. I hereby agree to let you have me for a present of £3 or £4. I will come to any address if you give me two days' notice. Name — D—, aged 16. Address No. 11, — Street, H—. (1885, Part 2: 7)

What is noticeably missing from the account is any notion of female sexual desire, and the presence or lack of it as justification for sex. Throughout Stead's text, females who consent lose their most precious possession; and so themselves are lost. The following excerpt, through which consent runs like a red thread, makes this clear. Stead is talking to a Scotland Yard policeman about his plans to buy a virgin:

'But,' I continued, 'are these maids willing or unwilling parties to the transaction – that is, are they really maiden, not merely in being each a virgo intacta in the physical sense, but *as being chaste girls who are not consenting parties to their seduction?*' ... I heard some strange tales concerning the precautions taken to render escape impossible for the girl whose ruin, *with or without her consent*, has been resolved upon. (1885, Part 1: 3, 7; emphasis added)

Stead's entire text is structured around the concern with female goodness and virtue and the lack thereof. Except for Stead himself, men play minor (if crucial) roles in the melodrama – they are abstract representations of the ruling class and one-dimensional, pantomime villains. Stead pits female sin against female goodness. The sinners are evil procuresses and drunken mothers, the sinned against maidens becoming the sinning almost as soon as they fall, as they lose both their most valuable commodity and their shame (shyness and shame associated with having a hymen, brazenness with losing it). Yet the text undermines itself, as both the innocent victims and brazen harlots refuse to stick to their allocated (melodramatic) roles, emerging, despite Stead's overt framings – as three-dimensional figures with compli-cated relations to, and opinions about, the meaning of consent and the value of virtue. Side by side with lurid accounts of the debauching of virgins are matter-of-fact stories by prostitutes. Despite Stead's efforts to write these stories into his melodrama, their meaning spills over the narrative con-straints of his melodrama, producing an 'unstable text and a contradictory, obsessive discourse around sexuality' (Walkowitz 1992: 85).

Stead records his conversation with a fourteen-year-old girl whom he had arranged to purchase from the 'firm' of 'Madame X and Z'. The girl had been approached by 'Madame X' and had agreed to meet Stead and allow him to arrange a 'seduction' with a 'gentleman' for a certain sum.

But the girl was quite incapable of forming any calculation as to the conse-quences of her own action. This will appear from the following conversation.

'Now,' said I, 'if you are seduced you will get £2 for yourself; but you will lose your maidenhood; you will do wrong, your character will be gone, and you may have a baby which it will cost all your wages to keep. Now I will give you £1 if you will not be seduced; which will you have?' 'Please sir,' she said, 'I will be seduced.' 'And face the pain, and the wrong-doing, and the shame, and the possible ruin and ending your days on the streets, all for the difference of one pound?' 'Yes, sir,' and she burst into tears, 'we are so poor.' Could any proof be more conclusive as to the absolute inability of this girl of sixteen to form an estimate of the value of the only commodity with which the law considers her amply able to deal the day after she is thirteen? (1885, Part 3: 6)

Stead picks out for special vituperation the women who lead girls astray:

There are no subterfuges too cunning or too daring for them to resort to in the pursuit of their game … Every brothel-keeper worth her salt is a procuress with her eyes constantly on the look-out for likely girls, and she is quite as busy *weaving toils in which to ensnare fresh women* as she is to command fresh customers. When a keeper has spotted a girl whom she fancies will be 'a good mark' she – *for in most cases the creature is of the feminine gender* – sets to work to secure her for her service. (1885, Part 1: 7; Part 2: 2, emphasis added)

However, just as in his interviews with prostitutes, his conversations with the 'evil procuresses' Madames X and Z can also be read differently (and not just because we have twenty-first-century eyes). While their matter-of-fact attitude towards the monetary worth of virginity and their contempt for 'silly girls' who 'make a fuss' when it is so much easier to remain quiet and get the money are not exactly overwhelming in their compassion or empathy, neither are they the purely evil machinations of the hunters for sacrificial victims.

Just how were Stead and his public to distinguish between white slaves and venal whores? One marker of the purity deserving of pity was youth: the younger the victim, the more likely it would be that she was as yet untainted by venality or by destructive female sexuality. The victims in Stead's accounts were all young, often prepubescent. As Walkowitz remarks: 'Because of their extreme youthfulness and inexperience, Stead's violated maids lacked the practical resources of Butler's prostitutes; as prepubescent, they were devoid of the sexual agency that might threaten the ascendancy of male desire' (1992: 84). Yet the purity of the girl-victim proves as impossible to guard in the narrative itself as in Stead's version of the evil city: her status as pure, blameless victim remains ambivalent.[28]

CONTRACT, CONSENT AND CLASS

In keeping with melodramatic convention, the narrative of 'The Maiden Tribute of Modern Bablylon' centres around the figure of the young, innocent 'girl of the people', who is the helpless victim of the depraved sexual appetites of aristocratic roués.[29] According to Walkowitz, this form reflected melodrama's traditional role as an expression of working-class desire and frustration, 'a form that allowed the weak to speak out and gain agency in their own defense' (1992: 85). She explains that Stead's intent with the *Pall Mall Gazette*, and especially with 'The Maiden Tribute of Modern Babylon', was to expand the public sphere of debate to include the working class. Melodramatic narrative had an essential role to play. Newspapers were already 'incorporating narrative codes of popular literature, organized around themes of sex and crime ... in the process, these newspapers linked sexual concerns to national and class concerns' (Walkowitz 1992: 84).

Stead argues that a girl between the ages of thirteen and sixteen is in danger of losing her most valuable asset through the inability to be fully appreciative of its value:

> The moment a child is thirteen she is a woman in the eye of the law, with absolute right to dispose of her person to any one who by force or fraud can bully or cajole her into parting with her virtue. It is the one thing in the whole world which, if once lost, can never be recovered, it is the most precious thing a woman ever has, but while the law forbids her absolutely to dispose of any other valuables until she is sixteen, it insists upon investing her with unfettered freedom to sell her person at thirteen. (1885, Part 2: 1)

In his text, the ability of a woman to consent to sex is explicitly linked to class relations.

> If the daughters of the people must be served up as dainty morsels to minister to the passions of the rich, let them at least attain an age when they can understand the nature of the sacrifice which they are asked to make ... That is surely not too much to ask from the dissolute rich. Even considerations of self-interest might lead our rulers to assent to so modest a demand. For the hour of Democracy has struck, and there is no wrong which a man resents like this ... But the fathers and brothers whose daughters and sisters are purchased like slaves, not for labour, but for lust, are now at last enrolled among the governing classes – a circumstance full of hope for the nation, but by no means without menace for a class ... unless the levying of the maiden-tribute in London is shorn of its worst abuses ... resentment, which might be appeased by reform, may hereafter be the virus of a social revolution. It is the one explosive which is strong enough to wreck the Throne. (1885, Part 1: 2).

Women's consent becomes the sword of revolution, the rallying cry of republicanism. Stead's pleas for 'consensual' sexual relations to be left alone by the state also involve a vision of the state, a democratic state, actually built upon the ire of the working class at the misappropriation of women's consent. From free-market bargaining chip, to a republican threat to the throne, Stead places women's consent as central to the relationship of the citizen to the state.

Empire and race in the construction of white slavery

Discourses of white slavery/prostitution mirrored changes in relationships between men and women and between the classes in Britain. The unwilling, innocent victim and the 'consensual' bringer of chaos were not only constructed through presumed essential differences between the sexual natures of men and women, or through class prejudice. The narratives of white slavery attempt to mark the purity and innocence of the white slave through inscribing her with characteristics symbolic of purity. These symbols, which represented also the meaning of consent, shifted according to the larger discursive context of which it was a part. This discursive framework took in the relations of race and colonialism, as well as those of gender and class. The attempts to police purity – to establish the boundaries of consent – were also attempts to mark and maintain national and racial boundaries, as these boundaries constantly shifted in the politics of empire. 'Real-life' consent may have been fluid and shifting, but the narratives of white slavery attempted to fix and pin down not only gender and class boundaries, but those of nation, colony and 'race' as well.

The intertwining of discourses of white slavery with concerns of empire can be seen in that part of the campaign against white slavery that focused on the international traffic in white slaves. In Stead's narrative, the city was a representational space symbolizing the ruin of innocent girls (and opportunity for wayward ones!) (Walkowitz 1992). This 'ruinous place' in international traffic was located outside the borders of the nation. Most of Stead's account concerns prostitution in London; the last article in the series, however, does deal with 'the foreign traffic', described in typically overwrought fashion:

> Prostitution in England is Purgatory; under the State regulated system which prevails abroad it is Hell. The foreign traffic is the indefinite prolongation of the labyrinth of modern Babylon, with absolute and utter hopelessness of any redemption. When a girl steps over the fatal brink she is at once regarded as fair

game for the slave trader who collects his human 'parcels' in the great central mart of London for transmission to the uttermost ends of the earth. They move from stage to stage, from town to town – bought, exchanged, sold – driven on and ever on like the restless ghosts of the damned, until at last they too sleep 'where the wicked cease from troubling and the weary are at rest'. (1885, Part 4: 7).

Abolitionists were convinced that the system of regulated brothels in Europe and in Latin America were at the root of white slavery. The role of melodrama's villain in this version of the story was a two-hander: split between Jewish and other 'foreign' men as the procurers and panderers (with the occasional 'foreign' woman playing a supporting role) and wealthy European aristocrats, 'Arab sheiks' (Malvery and Willis 1912) and Jews and Latins in Buenos Aires (Coote 1910; Bristow 1982; Guy 1991) alternately playing the part of the client.[30] Donna Guy (1991), in a study of anti-white-slavery activity concerned with the 'traffic' from Britain to Buenos Aires, examines how white slavery discourses drew on and developed ideas that linked female honour to that of the nation:

> the central issue that united anti-white slavery campaigns in Europe and Argentina was the way unacceptable female sexual conduct defined the behaviour of the family, the good citizen, and ultimately national or religious honour ... Rather than reflecting a completely verifiable reality, white slavery was the construction of a set of discourses about family reform, the role of women's work in modernizing societies, and the gendered construction of politics (1991: 35).

The equation of female purity – the ability to withhold consent until marriage – with national pride was used by feminists in their campaigns for suffrage. Consent in sexual terms spilled discursively over bodily boundaries into the political arena: women's lack of sexual passion translated into a higher morality than that of men, a morality which then became the basis for women's participation in empire. In *Burdens of History: British Feminists, Indian Women and Imperial Culture, 1865–1915* (1994), Antoinette Burton has examined, the manner in which Victorian feminists utilized the position of the prostitute in Britain and in colonial India as part of their campaign to prove that English women were fit subjects for political enfranchisement. This was through their supposed specifically gendered ability, based on essentialized feminine characteristics, to identify with suffering, and therefore to represent the sufferers politically.

Victorian feminists' arguments around prostitution were grounded in discourses of slavery (Irwin 1996). According to Burton (1998), the extension of anti-slavery discourses by Victorian feminists beyond their original political context in the early anti-slavery movement points to the importance of 'suffering others' for Victorian feminists in establishing their claim to be included in the body politic.[31] While early campaigns against prostitution made metaphorical use of the slavery trope, with the advent of the anti-white-slavery campaigns slavery became a literal description of the condition of prostitution. 'Slavery', as used by feminist abolitionists, served to demonstrate the need for feminist intervention: 'Ideologies of slavery, whether pro- or anti-, were premised on the notion that the slave, even when capable of resistance, was most often helpless in the face of either natural incapacity or culturally sanctioned constraint' (Burton 1998: 341). The use of 'slavery' by feminist and non-feminist campaigners was extremely powerful: as a site of 'irrefutable injury' it served to demonstrate the need for women's involvement: first in public philanthropy, and later directly in politics (Burton 1998). The purification of the state, these feminists argued, could only be achieved through women's suffrage (Walkowitz 1980).

Narrative, ideology and political effects

The political campaign against white slavery was an attempt to fix the meaning of white slavery, to furnish the empty framework of the melodrama with meaning. The key term in this fixing of meaning was that of consent. Consent can be seen, then, as a 'floating signifier': an empty category whose meaning shifted according to the social demands and the implied vision of the proper social order that accompanied it. If so, it follows that there was no single dominant version of the myth of white slavery, but multiple versions motivated by disparate ideologies.

The image of the prostitute was not fixed by the unwilling white slave: the spectre of chaos, her inverted double, her consenting evil twin, was lurking behind (and sometimes to the fore), leaking in, contaminating her purity, blurring her outlines, confounding all attempts to fix the meaning of white slavery. Campaigns against white slavery were constant attempts to pin down and fix the image of the prostitute – an attempt at closure that was always already thwarted by the image of chaos. Her ghostly presence made it impossible to fix the boundaries between acceptable and unacceptable female sexuality and to establish a point of consent beyond the vagaries of interpretation.

We have seen that within the myth of the unwilling slave, produced and suppressed but never contained by it, was the counter-myth: the woman who consents to sex and thus brings about her own ruin as well as threatening the social order. It then follows, contrary to the emphasis in historical approaches such as those of Grittner (1990), Connelly (1980) and Haag (1999), that it is not in the monomythic image of the prostitute as white slave/victim that the production and contestation of meanings is to be found. In the attempts to define white slavery it was not only the white slave who was constructed, but also the prostitute, the one who consented to her own fall. The presence of the white slave finds echoes down the centuries in the halls of the UN in Vienna. Chapter 5 takes up the trope of absences/disappearances in Vienna, showing the uncanny mirroring effects of current trafficking discourses, both in their textual and in their material forms. Before turning to the present-day manifestations of the ghost of the white slave, however, it is necessary to examine another significant aspect of myth: its function as metaphor. Chapter 3 turns to the production of the white slave myth in the USA, exploring the ways in which white slavery could be seen as a metaphor for social anxieties produced by contemporary changes in American society.

Unless we make energetic and successful war upon the red light districts and all that pertains to them, we shall have Oriental brothel slavery thrust upon us from China and Japan, and Parisian white slavery, with all its unnatural and abominable practices, established among us by the French traders. Jew traders, too, will people our 'levees' with Polish Jewesses and any others who will make money for them. Shall we defend our American civilization, or lower our flag to the most despicable foreigners – French, Irish, Italians, Jews and Mongolians? We do not speak against them for their nationality, but for their crimes ... On the Pacific Coast eternal vigilance alone can save us from a flood of Asiaticism, with its weak womanhood, its regimen of scant chivalry, its polluting vices and its brothel slavery ... On both coasts and throughout all our cities, only an awakening of the whole Christian conscience and intelligence can save us from the importation of Parisian and Polish pollution, which is already corrupting the manhood and youth of every large city in this nation. (Bell 1910b: 259)

Metaphor and myth

'Metaphor' is a term used by a number of white slavery historians to explain the effectiveness of the myth of white slavery. For example, Grittner (1990) and Irwin (1996) both rely on Geertz's notion of metaphor, developed in his 'Ideology as cultural practice'. In this highly influential 1969 essay, Geertz champions the application of literary theory to cultural analysis (a defining feature of structuralism), in particular, the role of metaphor in ideology. Metaphor, argues Geertz, works in ideology because it makes complicated reality intelligible (1969 [1973]). Grittner's exploration of the metaphorical meanings of white slavery combines this interpretation with Connelly's (1980) psycho-social approach. Connelly argues that white slavery, and the larger movement to eliminate prostitution of which it was a part, reflected American social angst: 'The central argument [of Connelly's book] is that antiprostitution had at least as much to do with the anxieties produced by the transformation of American society occurring in the progressive era as with the actual existence of red-light districts' (1980: 6).

These approaches are valuable in that they move our attention from a misguided search for the 'facts' of white slavery to an exploration of the function of the myth of white slavery in society. However, there are a number of problems with the 'myth as metaphor' approach, which are not dealt with by white slavery historians in their appropriation of the conceptual apparatus of myth and metaphor. By pointing out these problems, I do not mean that the metaphor approach should be discarded. These analyses point to the need for more careful attention to the relationship between metaphor and myth, to allow the idea of the white slave as a symbol and the myth of white slavery as metaphor to retain analytical value; in particular when applying these to trafficking in women.

First, the correspondence between the metaphor and the social anxiety that is claimed to have prompted it seems arbitrary.[1] Why would concerns about urbanization, for example, take the form of a myth about white slavery? Wouldn't some other myth have done as well? Why that particular myth, at that particular time? Equally, it is possible to ascribe any number of plausible metaphorical meanings to the myth of white slavery – so the white slave has been argued to symbolize everything from fear of women's sexuality to the growing commercialization of labour.[2] Second, as explored in Chapter 1, these approaches remain rooted in the idea of myth as distortion, of white slavery as mythical because it hid the truth. Third, as Chapter 2 demonstrated, these approaches also fail to account for the instability of the white slavery myth, for the need for the discursive purity of the white slave to be preserved through anxious attempts to place her always on the right side of consent. As Stead's text so clearly shows, female virtue was ever in danger of transforming into vice. The demarcation line of consent had to be vigorously policed (literally), if all women were not to slip into the chthonic, chaotic, inverted underworld of prostitution; invoking the terrifying vision of the community itself inverted, topsy-turvy, the back-to-front morality of carnival come to stay for good.[3]

Finally, there is the simplest but perhaps most serious problem: why dress up practical concerns in symbolic language at all? Why weren't the concerns – with urbanization, immigration, et cetera – addressed directly? Geertz (1969 [1973]) and other proponents of the metaphor approach argue that it is because myth simplifies a complicated reality. But, as Chapter 2 has shown, the myth of white slavery was anything but simple, with a great number of possible meanings and interpretations, and used by a great variety of actors in society. Myth is powerful not because it simplifies reality, but because it carries a vision of how that reality could be.

This point, as well as a more satisfactory account of the nature of the relationship between metaphor and myth, is made clear in Laclau's work on metaphor and ideology, as explored in Chapter 1. Myth, as set out by Laclau in *New Reflections on the Revolution of Our Time* (1990), *is* metaphor: the 'metaphor for an absent fullness' (Torfing 1999: 115), the fullness of the community. Applying Laclau's framework to the notion of metaphor used by Connelly and Grittner enriches our understanding of the term and provides a clearer link between the concepts of myth and metaphor. In 'The Death and Resurrection of the Theory of Ideology' (1997) Laclau applies Derrida's deconstruction to the notion of 'community': community is both impossible and necessary. Impossible, because all of the certainties and fixed characteristics that make up a 'community' can only be understood in relation to a 'constitutive outside'. For Laclau, community only exists in relation to what doesn't belong to it, an idea made familiar by Said's (1976) concept of 'the Other'. The 'impossibility' of community comes about as the community strives for completeness, for closure, for 'fullness' in Laclau's terminology. However, this 'fullness' can never be achieved because community only exists through defining itself against something else. The essence of community is its incompleteness, hence, the 'complete community' is what Laclau calls 'the necessary but impossible object' (1997: 298). The impossible community is a political struggle for hegemony: a conflict between a discursively constructed 'us' and 'them'. At the same time, community is necessary, because humans create and maintain identities through this impossible object. From this paradoxically impossible and necessary space arises myth.

According to Laclau, myth serves a function in the political struggles which define communities: it provides a 'surface of inscription' on which 'dislocations and social demands' can be written (Laclau 1990: 65, 68). At the same time, myth is used by groups in the social struggle to provide a vision of their version of the ideal society, a society in which their 'community' is complete and the threatening 'Other' no longer exists. Myth serves to 'suture' social dislocations through a representation of how society could be (Laclau 1990: 62). So we can see that for Laclau myth operates in two manners: it is both the surface on which social demands are inscribed and at the same time a model of how society should be. This representation of society – the model of the ideal society – is what Laclau terms 'metaphor'.

76

And, like the 'impossible communities' they represent, 'social myths are essentially incomplete: their content is constantly reconstituted and displaced' (Laclau 1990: 63). So Laclau helps us look for meaning in the very contradictions and variations within the myth of white slavery.

This chapter traces the genealogy of the trafficking myth through examining the metaphor of white slavery as it functioned in the US. As a preliminary formulation, I will suggest that in Progressive-era America, the myth of white slavery was a metaphor in which American society struggled to realize itself through discursive constructions of race and gender.

The American anti-white slavery campaign

According to one estimate, over one billion pages on the subject of prostitution were written in the US between 1900 and 1920 (Haag 1999). Forty cities formed so-called 'vice commissions' to investigate the extent of prostitution in their municipalities. White slavery laws were adopted to halt the feared national and international trade in women. The white slave herself became the subject of a huge number of books, articles, plays and sculptures. Across the US, groups were set up to abolish 'the social evil': prostitution. The groups involved in fighting prostitution were varied, and included women's groups, temperance organizations, religious groups and medical associations. These organizations often differed in their ideologies and goals, but were able to unite around one issue: the elimination of prostitution. In their efforts to root out 'the social evil', they were greatly influenced by the British campaign against white slavery. However, while the British experience may have provided a template for activism, there was also a home-grown tradition of purity reform for American campaigners to draw on.

EARLY PURITY

While campaigns against prostitution in the US have a long history, in the early nineteenth century a new approach to prostitution emerged. This approach, according to Connelly, was a result of urbanization, which made prostitution more visible, and was 'influenced ... by evangelical and perfectionist notions of social reform' (Connelly 1980). Groups such as the Women's New York Female Reform Society, founded in 1834, combined evangelical zeal with crusading efforts at social reform, in their attempts to convert prostitutes and close New York City's brothels (Smith-Rosenberg 1985). However, before the American Civil War, prostitution as an issue for social reform was less important than slavery and temperance. In the 1860s and 1870s, concern around prostitution led to a 'purity crusade'. Groups of women, anti-slavery campaigners, religious groups and temperance organizations joined in a fight dedicated to 'the regeneration of American sexual morality' (Connelly 1980: 5). Their main efforts were directed against 'regulationists'. Led mainly by doctors concerned with what was then called venereal disease, inspired by European experiences, they attempted to establish regulation of prostitution in Chicago, St Louis and New York.

By the mid-1880s, the purity agenda had grown to include other issues. Prostitution was still important, but it remained mainly a local issue: 'The suppression of prostitution was one plank in a broad platform of social purity: child rearing, sex and moral education, social hygiene, and temperance were elements of a moral vision that emphasized self-control and moderation' (Grittner 1990: 43). It wasn't until the first decade of the nineteenth century that prostitution was to become a national issue.

MODERNIZATION

Between 1890 and the outbreak of World War One, US society underwent a great transformation, from 'a predominantly rural-minded, decentralized, principally Anglo-Saxon, production-oriented and morally absolutist society to a predominantly urban, centralized, multi-ethnic, consumption-oriented, secular and relativist society' (Connelly 1980: 7). In the 1870s, the US both saw itself as, and actually was, still a nation of farms and small towns. The dominance of agriculture in the economy was challenged by the industrial revolution. 'By the 1880s and 1890s, the structure of American industry had changed dramatically. Centralized, large-scale manufacturing, national markets, giant corporations, finance capitalism, had concentrated economic power in a few cities' (Smith-Rosenberg 1985: 170).

The nature of immigration to the US also changed dramatically between 1890 and 1914, when changes in Europe meant changes in the nature of immigration. Whereas nineteenth-century immigration was mostly from northern Europe and Scandinavia, the new century saw the arrival of increasing numbers from southern Europe, Russia and the Austro-Hungarian empire. Connelly (1980) calls the arrival of 'over thirteen million immigrants' between 1900 and 1914: 'one of the most profound social and demographic transformations in American history' (p. 48). These changes inspired a range of reactions across the spectrum of US politics.

The massive economic and social changes, though in one sense the pride of an America which viewed itself as the most modern of societies, were also in tension with a society that prided itself on its traditional values. As Smith-Rosenberg (1985) colourfully describes it: 'Small-town Americans had become flotsam and jetsam in the ongoing maturation of American capitalism' who viewed the cities as 'Sodoms and Gomorrahs of sexual excess and sybaritic indulgence, Babels of conflicting languages, religions and customs; chaotic, ungovernable, the great cities epitomized the foreign, the unknown, and the dangerous'(pp. 171–2). But it was not only small-towners who experienced a heady mixture of anxiety and the sense of new possibilities afforded by America's modernization. In the cities and suburbs, new political actors emerged whose ideologies combined bold hopes for remedying societal ills with traditional prejudices. Their reforming zeal characterized the first decades of the twentieth century in the United States, which is known as the Progressive era.

PROGRESSIVISM AND PROSTITUTION

The reforming impulse of the Progressive era captured the ambiguities between tradition and progress, fear and fascination, resulting from the rapid social changes in the decades around the turn of the century. Middle-class, educated men and women turned their attention to the plight of the city's working classes and immigrants, tackling a range of issues including housing, delinquency, child labour and women's wages. While the range of organizations and individuals had differing, and even conflicting, ideas about why, how and which situations needed reforming, they had a number of things in common. These included a belief in 'expert' knowledge and the power of statistics, and a new notion of the relationship between the state and the citizen. According to Hobson (1987), this notion had two key elements: first, 'the state had to take a more active role in regulating the social welfare of its citizens' and, second, 'the private and public spheres of activity could not be disentangled' (p. 140).

It was in the context of great social upheaval and the anxiety and hope that these changes brought that prostitution became a nationwide issue of concern. According to Connelly (1990): 'What produced the full-throated alarm of the progressive years was a new evaluation of prostitution's significance ... [D]uring the progressive years ... [prostitution's] inherent capacity to provoke fear and alarm was greatly expanded' (p. 6). It was not all fear and alarm, however: the Progressive rejection of regulation, of the idea of prostitution as 'a necessary evil', embodied a great, hopeful optimism about the possibilities of radical social change. As Hobson (1987) describes it, Progressive views of prostitution involved 'a belief that the state should create a net to catch those fallen outside its protection and should suppress rather than manage the business of prostitution' (p. 140).[4] Prostitution reformers combined Progressive ideals such as improved health and better working and living conditions for the working class with social purity ideals of sexual continence. This led, according to Nicky Roberts, to an equation between poor working/living conditions and immorality (Roberts 1992). Individual prostitutes were also ideal candidates for reformers of all ilks, from conservative religious to feminist activists. Well-meaning but intrusive and restraining on the lives of prostitutes, the reforming activities embodied another formative tension within the Progressive spirit: that between social justice and social control (Hobson 1987).

Here we can plant the first genealogical signpost. The societal changes occurring during the Progressive years in the US were not happening in isolation. While hardly today's so-called 'global village', the world in this period was undergoing a number of disruptions which parallel those of today. These included mass migration, industrialization and, the most significant, the seeds of the disintegration of the old global order of British-dominated colonialism. Historians using the metaphorical approach to white slavery have argued that it was precisely the anxiety produced by these changes that gave the myth its potency and power.

THE WHITE SLAVE AS SYMBOL

The actions led by local purity groups against regulation in cities such as San Francisco, New York and Chicago, were largely successful. However, dedicated as purity campaigners were to abolishing prostitution entirely, the fight against regulation never became a national issue, simply because regulation itself never became a national issue (Hobson 1987). This was largely a consequence of a lack of enthusiasm on the part of doctors. US medical opinion, after some support for regulation, moved towards favouring the suppression of prostitution as the best route to stopping the spread of 'venereal' disease. The issue that sparked national concern was white slavery. However, it is a mistake to see 'white slavery' as a distinct, bounded area within the larger area of concern with prostitution.[5] For campaigners, policy makers and the public, the distinctions between prostitution and white slavery were blurred or nonexistent: for many, white slavery was synonymous with prostitution. (This will be explored further below.)

Nonetheless, it was when prostitution was grasped through the myth of white slavery that it began to resonate with the national conscience. British campaigners' success in whipping up public support for the cause of eliminating prostitution through horrific tales of white slavery inspired American reformers. According to Grittner (1990), 'American efforts to abolish prostitution foundered, but the efforts of British purity leaders to outlaw the practice they defined as "white slavery" soon gave American reformers hope' (p. 43). It was, however, the more sensationalist and repressive elements of the British campaign against white slavery that were to prove more influential in the US. William Stead's 'The Maiden Tribute of Modern Babylon' (1885) was published in the US and was widely read and commented on; Stead himself visited Chicago to meet anti-prostitution campaigners. The 'home grown' US campaign for moral reform, of which the elimination of 'vice' was a chief element, was helped along by British 'social purity' campaigners such as William Coote. In 1911 Coote set up the National Vigilance Association (NVA) with a repressive moral agenda that focused on the sexual behaviour of young people. The NVA was very active in the British campaign against white slavery and, according to Walkowitz (1980), was responsible for the increasingly repressive turn the movement took. Josephine Butler resigned her membership in the NVA in protest. Coote was instrumental in turning the American purity movement's attention to 'the white slave trade'. On a visit to the US in 1906, he led a 'successful campaign' to establish a US version of the NVA (Grittner 1990).

All this activity around white slavery led to a huge outpouring of narrative material. As in Britain, the white slavery narratives in the US took various forms, from books, newspaper articles and reports to films, paintings and sculptures. As in Britain, these representations used a variety of narrative conventions such as crime drama and gothic fiction. Throughout these ran melodrama, in which virtue was pitted against vice in an uncomplicated moral tale (Grittner 1990). As in the present-day accounts of trafficking in the Introduction, the victim's virtue was rhetorically achieved through a number of devices: by stressing the youth of the victim, her whiteness, and her unwillingness to be a prostitute. In line with melodramatic convention, virtue had her counterpart, the evil 'white slave' trader. Like the British version of the white slave myth, the innocent victim was constructed through the ghostly presence of her opposite: the prostitute as symbol of social disorder. However, melodrama's cardboard cast of characters was filled out by particularly American concerns.

Considering this particular historical juncture in terms of Laclau's (1990) formulation of myth, we may say that the social disorder that the myth attempted to suture was caused by the 'dislocation' of US society as a result of changing patterns of work, living and gender, race and class relations. The white slave, in the American symbolic incarnation, stood for more than the loss of sexual innocence. She stood for loss of an entire, disappearing, and imagined 'American way of life': imagined because the notions of gender, race, class, and geography on which this way of life depended were never stable, were never just 'the way things were'. The myth of white slavery was an attempt to reassert the 'fullness of the community' in order to shore up faltering certainties, through naturalization of their ideological suppositions. This will be demonstrated by an examination of some of the key documents and political events that shaped the white slavery debates in the US.

How white was white slavery?

In the US, as in Britain, the campaign against white slavery derived much of its rhetorical strength by presenting its fight as one against slavery: borrowing both the language and the sense of moral outrage generated by anti-slavery activism (Irwin 1996; Burton 1994). Jane Addams begins her 1912 polemic against white slavery, *A New Conscience and an Ancient Evil*, with a chapter entitled 'An Analogy'. The analogies she makes is between 'the social evil' of prostitution and black slavery, and between the work of anti-prostitution groups and that of the American anti-slavery abolitionists:[6]

> Those of us who think we discern the beginnings of a new conscience in regard to this twin of slavery, as old and outrageous as slavery itself and even more persistent, find a possible analogy between certain civic, philanthropic and educational efforts directed against the very existence of this social evil and similar organized efforts which preceded the overthrow of slavery in America. (p. 4)

But reflected through the mirror of the myth of white slavery, anti-slavery abolitionism came to be inverted, twisted and distorted, as white women perversely came to occupy the victimized narrative space formerly occupied by the black slave. Here we can posit a second signpost: contemporary anti-trafficking efforts also use the language of slavery, lending urgency and historical significance to their campaigns. And, like the twisted history of the appropriation of black slavery in white slavery narratives, the present-day twinning of the two has dubious results, explored in Chapter 4.

The white slave in US narratives was both literally and metaphorically white. That is, the young, innocent virgin in the white slavery narratives was most often presented as having white skin (literal meaning). At the same time, her whiteness symbolized her state of unsullied virtue (metaphoric meaning). The symbolic power of whiteness for Americans provided a reading principle (in Laclau's [1997] sense, a recognition that interpellates identity) which was especially potent for white Americans after the dislocations of the Civil War: 'The traditional Western connotation that whiteness equals purity and blackness equals depravity flourished in a myth that appealed to the moral and prurient natures of its audience' (Grittner 1990: 131). In American white slavery narratives, the role of virtue's downfall was very often played by immigrant men and freed male slaves. As 'white slavers', pimps and clients, 'racially other' men were charged with perpetrating a vast immoral network which threatened not only innocent American girlhood, but the very moral fibre of the nation. This was a perverse inversion of the historical reality of black slavery in America, an attempt to reconfigure its horrifying meaning by recasting the sexual violation of white women at the hands of dark men as 'more terrible than any black slavery that ever existed in this or any other country' (Grittner 1990: 74).[7]

Most historians consider the phrase 'white slavery' to be of little significance in racial terms. Hobson (1987), for example, calls white slavery a 'misrepresentation', as the 'real' traffic also involved Asian and African women, or, as she calls it, 'non-white slavery'. This phrase, which has no sort of sexual connotation, or any actual meaning at all, exposes the non-arbitrary nature of the term '*white* slavery'. In another example, Haag (1999) maintains that white slavery was a 'misnomer' because 'white slavery was not an idea focused principally on the enslavement of *white girls*' (p. 69, emphasis added).[8] She argues that a number of anti-white-slavery reformers were also concerned with the traffic in immigrant women. However, the concern with immigrant women did not negate the racial implications of white slavery. As explored below, immigrant women entered the debate on terms which both contested and reiterated racial prejudices. It remains the case that white slavery in the US could only, and did only, take shape through discursive opposition to black slavery. White slavery was an inherently racist discourse.

Prominent anti-white-slavery reformers, such as Roe and Turner, expressly configured their arguments in racial terms.[9] For example, US District Attorney Edwin W. Sims described the crime as follows: 'The white slave trade may be said to be the business of securing white women and of selling them or exploiting them for immoral purposes' (1910a: 14). Sims was highly influential in shaping the public debate on white slavery. The frontispiece of Illinois Vigilance Association secretary Ernest A. Bell's edited compendium on white slavery *Fighting the Traffic in Young Girls, or, War on the White Slave Trade* (Bell 1910b, the origin of the above quote by Sims), has a picture of Sims captioned 'Hon. Edwin W. Sims: The man most feared by all white slave traders'. Along with other Chicago-based activists such as Clifford Roe and Ernest Bell, he led sustained campaigns against 'vice chiefs' (Grittner 1990), and helped draft the 1910 Mann (White Slave Trade) Act (Grittner 1990: 87). He was much admired by prominent women's rights activists such as Jane Addams (Addams 1912). As Chicago's district attorney, he prosecuted the majority of the white slavery cases in Chicago. Thus it could not be said that his views were inconsequential.

The cause of historians' failure to appreciate the racial significance of 'white' in the term 'white slavery' is, I believe, a result of a confusion between the literal and the symbolic meaning of white slavery.[10] The correct approach to assessing the significance of 'white' is not to ascertain, like Hobson (1987), whether this misrepresented reality, or, like Haag (1999), the extent of reformers' concern about immigrant women, but to investigate the symbolic power carried by 'white' when linked to 'slavery' in a sexualized context. Whatever the historical circumstances in which the term 'white slavery' came into being, by the time it was picked up by American purity reformers, 'white' was indelibly attached to 'slavery'.[11] The adjective gave the concept its meaning; it was not simply an anachronistic hanger-on. It is clear from reading the most influential white slavery narratives, such as those of the Chicago reformers, that 'whiteness' was most often explicitly employed to emphasize the horror of the white slave's fate.

FEAR OF EROSION OF RACIAL BOUNDARIES

The myth of white slavery embodied the fear of the erosion of racial boundaries, the fear of the contamination and eventual disintegration of the illusionary 'wholeness' of the community of white America: whether by freed black slaves or 'dark' foreigners. The fear of the freed slaves and desire to preserve racial boundaries between American whites and blacks was highly evident in the writings of prominent anti-white-slave campaigners such as Samuel Painter Wilson. Wilson's writings, according to Grittner (1990), marked the high point of lurid rhetoric among the group of moral reformers who emerged in Chicago in the first decade of the twentieth century. In his 1910 narrative of white slavery in Chicago, *Chicago and Its Cess-Pools of Infamy*, Wilson wrote that compared to white slavers, 'the Congo slave traders of the old days appear like Good Samaritans' (quoted in Grittner 1990: 70) and goes on to describe his experience in Chicago: 'I have heard shrieks and hear cries and groans of agony that have never been surpassed at any public slave auction America has ever witnessed' (quoted in Grittner 1990: 70).

Wilson's narrative presents blacks and foreigners as interrelated threats to American white womanhood. The two played complementary roles:

> Wilson's description of the problem made non-WASPs the source of the greatest sexual danger. If the 'brutal Russian Jewish whoremonger' was a villain, so were the blacks and Chinese who joined white men in the brothels. The image of 'young white girls, huddled in with the worst mob of negroes' gave Wilson his proof that Chicago was fouled by cesspools of immorality. (Grittner 1990: 69)

MYTH OF THE BLACK MAN

The white slave myth also worked through that of another, extremely potent US myth: the black man as brutal and sexually rapacious, as raper of white women (Grittner 1990). The 'social dislocations' of the Civil War and the end of slavery were inscribed in mythical tales of black men lying in wait to rape white women. The real effect of these beliefs was a dramatic rise in the lynching of black men in the US South in the 1890s. According to Martha Hodes (1997), while beliefs in black men's super-potent sexuality and sub-human nature were prevalent (indeed were a cornerstone of slavery), it was not until the ending of slavery threatened the stability of the dividing lines between white and black that the myth of the black rapist became so prevalent, with such horrific consequences. The black man's sexual danger was linked to his political threat to the white community which, as Hodes records, was recognized by anti-lynching campaigners Frederick Douglass and Ida B. Wells. Douglass wrote, 'It is only since the Negro has become a citizen and a voter ... that this charge [of raping white women] has been made' (quoted in Hodes 1997: 6).

As the demise of slavery shook the foundations of white supremacy, 'interracial' sex between black men and white women became the paradigmatic expression of sexual violation. As in Victorian Britain, acceptable sexual behaviour was expressed in terms of consent. Sex between a black man and a white woman became that which by definition could not be consented to (Hodes 1997). In 1911 the sociologist Lester Ward stated in his 'four laws of consent' that, 'The women of any race will vehemently reject the men of a race which they regard as lower than their own' (quoted in Haag 1999: 143). Somewhat strangely, the interworking of racialized discourses of citizenship and sexual consent do not figure in Haag's analysis of white slavery, which is limited to shifting notions of the role of the state in labour contracts. However, it is possible to see from the work of other historians the ways in which the victim, who (crucially) played no part in her own downfall, was inscribed with whiteness. By writing her 'slaver' as black/'dark', any suggestion of complicity in her own fall was removed.

White slavery's racialized nexus of sexual innocence and sexual violation was constructed not only through narrative contrast with black men, but also through unwritten opposition to black women – a point barely touched on by historians of white slavery. The white slave's metaphorical shadow was 'coloured'. In discourses of slavery, black women were differently positioned than white women in relation to a notion of consent. While Christian morality frowned on white male sexual licence, 'rape' as the possible description of a sexual encounter between a white man and a black woman could not be conceptualized. Not only was she barred from considerations of consent because of her nonhuman, 'property' status, but black women's sexual nature was considered voracious, indiscriminate and animalistic. Ward's consent laws had their corollary for a sexual relationship between a black woman and a white man: 'The women of any race will freely accept the men of a race which they regard as higher' (in Haag 1999: 143). For many white Americans, including anti-white-slavery campaigners, it was unthinkable that a black woman would not consent to sex with a white man: how could a black woman become a 'white slave'? The absence of mention of American black women in anti-prostitution campaigns, like the absence of consideration of this gap in historians' account of this time, is notable.[12]

Where champions of reform twisted and turned over what constituted genuine white slavery as opposed to 'willing prostitution', American black women fell outside this consideration altogether. As Gail Pheterson has examined in *The Whore Stigma* (1986), the term 'whore' carries specific racial connotation (as does 'pimp'). By virtue of her literal blackness, in the eyes of much of white America the black woman had no claim to virtue.

White slavery 'worked' as a metaphor because the connotations of 'whiteness' – purity, innocence and virtue – were juxtaposed in a melodramatic framework with its opposite, 'blackness' – impurity, guilt and vice (Geertz 1969 [1973], Grittner 1990). This opposition was both visible and invisible, present and absent: the melodramatic presence of the black villain/'dark' man, whose darkness was also both literal and symbolic; and the supplementary absence of the 'dark' woman, whose 'shadiness' was sexually and racially constructed. Thus the white slave was able to exist mythically precisely because she was not a 'black slave'.

86

BAD GIRLS AND 'BAD NIGGERS': JACK JOHNSON AND THE MANN ACT

The story of the prosecution of Jack Johnson, a black heavyweight boxing world champion, under the US 1910 White Slave Act (Mann Act), is an example of the narrativization of 'race'/sex, in which the shape of the 'innocent white slave' is thrown into relief against the blackness of the boxer. Randy Roberts's *Papa Jack: Jack Johnson and the Era of White Hopes* (1983) documents the trial of Johnson under the Act. Roberts's main argument is that Johnson symbolized the threat of the disorder whites feared from the destabilizing of racial boundaries. During his trial, the melodrama of white slavery was actually performed, as Jack Johnson became the living embodiment of the 'white slaver', whose congress with white women had to be punished.

Jack Johnson was a heavyweight boxer from Galveston, Texas, born in 1878. When Johnson began his career in the 1890s, whites and blacks did not fight against each other in heavyweight matches (though black–white fights in the lower-profile lightweight divisions did occur). Why was this the case? To answer that, we have to look at the racial significance that boxing carried at that time in the US. America's boxing chauvinism reveals how nation and race were linked for many white Americans: the American community was white, thus American superiority meant white superiority. White Americans saw the dominance of white Americans in the boxing ring as evidence of American superiority: it proved that 'in the social Darwinist sense, Americans were the most fit people in the world' (Roberts 1983: 17). Johnson the black fighter possessed American citizenship in name, but he was excluded from the 'real' America, the nation, the community that was white. 'Whites also feared racial unrest in the "unlikely event" that a black fighter should win a fight against a white man' (Roberts 1983).[13] It was not only a win that was feared: even the sight of a black man and a white man on equal footing in a boxing ring was seen as enough to bring down the walls of racial separation (Roberts 1983).

Until 1908, Johnson fought only other black heavyweights or low-profile white heavyweights – 'white fighters so unimportant that they had no reputations to lose to black boxers' (Roberts 1983: 19). Today, when heavyweight boxing is so dominated by black men, it is surprising to find out just how threatening Johnson's ring prowess was to white America. When he won the world championship from white Briton Tommy Burns in 1908, white commentators spoke in apocalyptic tones about the end of Caucasian race dominance. Blacks regarded the victory as a portent of their advance; as the black newspaper the *Richmond Planet* wrote, 'no event in forty years has given more genuine satisfaction to the colored people of this country than has the signal victory of Jack Johnson' (Roberts 1983: 55). For whites and blacks, Johnson was more than a boxer, and boxing was more than a sport: the boxing ring became the place where the 'race war' was fought.

The sense of white doom at the Burns fight was nothing compared to the devastation caused by Johnson's defeat of the 'Great White Hope': former American heavyweight champion of the world John Jeffries. The fight, held in Reno on 4 July 1910, generated intense interest nationwide: Roberts records that 100,000 words of commentary per day were sent from Reno in the pre-fight weeks. 'From the very first, it was advertised as a match of civilization and virtue against savagery and baseness' (1983: 85). The belief among many whites was that 'race relations remained most stable when blacks remained in their clearly defined, circumscribed place and when there was no nonsense about equality' (1983: 110). For whites, a black world champion 'challenged the old notion of the blacks as an inferior race and raised once more the spectre of black rebellion ... Johnson was transformed into a racial symbol that threatened America's social order' (1983: 110–11).

Johnson compounded the 'threat' to white American manhood by 'poaching on' white American women. Johnson had relationships with a number of white women, all prostitutes, one of whom, Lucy, he married in 1910. He was the black man who beats white men in that most masculine of pursuits – heavyweight boxing – and then 'takes his women'. Johnson menaced not only his white opponents in the ring, but white American manhood and the white American nation. Roberts suggests (following Wiggins 1971) that Johnson was an example of what was then called 'the Bad Nigger': 'a black man who chose a different attitude and station from the ones prescribed by white society' (1983: 118). The Bad Nigger was celebrated in African-American folklore, but to white society he represented the subversion of racial order.

Johnson's threat to the moral and social order was not taken lightly by the government. His deliberate flouting of racial boundaries through his marriage was too provocative to let pass. After one failed attempt to bring Johnson to trial for abducting his wife (Lucy was incarcerated for a number of months 'for her own protection'), in 1912 Johnson was brought before a grand jury on white slavery charges regarding a former girlfriend, a white prostitute named Belle. The 1910 Mann Act had been designed to act primarily against domestic white slavery, and forbids the transport of any woman or girl across state lines for 'prostitution, debauchery or any other immoral purpose' (Grittner 1990: 87). Belle, Johnson and a few other prostitutes had travelled together to and from Johnson's fights, living it up in cities including Chicago, New York and Minneapolis. During the trial, the state was unable to prove that Johnson had in any way profited from Belle's prostitution, or that he had 'induced' her to cross state lines. Nonetheless, Johnson was convicted and sentenced to five years in prison.

Roberts argues cogently that the trial was about more than just Johnson's guilt or innocence. Assistant district attorney Parkin, prosecuting, made this clear in his comments after the verdict was passed:

> This verdict ... will go around the world. It is the forerunner of laws to be passed in these United States we may live to see – laws forbidding miscegenation. This negro, in the eyes of many, has been persecuted. Perhaps as an individual he was. But it was his misfortune to be the foremost example of the evil permitting the intermarriage of whites and blacks. (quoted in Roberts 1983: 177, ellipses in Roberts)[14]

Roberts concludes: 'Johnson the symbol had to be punished, even if Johnson the man was technically innocent of violating the Mann Act' (p. 178). In the words of a journalist of the time, Johnson was being 'meted out a terrible punishment for daring to exceed what is considered a Negro's circle of activities' (quoted in Roberts 1983: 178). The Ku Klux Klan (KKK) capitalized on the result of the trial, attempting to stop Jackson from taking part in a boxing match in Indiana because he was a 'white slaver'. They also used fears of 'white slavery' in their recruitment pamphlets (Blee 1992).

If Johnson was the symbol of transgressive black manhood, what did his counterpart in the actually performed melodrama symbolize? This is a question that Roberts does not explore. Both Lucy, Johnson's wife, and Belle, his girlfriend, were prostitutes who had already worked for a number of years before he met them. In the court proceedings it was impossible to portray them as betrayed innocents. This, however, did not matter to the outcome of the trial: Judge Carpenter, in his instructions to the jury, stated: 'The law does not apply solely to innocent girls. It is quite as much an offence against the Mann Act to transport a hardened, lost prostitute as it would be to transport a young girl, a virgin' (quoted in Roberts 1983: 177).

While this is technically true, it is a curious statement for the time, highly out of keeping with the tone of the most strident advocates of the White Slavery Act, who made much of the innocence of the girls, and the deception and violence needed to accomplish their ruin (see Connelly 1980: 128).[15] In most cases, an 'immoral' woman did not have the sympathy of the public, and was not likely to be believed in court. White slavery reformer Charles Nelson Crittenton decried a Missouri law that declared that 'a woman of immoral life was debarred from giving testimony in the courts of that state, as the fact of her immorality prevented her from being a credible witness' (Crittenton 1910: 135).[16] Yet, in the trial, Belle's immorality was rubbed out by the whiteness of her skin. Her whiteness was enough to convince the jury of Johnson's guilt. Though a 'hardened prostitute', she symbolized the purity of white womanhood that needed to be avenged: through Johnson's blackness, she was transformed into a piteous white slave. It is a horrible irony that Johnson, whose parents had been slaves, was himself convicted of being a slaver in the acting out of this perverse melodrama.

That white slavery was the axe that felled Johnson could not be more significant. Progressive reformers had prize fighting down on their list of societal ills, along with drinking, gambling and prostitution; in all these cases high-minded concern with social welfare went hand in hand with repressive moralism. Roberts records that Progressive reformers considered prize fighting to be un-American: 'prize fighting, they argued, was as alien to those [traditional, rural American] values as an illiterate Jewish immigrant from Russia' (1983: 93). Prize fighting was 'an immigrant sport that attracted Irish and Polish Catholics, Russian Jews, and other undesirable sorts'(1983: 93). It is striking how similar these sentiments are to those linking immigration to prostitution through the trope of white slavery. Johnson's role in the melodrama of white slavery illustrates perfectly the fear of disorder expressed in the myth. Johnson himself symbolized many of the anxieties of the Progressive era. He was a symbol squared: all of his attributes and characteristics worked together to amplify the symbolic significance – the black man, the black boxer, the lover of white women – disorder upon chaos upon dissolution and devastation. As Roberts records: 'He embodied the white man's nightmare of racial chaos' (1983: 6).

Immigration and white slavery

Haag (1999) and Hobson (1987) are partially correct in their observations about the concern of campaigners for 'non-white' women involved in the trade. Immigrant women did feature in many campaigns around white slavery. As with other symbolic placings in the myth, the immigrant woman took up an ambiguous, even paradoxical, position. On the one hand, the immigrant woman's plight was seen as the result of the backwardness of her own culture, and the failure of immigrants successfully to adopt or adapt to

American 'civilization'. On the other, the helpless immigrant girl served as a powerful symbol of outrage for campaigners against the low wages and poor living conditions of immigrants. The mythical tide of immigrant prostitution was used both by those who championed the cause of immigrants and those who sought to keep them out.

The changes in immigration to America inspired a range of reactions across the spectrum of US politics. Haag divides these reactions into two principal camps: 'one that espoused a romantic-racial "uplift" of the immigrant to citizenship and another that endorsed the exclusion of "savage" races' (1999: 95): or, an 'assimilationist' and a 'eugenicist' tendency. The official and public reaction to white slavery took shape in conversation with both of these tendencies. These tendencies still prevail in much discussion of migration today, and hence we can put down another signpost here: the supposed threat to the nation by immigrants is one of the most potent aspects of the contemporary trafficking myth.

According to Grittner (1990), vice reform did not really catch fire in the US until the myth of white slavery turned the blame for the country's moral downfall on to a network of immigrants engaged in the traffic in women. 'Muckraking' journalist George Kibbe Turner was a key figure in setting up this interpretive framework, which was judicially fixed in the US Immigration Act of 1910 and the 1910 Mann Act (Connelly 1980; Grittner 1990). In two articles in *McClure's Magazine* (G. K. Turner 1907; 1909) he linked corruption in city politics in Chicago and New York to a network of foreigners, primarily Jews, whose nefarious deals included white slavery. Turner was successful in arousing mass concern for the issue of white slavery through combining it with other Progressive concerns: 'By nimble transpositions Turner placed virtually all aspects of urban corruption and political chicanery that interested middle-class, Progressive reformers in conversation with one another through the interlocutor of white slavery' (Haag 1999: 68).

Anti-semitism was a common theme in anti-white-slavery tracts, reflecting the anti-semitism that was prevalent in the Progressive years. According to Connelly (1980), George Kibbe Turner 'expressed most fully' the anti-semitic outlook, detailing 'the cabalistic machinations of the caftan-cloaked latter-day Shylocks ... without documentation or the mention of sources' (p. 62). His report on Chicago blamed Russian Jews for supplying women for prostitution in that city (Turner 1907). 'Daughters of the Poor', his 1909 article on New York, allegedly uncovered the links between international Jewish white slavery rings and corruption in New York's

Tammany Hall, centre of the Democratic government of the city and a by-word for political corruption. When railing against the spread throughout the country of New York Jewish 'cadets' (young men, connected to Tammany Hall, who supposedly lured young women into white slavery), he evokes with chilling prescience images of insects or rats who needed to be exterminated: 'To-day they are strong in all the greater cities, they swarm at the gateway of the Alaskan frontier at Seattle; they infest the streets and restaurants of Boston; they flock for the winter to New Orleans … they abound in the South and Southwest, and in the mining regions of the West' (1909: 52). This statement plays on the well-known anti-semitic sentiment of the Jew as pollutant, spreading his pestilence from the already corrupt New York throughout the rest of the US. This anti-semitism, 'the myth of a national Jewish conspiracy' (Grittner 1990: 90) was pervasive in the US Immigration Commission Report of 1909 (US Senate 1909), which served as a basis for the 1910 Immigration Act severely restricting immigration to the US.[17]

Grittner (1990) claims that one of the effects of Turner's work was to cement the perception of the immigrant man as the white slaver, with the innocent American woman his helpless victim: 'Native-born women, not immigrant women, were presented as the chief victims. The alien man assumed the role of villain' (p. 63). While my reading of Turner supports Grittner's claim about immigrant men, I disagree about the victims of white slavery. In Turner's anti-Tammanay Hall diatribe, Jewish white slavers, and to a much lesser extent Polish and French traders, preyed nearly exclusively on women of their own nationality or ethnicity: 'The victim of the cadet is usually a young girl of foreign birth, who knows little or nothing of the conditions of American life' (Turner 1909: 49).

BEAUTIFUL, YOUNG AND INNOCENT: POOR LITTLE GIRL IN THE BIG BAD CITY

… white slavery is an existing condition – a system of girl hunting that is national and international in its scope, that … literally consumes thousands of girls – Clean, innocent girls, every year; that … is operated with a cruelty, a barbarism that gives a new meaning to the word fiend; that … is an imminent peril to every girl in the country who has a desire to get into the city and taste its excitements and its pleasures. (Sims 1910a: 5)

Turner was convinced that immigrant Jewish girls from New York were the major source of prostitutes throughout the US:

... the East Side of New York ... which has now grown ... to be the chief recruiting-ground for the so-called white slave trade in the United States, and probably in the world. It can be exploited, of course, because in it lies the newest body of immigrants and the greatest supply of unprotected young girls in the city. (1909: 54)

Others, such as Chicago district attorney Sims, were convinced that the number of foreign girls were a 'mere fraction' of the number of American girls involved in the trade. White slavery narratives, such as those by Sims, are full of dire warnings to parents of the dangers of the city for young, innocent girls – the flower of American womanhood – fresh from the country:

... literally thousands of innocent girls from the country districts are every year entrapped into a life of hopeless slavery and degradation because parents in the country do not understand conditions as they exist and how to protect their daughters from the 'white slave' traders who have reduced the art of ruining young girls to a national and international system. (Sims 1910c: 48)

The fate of the white slave in the city carried metaphorical resonance in a number of directions. As Connelly (1980) describes it, white slavery, the corruption of the innocent American girl, came to symbolize the demise of rural America, all that was 'pure and innocent' in America.[18] In many narratives, the city was portrayed as a place of entrapment – Sims (1910b) describes the dangers of the ice cream parlor:

... a spider's web for her entanglement. This is especially true of those ice cream saloons and fruit stores kept by foreigners ... I believe that there are good grounds for the suspicion that the ice cream parlor, kept by the foreigner in the large country town, is often a recruiting station and a feeder for the 'white slave' traffic (p. 71).

He claims that foreign proprietors of ice cream parlors have a kind of 'free-masonry' among them, so they can 'pass girls along'. Sims concludes that 'the best and the surest way for parents of girls in the country to protect them from the clutches of the "white slaver" is to keep them in the country'. (p. 71)

Connelly (1980) writes that the foreign white slaver 'assumed the role formerly occupied by the Indian' (p. 84) in one of the literary precursors of the American white slavery myth: Indian captivity stories. Connelly argues that, 'This depiction of the white slavers served several functions'; it was psychologically easier to hate someone if they were racially 'other', but on a deeper level, it was the 'projection of native America's deepest sexual fear:

immigrant males possessing the daughters of the land while their men stand unable to help or protect' (p. 85). Sims's use of a 'Little Red Riding Hood' metaphor – 'their warfare upon virtue is as persistent, as calculating, and as unceasing as was the warfare of the wolf upon the unprotected lamb of the pioneer folk in the early days of the Western frontier' (1910b: 68) – exposes its meaning when seen in the light of Connelly's suggestion that the white slave metaphorically represented 'virgin' American territory.[19]

However, while I agree with Connelly in this interpretation, I do feel that it limits the various meanings that the simple melodramatic theme of 'young girl in the big city' had for its various audiences. It was not only American country girls who met fates as 'white slaves: the worse fate that can befall a woman' (Sims 1910b: 68) in the big bad city. Newly arrived immigrant girls were also seen as likely to meet their downfall in the urban mire. The country girl and the newly arrived immigrant shared the narrative characteristics of youth, beauty, innocence, mobility and a lack of parental supervision.

'INNOCENCE LURED, BETRAYED, DESTROYED': (PARADISE LOST)

The stress on the beauty of the victim is a common feature of white slavery narratives. These physical descriptions function both as a mildly salacious stimulant and to provide narrative contrast with the tragic, wasted figure at the end of the tale: as in a fairy tale, goodness is associated with beauty and ugliness with evil and immorality.[20] Sims (1910b) describes a country girl returned home by Ernest A. Bell of the Illinois Vigilance Association:

> They, however, welcomed a very different person from the pretty girl who went out from that home to make her way in the big city. She was pitifully wasted by the life which she had led, and her constitution is so broken down that she cannot reasonably expect many years of life, even under the tenderest care. What is still worse, the fact cannot be denied that her moral fibre is shattered and the work of reclamation must be more than physical. (p. 67)

Bell, with the lush rhetoric common to many white slavery narratives, contributes a story to the same volume:

> These murderous traffickers drink the heart's blood of weeping mothers while they eat the flesh of their daughters, by living and fattening themselves on the destruction of the girls. Disease and debauch quickly blast the beauty of these lovely victims. Cannibals seem almost merciful in comparison with the white slavers, who murder the girls by inches. (1910a: 75)

Often, the beautiful innocent pays with her life: racked with disease (presumably syphilis, but rarely mentioned by name), she decries from her hospital bed her slaver and praises the good reformer who tells her tale.[21] A series of photographs in Bell's *Fighting the Traffic* (Bell 1910b) illustrates perfectly the 'Harlot's Progress' from innocence, through ruin, to death. The captions in the text itself describe the first two photos – 'Daisy at fourteen', above a photo of 'Daisy at seventeen "Young and So Fair"' – with these words underneath: 'The top picture shows a pure, winsome girl of fourteen going to school in a little country town. The bottom one is the same girl who left her home town to take a position in the city. The man she trusted deceived her' (photo next to p. 99). The next photo in the series shows a crop-headed girl in an institutional bed, with the caption: 'Daisy under twenty, dying in the poor-house. Less than three years after leaving her home she was found in the poor-house, forgotten by (sic) and friends, and dying of a loathsome disease' (photo next to p. 146). The next photo shows a funeral carriage on the street: 'Daisy's lonely funeral paid for by charity. The charity nurses took up a subscription and saved her from the potter's field. No flowers. No friends. No relatives. Only the undertaker and his assistants' (photo next to p. 147).

The horror and titillation of white slave narratives was magnified by stressing the youth of the victim. Youth and beauty combined to produce a delectably innocent victim. Bell (1910a) recounts the story of a white slave rescued in Chicago from the 'den' of the 'notorious French trader and his wife, Alphonse and Eva Dufour':

> In this glittering den, with its walls and ceiling of mirrors, was a sweet Russian girl, perhaps sixteen years old, whose fate made my heart bleed. She was of the best Russian type, blonde, of medium height, peach-blossom complexion, roundish, and of exceedingly gentle and loving disposition. (p. 75)

This lingering description links racial stereotypes to beauty and sexual attractiveness, as does Sims (1910b) in his tale of 'a little Italian peasant girl':

> At this time she was about sixteen years old, innocent and rarely attractive for a girl of her class, having the large, handsome eyes, the black hair and the rich olive skin of a typical Italian. (p. 55)

This 'pretty victim's' loss of virtue is paralleled by her violent disfigurement: in an attempt to escape she is slashed with a razor that disfigures her completely so that 'to look upon her is to shudder' (p. 56).

Sims tells the above tale as if he had personally met the girl and heard her story (which would make it impossible to know she was once pretty), a typical narrative device in the white slavery stories, lending authenticity to the melodrama. Even more 'authentic' are the first-person tales from the

'victims' themselves, such as 'A White Slave's Own Story', a letter supposedly written to Ernest A. Bell from a victim of the French traders. The
letter begins with a description of the victims ('Here we were, always from
fifteen to eighteen girls, most of us very young'; p. 77) traces their fate, and
ends with expressions of gratitude to the good men who saved them:

> Some one ought to do his duty and make war on those horrid men. They simply
> take girls for their slaves in all the country. For even if we are weak, some one
> with courage ought to help us not to be persuaded by those men. I am certainly
> glad that all the men are not bad, that some one (sic) takes our part. You can be
> sure that most of the girls are happy that some one came to make us strong. (Bell
> 1910a: 78)

It was by no means only men who lingered on the youth and beauty of
the victim. Florence Mabel Dedrick, a rescue worker in Chicago, wrote:

> One father, not long ago, after some striking warnings, wrote saying he had been
> aroused to inquire after his little girl, her letters had been more and more
> infrequent ... When rescued, it was a girl with a blighted, pitifully wasted life, a
> sad return, indeed, to the old home. Once a pretty pure, innocent girl. I find a
> majority of girls gone astray are from the county towns, villages and hamlets.
> There is need for the small communities to awake. (Dedrick 1910)

THE MINOTAUR'S LABYRINTH

In white slavery narratives, as shown in Chapter 2, the moral geography of
the city was hazardous for the young girl, and the places that might lead to
her irredeemable loss were very numerous. A drawing in *Fighting the Traffic
in Young Girls* (Bell 1910b) shows the door of a dance hall blazing with light,
with a young women poised outside. It is captioned,

> Dangerous amusements – the brilliant entrance to hell itself. Young girls who
> have danced at home a little are attracted by the blazing lights, gaiety and appar-
> ent happiness of the 'dance halls,' which in many instances leads to their down-
> fall. (across from p. 35)

Other 'dangerous amusements' that parents are urged to be continually on
guard against include 'five-cent theaters', amusement parks and 'restaurants
selling wines and liquors where many young girls go as waitresses, which
hold dangers for any girl' (Dedrick 1910: 11) and of course the foreign-run
ice cream parlor and fruit store. Clifford Roe warned that

> ... so many and varied are the ways of procuring girls that it is quite impossible to
> tell all of them ... Schools for manicuring, houses for vapor and electric baths,

large steamboats running between the city and summer resorts, amusement parks, the nickel theaters, the rooms in the depots and stores are all haunts and procuring places for the white slave traders. (1910: 173)

In white slavery stories, the American countryside and the foreign land both figured as a sort of prelapsarian rural idyll, a garden of Eden expulsion from which is guaranteed by the serpent of sexual knowledge. Often, the tales have the 'serpent' himself visiting the garden to tempt the innocent young beauty with the apple of an easy life and pretty clothes. In other tales, such as that of Sims's 'little Italian peasant girl', the tempter is a woman:

A 'fine lady' who wore beautiful clothes came to her where she lived with her parents, made friends with her, told her she was uncommonly pretty (the truth, by the way), and professed a great interest in her.[22] Such flattering attentions from an American lady who wore clothes as fine as those of the Italian nobility could have but one effect on the mind of this simple little peasant girl and on her still simpler parents. Their heads were completely turned and they regarded the 'American lady' with almost adoration. (1910: 54)

In these stories, a complicated tale of American pride and American shame is being told. The 'American lady' is presented in sharp contrast to the backward peasants, and 'free America' is seen as the natural desire of any foreign girl. On the other hand, this innocence is destroyed once it reaches the promised land, as America fails to live up to her promise:

What mockery it is to have in our harbor in New York the statue of Liberty with outstretched arms welcoming the foreign girl to the land of the free! ... What a travesty to wrap the flag of America around our girls and extol virtue and purity, freedom and liberty, and then not raise a hand to protect our own girls who are being procured by white slave traders every day! (Roe 1910: 153)

Other tales of foreign girls in peril focus on the debased cultural practices of other countries, exhorting foreigners to reach American standards and decrying Americans who themselves fail to uphold American values. Even if the immigrant woman in a narrative lacked literal whiteness of skin, she still partook of symbolic whiteness: partially through her childlike sexual innocence, but most significantly by her positioning opposite the 'dark' slave trader.

There is no more depraved class of people in the world than those human vultures who fatten on the shame of innocent young girls. Many of these white slave traders are recruited from the scum of the criminal classes of Europe. And in this lies the revolting side of the situation. On the one hand the victims, pure, innocent, unsuspecting, trusting young girls – not a few of them mere children.

> On the other hand, the white slave trader, low, vile, depraved and cunning – organically a criminal. (Sims 1910a: 16)

The foreign white slave trader is one so foul that he would not hesitate to apprehend and ruin women of his own 'race':

> The immigrant girl is thus exposed to dangers at the very moment when she is least able to defend herself. Such a girl, already bewildered by the change from an old world village to an American city ... Those discouraged and deserted (by lovers) girls become an easy prey for the procurers who have sometimes been in league with their lovers. (Addams 1912: 28)

The discourse of the oppression of immigrant women by immigrant men was linked to notions of citizenship in narratives of immigrant prostitution and concurrent concerns about fraudulent, 'forced' marriage (Haag 1999). Tales of sexual coercion involving men and women of the same 'lower race', reaffirmed the superior morals of the white American, *national* community.

Feminism and white slavery in the US

As in Britain, in the US at the turn of the twentieth century, certain feminists were a major force in the campaigns against prostitution, including in anti-white slavery campaigns. These feminists, too, took up the anti-corruption line in campaigns against prostitution and campaigns for political enfranchisement. In the US as in Britain, female sexual purity was translated into a higher moral sensibility in all things, including politics. Women's 'good housekeeping' was needed to clean up the corruption in city, state and national government. Paradoxically, women's entry into the public sphere was predicated on the presumed moral conditions that kept her confined to home and hearth in the first place (Elshtain 1974).

A number of feminists concerned with prostitution in the US displayed the same ambiguous relationship to the figure of the prostitute as did many British and Continental feminists. A curious phrase from the inaugural resolution of the New York Female Moral Reform Society, one of the first female anti-vice societies, and dedicated to converting prostitutes and closing brothels in New York City, encapsulates this ambivalence: 'Resolved, That the licentious man is no less guilty than his victim' (Smith-Rosenberg 1985: 112). The notion of a 'guilty victim', oxymoronic as it may sound to our ears, expresses perfectly how these feminists (and others) struggled to harmonize their moral impulse to condemn a woman's loss of virtue with sympathy for her fall, as well as a desire to make men share the guilt. The ambiguities in this feminist relationship to prostitutes reflected tensions in Progressive ideology itself. Certain feminist desires to protect vulnerable girls – primarily working-class and immigrant girls – took shape through a disciplinary desire to control 'wild' tendencies. Desire to achieve equality for women partook of notions of women's moral superiority. The work of women's groups and prominent female campaigners highlights most starkly the contradictory tendencies in anti-white slavery campaigns. These ambiguities in the feminist response to prostitution persist in present-day anti-trafficking efforts, with feminists' calls for protection of young women often voiced in terms of disciplinary actions (explored in Chapter 4).

This ambiguity is clearly illustrated in the work of the notable US feminist campaigner Jane Addams. In her 1912 book on white slavery, *A New Conscience and an Ancient Evil*, Addams argues forcefully against police harassment of prostitutes and for improved wages for working women. While she relates with heart-rending pathos the stories of poor girls whose only hope of feeding their families is by giving in to the blandishments of wicked men, she is scornful and dismissive of those girls who would contemplate selling their virtue in slightly less desperate circumstances:

> Although economic pressure as a reason for entering an illicit life has thus been brought out in court by the evidence in a surprising number of cases, there is no doubt that it is often exaggerated; a girl always prefers to think that economic pressure is the reason for her downfall, even when the immediate causes have been her love of pleasure, her desire for finery, or the influence of evil companions. (pp. 47, 60)

According to Addams, these moral failings supposedly made young working-class and immigrant girls 'easy prey' for white slavers. What is certain is that belief in these girls' innate moral weakness made them the ideal target for the reforming impulses of certain middle-class feminists.

In Chapter 2, following Walkowitz (1992), I described how Josephine Butler cast herself as the loving and castigating Christian mother in the feminist melodrama of white slavery. American 'rescue work' in prostitution was historically both Christian and female: ' "women ministering to women" was one of the few fitting activities for women in the Church' (Smith-Rosenberg 1985: 72). In their writings, American Christian women tended to allocate themselves roles as melodramatic heroines, gently but firmly taming the wild chaotic girl to adopt the meek and grateful posture befitting her age and sex (Smith-Rosenberg 1985). A common referent in American white slavery narratives, but especially those written by women, is the Mother: her failure to protect her daughter must be compensated for by the intervention of mother-figure rescue workers. This is illustrated in a story by the Chicago rescue missionary Florence Mabel Dedrick:

> The danger begins the moment a girl leaves the protection of Home and Mother. One of these dangers, and the one that seems to be well nigh impossible for parents to realize, is the fact that there are watchers or agents, who may be either men or women, at our steamboat landings, railroad stations, everywhere, who seek attractive girls evidently unused to city ways, try to make their acquaintance, using inducements and deception of every conceivable kind, offers of helpfulness, showing her every kindness. I remember so well one dear girl whom I found in Cook country Hospital, brought there from a brothel, sold, led away, deceived, from another town, on the promise of work, who said to me, 'Every one in Chicago deceives you. No one told me the truth until I met you. You are the first real friend I could trust.' (1910: 109)

Mothers are exhorted to protect their daughters by Ophelia Amigh, Superintendent of the Illinois Training School for Girls:

> As one whose daily duty it is to deal with wayward and fallen girls, as one who has had to dig down into the sordid and revolting details of thousands of these sad cases ... let me say to such mothers: In this day and age of the world no young girl is safe! And all the young girls who are not surrounded by the alert, constant and intelligent protection of those who love them unselfishly are in imminent and deadly peril. And the more beautiful and attractive they are the greater is their peril! (1910: 119)

It is easy to see why anti-prostitution was such a potent symbol for many early feminists and female reformers. What more powerful way of denouncing a range of conditions that affected women, the poor, children and immigrants could there be than by connecting them with prostitution? The prostitute could embody, not just a range of repressive anxieties, but progressive ones as well. Prostitution and the harlot's miserable end represented the ultimate horror that resulted from a range of social ills these feminists were fighting against. What better way to decry the low wages paid to women than with a story of a poor girl lured into degradation with oily promises of an easy life and beautiful clothes? On the one hand, there was the department store – the symbol of the new urban marketplace – with all the consumer goods that young women desired; on the other hand, there was their own low-paid position. What better way to argue against slum living for the poor was there than to link these conditions to prostitution?

100

Jane Addams argued that slum overcrowding broke down the natural modesty of little girls, making it easier for them to go with 'bad men'. What better way to condemn child labour than through the pitiful figure of the sexually enslaved girl child? How better to illustrate the need for the integration of immigrants – or to close borders to them – than through the figure of the naïve immigrant girl tricked by her own countryman into marriage, and then deserted and degraded?

In conversations with racialized discourses of the American nation, white slavery fears fostered a range of feminist positions, some of which advocated eugenicist strategies for achieving racial purity and feminine equality. Feminist-produced white slavery campaigns and narratives never carried simply one message: often, they were 'an uneasy admixture of progressive opinion and eugenicist principle' (Beer and Joslin 1999: 15). Beer and Joslin compare the work of Jane Addams with that of her friend Charlotte Perkins Gilman to illustrate these conflicts in feminist politics.

While Addams's reforming work was concerned with the need to integrate immigrants, and to bring them up to an American standard of morality, Gilman believed that moral purity was linked genetically with race (Gilman 1991). Gilman combined her view of women's role as guardians of the species through the political space of their wombs with a condemnation of the system of women's economic dependence. Gilman's work (as looked at by Beer and Joslin) is a fine illustration of the way in which women created Laclau's necessary but impossible 'fullness of the community' through invocation of the white slavery myth. In Gilman's story 'His Mother' (1981), the standard figures of white slavery enact a eugenics morality play: 'Gilman's message is clear: the body politic will be cleansed of its perversions and distortions if women can refuse complicity in the accepted nexus of duty and sexual dependence and reconfigure it so as put the species above the individual' (Beer and Joslin 1999: 15).

Commercialization: 'the rise of the pimp system'

Hand in hand with beliefs about the rise of the immigrant-controlled 'vice trust' went beliefs in the increased large-scale commercialization of prostitution. This belief was an article of faith in white slavery stories, which is mirrored in today's discourses of 'nets' and 'rings' of immigrant-controlled organized crime: the 'Yakuzas', 'Triads' and mafias. The large-scale commercialization of present-day prostitution is an ideological motif that serves any number of causes: from anti-globalization advocates who

101

point to it as the most egregious example of the excesses of global capitalism, to American hawks who use it to justify America's 'war on terror' (see page 130). These contemporary uses of the mythical mafia are explored in Chapter 4, and their genealogy is examined below.

Hobson (1987) provides a good example of the belief in the increased commercialization of prostitution in the Progressive period. In this, she takes issue with the approach to white slavery as a metaphor, as a 'psychological clearinghouse for a host of social disorders' (p. 140).[23] While citing Connelly as the most 'coherent and subtle' (p. 140) practitioner of this approach, she still indicts him for failing to take sufficient account of campaigners' concern with the 'reality' of prostitution. Hobson's position is that white slavery discourses reflected real changes in the prostitution economy. Chief among these changes, according to Hobson, was the loss of control of the prostitution economy by women, or what she terms 'the rise of the pimp system' (p. 139). What were the characteristics of the 'rise of the pimp system' identified by Hobson? This involved a number of changes, most linked to the assumed growing large-scale commercialization of prostitution. According to this conception, prostitution was becoming 'more rationalized and organized' (p. 139), the role of middlemen was increasing, and there was a 'greater division of labor' which encompassed 'proprietors, pimps, madams, runners, collectors ... doctors, clothing dealers, and professional bondsmen' (p. 139). As a result of this deep commercialization, women were supposedly less able to work independently: 'Whereas in the past prostitutes had had bully boys or lovers who often exploited them, by the turn of the century more and more prostitutes' labor and wages were actively managed by pimps, who in some cases arranged clients or installed women in particular brothels' (p. 143).

Comparing Connelly's (1980) and Hobson's (1987) different interpretations of the matter of 'the rise of the pimp system' is a good way of examining how myths around prostitution can retain their performativity long after the social context in which they were active has changed. It is worthwhile to linger here, for assertions about the growing horrors of pimping are a staple feature of anti-prostitution campaigns to this day. First, Hobson overemphasizes the symbolic dimension in Connelly's view of anti-prostitution. Though Connelly sees anti-prostitution as a metaphoric response to various social anxieties, he does not consider prostitution itself to be a 'red herring': 'The grim reality of the vice districts and of streetwalkers plying their trade along the thoroughfares was the immediate occasion of the progressive concern over prostitution, and this study is in no way

102

intended to minimize that basic truth' (p. 6). Most interesting, however, is that Connelly's 'psychological' approach to a seminal white slavery document, the Chicago Vice Commission Report (1911) exposes the 'rise of the pimp system' as a potent myth in itself.[24]

The increasing control of prostitution by pimps was an essential element, and an article of faith, in anti-prostitution and anti-white slavery campaigns. Connelly (1980) notes the concern with commercialization in the 1911 Chicago Vice Commission report, *The Social Evil in Chicago*: 'The first truth ... is that fact that prostitution in this city is a *Commercialized Business* of large proportions with tremendous profits of more than Fifteen Million Dollars per year, controlled largely by men, not women' (p. 32, emphasis in the original). Clifford Roe argued that 'The power of free enterprise and competition had even reached the vice industry as cheaper sources of supplying women became widespread' (quoted in Grittner 1990: 67). For Connelly, this 'ominous' discovery was a symbol and symptom of other anxieties during the Progressive years: the corruption of the 'evil city', the supposed fear of underground criminal networks controlled by immigrants (vice-trusts) and the social dislocation during the Progressive years caused by the spread of factory labour and the consequent process of reification and alienation.[25]

One key difference between Hobson and Connelly is in their evaluation of source material. Connelly recognizes that 'The voice speaking in *The Social Evil in Chicago* was ... the voice of specific, identifiable, powerful and established groups in Chicago' (1980: 99). He notes that there were no representatives of prostitutes on the commission, the group 'which might have been the most knowledgeable about prostitution in the city ... [it] was, thus, the *official* version of prostitution in Chicago in the early twentieth century. This does not in any sense make it a less important source; it simply makes it a certain kind of source, a qualification of no mean importance'(p. 99, emphasis added). It is precisely this recognition of the location of the authority contained in the commission's report that is missing in Hobson. 'The rise of the pimp system', according to Hobson, 'was documented in nearly every study of prostitution during this period' (1987: 143). But what exactly were the nature of these studies? She relies heavily on the Chicago Vice Commission Report, and her main sources include Clifford Roe, a key member of the Chicago commission, whose manipulation of evidence was so blatant that it was marked even by his contemporaries in the anti-prostitution movement (Connelly 1980). Hobson casts no critical eye on these materials, and as a result, her analysis reflects the assumptions and anxieties of those whose material she uses, rather than a critical evaluation of them.

The lack of critical evaluation is especially striking in light of Hobson's close reading of other 'factual' accounts of the day, such as social workers' and doctors' evaluations of prostitutes, and testifies to the strength of the belief that prostitution is controlled by pimps. While Hobson is most keen to stress the 'real', rather than the symbolic, nature of anti-prostitution campaigns, she nonetheless acknowledges that there was a 'symbolic content' to the campaign, 'particularly in its obsession with the white slave trade ... White slavery as a metaphor captured a prostitute's growing dependence on a manager/pimp and her loss of the freedom to move in and out of prostitution to work part time or seasonally' (1987: 141, 144). In her attempt to re-suture the gap between 'actual conditions in prostitution' and campaigners' concerns over white slavery, however, she takes the 'rise of the pimp system' as the actual real 'event' that white slavery reflected, rather than seeing both the rise of the pimp and the fear of white slavery as two aspects of the same myth.[26]

Metaphor and myth redux

Throughout the above examination of the US genealogy of white slavery, I have signposted the links to today's trafficking debates. I have explored white slavery at such length so that it might become easier to decode the discursive statements that masquerade as descriptions of reality in today's discussions of trafficking. For example, reading that lack of parental protection was a cause of white slavery can help us to see claims about the lack of proper parenting in the Third World as more than simply inaccurate or discriminatory. The purpose of the examination, however, was not only to lay the groundwork for drawing parallels between white slavery and trafficking, but to establish more completely the framework of myth for looking at trafficking, taken up in the following chapters.

The purpose of the first section of this book has been to use theoretical perspectives developed by historians to interrogate current debates; to investigate accounts of white slavery as performatives, as ideology, as myth; and to set out an interpretive framework for understanding trafficking in women. In short, the aim has been to use the past to inform understandings of the present. The second section of this book, which takes the international as the level of analysis for understanding the myth of trafficking in women, will also inform our understanding of the past. This will set up a two-way conversation.

Up to this point, this book has examined the myth of white slavery by looking at its effects at the national level, foregrounding 'narrative' in a look at Britain, and foregrounding 'metaphor' in a look at the US. In this, the book follows the form of the histories of white slavery, which examine the myth in a national context, and explain its appeal, strength and believability through the particular, political/social configurations in each country.[27] So, as we have seen, for the US, Connelly (1980) gives particular explanatory weight to the American Progressive ethos, while Haag (1999) highlights the intermeshing of discourses of sexuality and liberalism. In the UK, Nead (1988) and Walkowitz (1980; 1992) emphasize class, while Burton (1994; 1998) examines the effect of colonialism. Considering that histories of white slavery have chosen in the main to focus on the myth in one country, it would seem at first glance that a major difference between then and now is the international nature of the current discourse. However, it was not only in Britain and the US that the myth flourished. Throughout Europe, in the colonial administrations in Asia, and in Brazil and Argentina, the myth of white slavery mobilized private concern and led to changes in national laws. This transnational concern also produced international organizations and international conventions. Most historians do note that the concern with white slavery went beyond national borders. A number mention the role of private organizations and governments in their country of focus in international action and legislation against the white slave trade. Yet there has been relatively little examination of the myth at a transnational level. The second part of this book looks beyond national borders at international and global social/political conditions that contextualize the myth of trafficking in women.

4 'Prevent, protect and punish'

'The men who consort with vile women lose their respect for all women ... Harlots and their patrons are the worst enemies in every way that good women can have.' (Bell 1910b: 267, 268)

The 'bare bones' of the simple melodramatic tale of feminine virtue destroyed by masculine evil informs narratives and political accounts of trafficking. Yet, as with white slavery, the myth of trafficking is also about much more. It is within the negotiations around the 2000 Trafficking Protocol – where trafficking was defined by both what literally appeared in the text and also, crucially, by what was left out – that the myth reveals its performative power. Demands, inscriptions, and political struggle: all were present in the feminist participation in the Protocol negotiations. Analysis of the negotiations shows myth in action, kinetic and powerful. The 'ideal society' imagined by political actors in the negotiations was represented by the 'trafficking victim'. The subject of the trafficking protocol is a mythical subject, constructed through sexual vulnerability, the vulnerability that creates the mythical female subject of trafficking in women.

Locating the myth

The language of the Protocol, in particular the language concerned with elucidating the crime of trafficking, is in large part taken directly from earlier international agreements on white slavery, as examined below. Thus the Protocol bears the genealogical traces of white slavery in the text of the document itself. Yet while it was clear that the negotiations were a manifestation influenced by the myth of trafficking, I struggled at the beginning of my research to 'locate' the myth in the language of the negotiations. The stories familiar from newspapers and NGO and government reports – the melodramas of innocence lost – were rarely heard or seen during the negotiations.

Combing through hundreds of pages of text-different versions of the Protocol, lobby documents, government statements, and notes of what delegates said both during sessions and in informal conversations with me and other Human Rights Caucus (HRC) lobbyists, I continued to hope I would find at least one example of the trafficking narrative, complete from village to brothel. Newspapers from all over the world were full of these narratives, and hundreds if not thousands could be found in NGO and government reports. Anti-trafficking campaigns were suffused with examples of narrative images: the story revealed in a series of tableaus or in a single image telling the entire tale.

It is here that the clue lies to the location of the myth in the negotiations. When I stopped looking for the complete story, I was finally able to see the myth itself working in the text. I realized that the narrative was indeed present: it appeared, fragmented, out of sequence, disguised in legalese or hidden in human rights language. Myth does not appear whole in the Protocol, but rather in synecdochal splinters, as examined in Chapter 2. Thus a word such as 'consent' or a phrase such as 'sexual exploitation' is able to conjure up the entire corpus of the myth.

Performing narrative

Yet it is not only as narrative that myth was present at the negotiations. Through returning, in the process of writing this book, to persistent problems of methodology in my work, I was able to discover another appearance of the ghost of white slavery. Textual examination can show the presence of myth, but in the process actually works to obscure an understanding of how myth functions. It is only by moving beyond narrative that we can begin to see myth as more than only moving words. My analysis shows that it is not simply that the myth inspired or influenced the negotiations: the entire process of the negotiations in itself formed the myth.

Most scholarly work dedicated to analysing examples of political myths, or bodies of myths, focuses on a given narrative or narratives that are taken as representative of the myth under examination. The newspaper account given at the beginning of the Introduction can be taken as an example of such a narrative. It describes the 'story' of the myth of trafficking.

A narrative analysis locates myth in a specific, usually textual, place. It captures myth and renders it analysable. If, as argued in Chapter 2, narrative is an essential element of myth, then close readings of these narratives must form part of the process of studying any myth. As indicated in Chapter 2, understanding the role of narrative in myth is essential. The benefits of a narrative approach to myth are many: such an approach facilitates understandings of how myths become meaningful, of how myth affects understandings, in recognizing motifs and patterns, as well as enabling comparisons between and among myths, and tracking changes over time.

However, while a study of narrative is essential for any given myth, I believe that it is insufficient. What is lacking? Which aspects of myth does it miss? The answer is found through looking at what the narrative approach *does* to myth: more precisely, where it *places* it. A narrative study of myth necessarily assigns myth a certain location, and this location is also of necessity a material one. How is this so? While discussion of a given myth or myths may take place at a very abstract level (reaching even the level of mathematical representation), these abstract musings are constructed upon a material foundation: mythical matter. As narrative, myth is collected and conveyed in actual, existing, objects that take up space. Narrative locates myth in *things* in artifacts; it gives an archaeological twist to a genealogical study. Mythical narrative is recorded and encountered in the typed words on the pages of a book, report or legislative record; in the tape-recorded words or hand-written notes of interview results; in the tape of a film; the disk of a DVD. From ancient oral tellings to new electronic formats, narrative myth remains material; whether seen or heard, it is through our physical senses that narrative myth becomes known to us.

The study of the narratives of myth is, as already stated, essential to understanding, yet close examination reveals that the core of its usefulness forms at the same time the barrier to a full appreciation/understanding of myth. In a way that recalls the Uncertainty Principle in physics, when myth is materially located, the way myth moves cannot be seen. What is necessary to reveal one aspect of myth, that is the materialization of myth in narrative, is also at the same time the very thing that obscures its performative aspect. In making myth matter, the narrative approach encourages stasis.

I believe that this static approach to myth prevents an understanding of the power of myth. For I began to see that myth was not only words but also actions, that myth not only instigated performance but was in itself performance. Rather than seeing the Trafficking Protocol negotiations as a process influenced by myth, it becomes possible through moving beyond a narrative approach to see the movements of people and things, the dance of the negotiations, as in itself the myth. Thus the actions of lobbyists, of states, the formal sessions and the late strategy meetings, all of these can be considered to form part of the myth of trafficking and can be seen as mythical. My study of the myth of trafficking as it appeared in the negotiations thus consists of two levels of analysis: one, a textual analysis of the Protocol and supporting documents, and, two, an action analysis of the actors involved in the negotiations.

This chapter begins with an exploration of the use of 'consent' in early-twentieth-century anti-white slavery agreements, and then moves to the negotiations around the 2000 Trafficking Protocol. The HRC focused much of its lobby efforts on convincing state delegates of the need for strong human rights protections for trafficking victims. This chapter takes a detailed look at the way delegates responded to the efforts of the HRC, and shows how the Protocol veers between treating the 'trafficked woman' as a victim and as a criminal. I examine how the Coalition Against Trafficking in Women lobby positioned the 'trafficking victim' in their lobby efforts. I argue that the lobby efforts of CATW, while ostensibly seeing the prostitute purely as a victim, actually worked to enhance the treatment by states of the prostitute as a criminal.

Interrupting the innocent victim

Both nationally and internationally, state response to white slavery was configured around the twin figures of the prostitute as chaos bringer and as defiled innocent. The identity that these responses attempted to pin down and fix in law was dominated by the need to define white slavery. The tension between the white slave as innocent victim and as anarchic border crosser became most clear in those arenas in which states attempted to reach agreement with each other over the conditions under which their own nationals would be treated in other countries, and how they would treat other states' nationals.

Wijers and Lin (1997), in their study of trafficking, have used the phrase 'from "coercion" to "even with her consent"' (p. 23) to describe the shift in the way white slavery is defined in international agreements up until World War Two. In 1899, the first international congress of voluntary anti-white slavery organizations took place in London. International regulationist groups, purity groups, prohibitionists and abolitionists met to debate what sort of international measures were needed to end 'white slavery'. This congress called upon states to enter into international agreements to stop the trade. The first international agreement against 'white slavery' was drafted in 1902 in Paris and was signed in 1904 by thirteen states.[1] Largely due to the input of regulationist countries such as France, this *International*

Agreement for the Suppression of the White Slave Trade did not equate 'white slavery' with 'prostitution'. Bristow (1977), in his examination of the development of the international agreements, demonstrates that they were a compromise between countries such as the Netherlands and Germany that had adopted an abolitionist position in response to domestic fears about white slavery, and those such as France that remained regulationist. As he remarks:

> The French always showered the white-slavery movement with attention in order to demonstrate the human face of state regulation ... there was considerable willingness to fulfil the spirit of the agreements. In regulationist countries it was a noncontroversial way to demonstrate a progressive attitude. (pp. 181, 183)

Accordingly, the 1904 agreement only addresses the fraudulent or abusive recruitment of women for prostitution in another country.

This agreement set the tone for two subsequent (supplementary) international agreements. In 1910, the *International Convention for the Suppression of the White Slave Traffic* broadened the scope of the crime to include recruitment for prostitution within national boundaries. According to this convention, a white-slaver was one who:

> to gratify the passions of others, hired, abducted or enticed for immoral purposes, even with her consent, a woman or girl under twenty years of age, or over that age in case of violence, threats, fraud or any compulsion. (1910 International Convention, cited in Derks 2000)

What is notable in this definition is that for 'a woman or girl under twenty', consent was nullified. For women of the majority age of twenty-one, however, force or deception must have been used for the act to be considered 'white slavery'. The 1921 *International Convention to Combat the Traffic in Women and Children*, adopted by the League of Nations, marked the change of language from 'white slavery' to 'traffic in women', as well as including children of both sexes.[2]

It was not until 1933 that an international agreement was drafted that reflected the abolitionist position, that is, that a woman's consent was irrelevant when a 'third party' was involved in recruitment and movement for prostitution. The 1933 *International Convention for the Suppression of the Traffic in Women* condemned all recruitment for prostitution in another country. It obliges states to punish

> Any person who, in order to gratify the passions of another person, procures, entices or leads away, even with her consent, a woman or a girl of full age for

immoral purposes to be carried out in another country (quoted in Wijers and Lin 1997).[3]

If we compare this definition with the one quoted above from the 1910 agreement, we see the significance: 'even with her consent' has shifted. No longer does it serve to mark the distinction between the consensual capacity of children and adults. The definition changes: from 'even with her consent, a woman or girl under twenty years of age' to 'even with her consent, a woman or a girl of full age'.

Yet this agreement only partially adopted the abolitionist position. The phrase 'even with her consent' only applied to international traffic, thus again leaving national regulationist systems intact. This meant that while an adult woman was deemed capable of 'consent' to prostitution within her own country, she could not consent to travel to another country to engage in prostitution. This situation was resolved in the 1949 *UN Convention for the Suppression of the Traffic in Women and the Exploitation of the Prostitution of Others*, which fully enshrined the abolitionist position. In its preamble, this convention states that 'trafficking and the accompanying evil of the traffic in persons for the purpose of prostitution are incompatible with the dignity and worth of the human person and endanger the welfare of the individual, the family and the community'. Wijers and Lin (1997) track the tricky transpositions of consent in the 1949 convention:

> art. 1 of the ... convention obliges State Parties to punish any person who 'to gratify the passions of another':
>
> 1) *Procures, entices or leads away, for purposes of prostitution, another person, even with the consent of that person;*
>
> With this paragraph the previous distinction between international and national 'trafficking' disappears: in both cases now 'trafficking' is punishable even with the consent of the woman concerned. Moreover, in the following articles the scope of the convention is broadened to include the exploitation of prostitution by calling State Parties to punish anyone who:
>
> 2) *Exploits the prostitution of another person, even with the consent of that person;*
>
> 3) *Keeps or manages, or knowingly finances or takes part in the financing of a brothel;*
>
> 4) *Knowingly lets or rents a building or other place or any other part thereof for the purpose of the prostitution of others.* (p. 2, emphasis in original)

The fact that the abolitionist position was not fully enshrined in international law until the furore around white slavery that led to the sequence of international treaties had subsided deserves further examination. Historians are agreed that the international concern with white slavery had all but died out by the start of World War One. According to Roberts (1992), by the time the League of Nations adopted the 1921 convention 'the issue no longer had the power to stir up the populace or the authorities ... The "white slave" myth remained a minor theme of popular melodrama, surfacing in many lurid films, for instance, but it had already done its worst in the hearts and minds of the people' (p. 279).[4]

Why did the 1933 and 1949 conventions extend and then fully embrace the abolitionist position? One reason is that, while public concern about 'white slavery' had died away, state and public concern about prostitution had not. The advent of World War One marked an increase in state repression of prostitution – meaning state repression of prostitutes – throughout Europe and the US as prostitutes were blamed for spreading disease and ruining the morale of the troops (Roberts 1992). Hobson (1987) gives a fascinating and horrifying account of the degree of persecution suffered by prostitutes in the US, who were viewed as a security threat. In the inter-war period, regulationist systems went out of favour as toleration of prostitution decreased.

Yet the question still remains, why did these conventions take an abolitionist position, rather than a prohibitionist one? It is because, as Corbin (1990) argues, prohibitionism and abolitionism were actually closer together than they might appear. Both approaches wanted to get rid of prostitution, and as such were arrayed together against regulationism, which tolerated prostitution. Though abolitionists claimed to absolve the female prostitute from blame, their position, as explored in Chapter 2, was actually ambiguous towards prostitutes, often blaming the prostitute herself for her condition. The repression of prostitutes under abolitionist laws formulated in response to white slavery is well documented, for example by Roberts (1992) and Walkowitz (1980). Many of these laws are still in place, causing extreme hardship for sex workers, and thus are the target of much sex worker activism.

It is also the case that prohibitionists, when campaigning against white slavery, had discovered how useful it was to adopt in their arguments the abolitionist language of 'protecting women' and 'saving women'. Bell referred in florid terms to the 1904 convention as 'The Woman's Charter' (Bell 1910a: 200). With their common desire to see an end to prostitution and their ambiguous attitudes towards prostitutes, abolitionists and prohibitionists formed natural allies in the fight against regulation and white slavery. As we shall see in Chapter 5, they continue to do so in the fight against trafficking.

After the 1949 convention, no new international agreement specifically addressing trafficking appeared until the 2000 Trafficking Protocol.

However, trafficking and prostitution were addressed in an increasing number of UN resolutions, declarations and statements. The abolitionist position continued to hold sway at the international level for more than three decades. An examination of relevant UN instruments shows that in the mid-1980s, however, there was a general (if uneven) shift away from abolitionist mechanisms towards those that recognized the capacity for adult women to consent to sex work (Doezema 1998). This is demonstrated by the adoption of language in these agreements that condemns only 'forced' prostitution, rather than prostitution *per se*. It would seem as if history was circling around itself – at one moment granting adult women consent, at another taking it away. Yet the arguments used to reassign to adult women the capacity for consent to prostitution had shifted subtly under the influence of feminism, sex worker rights movements, and the politics of AIDS. The 'old' regulationist position had as its bedrock the idea that prostitution was 'a necessary evil', and that a certain group of women, who 'consented' to be prostitutes, had to be put under extra state discipline and control. As examined in the Introduction, the 'new' feminist/sex worker position argued that prostitution was a profession, and that women and men who chose prostitution should be recognized as workers and given labour rights.[5] However, while the underlying view of sex work and women's sexuality was radically different in this position, arguments continued to be framed in terms of 'consent'.

The Protocol on Trafficking in Persons: background

The 2000 Protocol to Suppress, Prevent and Punish Trafficking in Persons, Especially Women and Children (the Trafficking Protocol) is a subsidiary treaty or 'optional protocol' to the United Nations Convention on Transnational Organized Crime. The body charged by the UN General Assembly with the task of developing this convention was the UN Centre for International Crime Prevention (also called the Crimes Commission), located in Vienna. The 'main convention' was negotiated during the same period as the Trafficking Protocol. The convention also had two other 'additional instruments', one related to weapons smuggling (the Arms Protocol) and one related to smuggling of migrants (the Smuggling Protocol).[6] The first drafts of the Trafficking Protocol were submitted by the United States and Argentina, which had taken the lead in the development of this instrument.[7]

The negotiations took place between January 1999 and October 2000, with eleven sessions in total. The Trafficking Protocol was discussed at eight of these sessions. Over 100 countries sent delegations to the negotiations. They were also attended by representatives of NGOs, including those in the HRC, and representatives of other UN organizations including the Special Rapporteur on Violence Against Women, the UN High Commissioner for Human Rights, the International Organization for Migration and the International Labour Organization. All sessions were translated into official UN languages using simultaneous interpretation.

The eleven sessions were a mixture of 'formal' and 'informal' meetings. Formal sessions were the place where the main negotiating occurred. NGOs were allowed to attend the formal sessions as observers, make use of the simultaneous translation, and sit in the back of the room while the delegates discussed the instruments. The actual negotiations took place only between state delegations. As with other international treaties, negotiations were aimed at achieving consensus among delegates on the wording of the text, in order that the largest number of states would be able to commit themselves to be bound by the final document. NGOs and representatives of other bodies were given the opportunity to address the sessions with prepared statements, but did not intervene in discussions between delegations.[8] In order to influence the proceedings, NGOs relied on speaking to delegates between sessions and giving them our documents. If NGOs urgently wanted to speak to a delegate while a formal session was taking place, they would hand a delegate a slip of paper with comments written on it, or whisper a suggested intervention in her ear.

The informal sessions were added to the agenda when it became obvious that the time allocated in formal sessions would not be enough to finalize the Protocol, because delegates could not agree on the definition of 'trafficking'. Informal sessions were intended only to clarify the language in the text that was being negotiated, and not to make any substantial revisions to the text. The power to clarify, however, proved to be very influential to the final outcome of the Protocol, as examined in Chapter 5. The addition of informal sessions caused controversy. A number of countries, especially developing countries, objected that they were effectively barred from an important sphere of influence, as these sessions were not translated and involved additional expense to delegates. NGOs were also in a more difficult position: they were not allowed to be present during informal session negotiations, and had to rely on contacts in the halls outside to follow the process and to exert possible influence.

An arena less conducive to melodrama than the ultra-formal context of a UN committee meeting is hard to imagine. At the negotiations, the subject of trafficking could not have been discussed in a more superficially rational, more dry, less apparently mythical way. The use of competing ideologies by feminist lobbies is an example of this, but so are the interactions between state delegations and between state delegations and lobbyists. Nevertheless, fierce ideological battles were waged around the definition of 'trafficking', battles which, when taken as the subject of examination, reveal that trafficking operated as a myth, a performative period piece with the power to shape international law and to transform reality.

The Ad Hoc Committee on the Elaboration of a Convention Against Transnational Crime (set up by the UN Centre for Crime Prevention) meetings began, in 1998: its meetings were were not high on the international political agenda. Unlike other UN meetings, such as the UN Conference on Environment and Development in Rio de Janeiro in 1992, the UN Conference on Women in Beijing in 1995 and the Population and Development Summit in Cairo in 1996, very few NGOs were in attendance. At the first session, in January 1999, there were only the handful of NGOs in the Human Rights Caucus, two delegates from the National Rifle Association in America (there to lobby concerning the Arms Protocol) and one from the International Abolitionist Federation (IAF).

RIGHTS VERSUS CRIME

The most obvious way in which the Protocol bears the genealogical traces of white slavery is in the text of the document itself. The language of the Protocol, in particular the language concerned with elucidating the crime of trafficking, is in large part taken directly from earlier international agreements on white slavery. Both nationally and internationally, state response to white slavery had been configured around the twin figures of the prostitute as chaos bringer and the prostitute as defiled innocent. The Protocol, like previous international legislation, encodes this duality, which is also the formative internal tension of the white slavery myth. The chaos bringer and the innocent victim function as the magnetic poles of the myth, the pull they exert on each other being not magnetism but consent. Without it, the myth would lose its form, its structural integrity, and collapse flat.

This tension was reflected in the Protocol negotiations. As experienced by the Human Rights Caucus, this tension found expression in differences of opinion between states and (certain) NGOs and inter-governmental organizations (IGOs) around who needed protecting from what. Was it the state which needed to protect itself against organized crime or the trafficked person who needed protection from the state against organized crime? Or, as

115

argued by the HRC, was the draft Protocol in fact concerned with 'protecting the state instead of preventing and combating trafficking in persons by protecting the human rights of the persons being trafficked' (HRC, *Recommendations and Commentary*, January 1999: para. 2). In order to make this distinction clearer for delegates, the HRC translated it into the shorthand of a 'human rights approach' versus the 'law enforcement approach'.

THE FAILURE TO ACHIEVE STRONG HUMAN RIGHTS PROTECTIONS

One of the HRC's two main lobby goals was to shift the focus of a Protocol from a law enforcement approach to a human rights approach (the other goal, to ensure a definition of trafficking that was not linked to prostitution, is examined in Chapter 5). However, as state delegations were primarily concerned with organized crime, the HRC needed to find ways in which its arguments for human rights could allay these fears. The HRC did this through making the two positions complementary: stronger human rights protections, it argued, would serve to make prosecutions of traffickers easier. Trafficked persons would be more likely to come forward and to testify in court if they did not themselves fear prosecution and deportation.

The HRC failed in a large part to achieve the goal of strong human rights protections, as the final Protocol to Suppress, Prevent and Punish Trafficking in Persons, Especially Women and Children contains much stronger law enforcement provisions than human rights protections. Why was this so? Ann Jordan, a member of the HRC, wrote a commentary on the Protocol after it was completed in which she explains that the Protocol is weak on human rights protections because the Crimes Commission is a law enforcement rather than a human rights body.[9] According to Jordan, the Crimes Commission was given charge of the instrument because:

> the impetus for developing a new international instrument [on trafficking] arose out of the desire of governments to create a tool to combat the enormous growth of transnational organized crime. Therefore, the drafters created a strong law enforcement tool with comparatively weak language on human rights protections and victim assistance. (2002: 2)

This is certainly a valid argument. However, there is a more profound, more subtle reason that states were reluctant to opt for strong human rights protections for trafficked persons, as advocated by the HRC. Recalling earlier international agreements, we remember that the foreign prostitute was viewed as a moral threat when her migration was determined to be voluntary – as an accomplice of, rather than victim to, the pimps and procurers. Documents such as the US Immigration Report of 1909 – whose section on trafficking was directly inspired by the 1904 Agreement on White Slavery – used graphic, heart-rending stories about young innocent victims and at the same time denounced the threat posed by immigrant prostitutes and their procurers. As Haveman (1998) writes in relation to the Netherlands, Dutch negotiators on bilateral and international agreements on white slavery were preoccupied with the question of how to stem the tide of immoral women. The situation was similar in other European countries, as the white slave collided with the immoral foreign prostitute.

Thus the weakness of protections and the strong law enforcement focus are not new in international approaches to prostitution. They come about because of the schism between the prostitute/white slave/trafficked person as victim and as threat. As in white slavery legislation, foreign prostitutes are seen as both victims and threats to the nation.[10] Or, to put it in terms of the title of the Protocol: who exactly is to be protected, who is to be punished, and what is to be prevented?

THE STATE AND ORGANIZED CRIME

The fear of organized crime on the part of the 'international community' formed the background to the development of the Trafficking Protocol.[11] The perceived transnational nature of the 'criminal networks' demanded a 'transnational' response: for states to join together to fight against what was seen as a cross-border problem. In the view of the HRC, this led to a draft Protocol that was too heavily weighted towards combating organized crime.[12] The HRC argued that:

> combating international trafficking in persons requires a two-fold approach: one, a criminal response (prevent the crime and punish the trafficker) and, two, a human rights response (protect the rights of trafficked persons). As written, the Preamble [to the Protocol] places a disproportionate emphasis upon the criminal response. Prevention, punishment and (human rights) protection must all be given equal weight if the stated objective of halting criminal and human rights abuses of trafficked persons is to be met. (HRC, *Recommendations and Commentary*, January 1999: para. 1)

PROTECTING TRAFFICKED PERSONS: 'THE HUMAN RIGHTS APPROACH'

The HRC called its general philosophy about trafficking 'the human rights approach'. The term and the approach reflect the influence of the Dutch

Foundation Against Trafficking in Women (STV), a feminist anti-trafficking organization begun in the 1980s in Utrecht. This organization was very influential in setting the agenda for anti-trafficking policy in the Netherlands. It was also very active in helping to set up and advise anti-trafficking organizations throughout the world, and was, with the Thai Foundation for Women, a key force behind the establishment of GAATW. The liberal feminist approach to trafficking was based on the distinction between voluntary and forced prostitution, a distinction developed by feminists and sex worker rights organizations, as examined in the Introduction. STV and the Dutch sex worker rights organization, the Red Thread, had an ongoing and generally positive relationship (though not without differences of opinion), which was reflected in the 'human rights approach'. The approach also bore the hallmarks of the Dutch approach to prostitution, which was similarly based on an adult woman's right to choose prostitution as work.[13]

The most comprehensive source for the 'human rights approach' are the 'Human Rights Standards for the Treatment of Trafficked Persons' developed by GAATW (GAATW 1999). The essential elements of this approach are:

- giving the trafficked person the right to temporary residence in the country of destination, regardless of that person's status as a (potential) witness in a criminal trial;
- the provision of safe housing and educational opportunities during the temporary residence;
- the opportunity for residency to become permanent if there are strong chances of reprisals by traffickers or by governments in countries of origin;
- strong protection of trafficked persons during criminal trials against traffickers, such as protection of identity;
- no punishment for crimes committed while being trafficked (such as travelling under false papers or working in prostitution);
- the right of the trafficked person not to be treated solely as a 'victim'; recognition of the agency of trafficked persons, and the obligation to base their treatment not on sympathy or pity but on internationally recognized human rights norms;
- the distinction between 'forced' and 'voluntary' prostitution.

The HRC and the IGOs who argued for a human rights approach to trafficking at the negotiations did not dispute that trafficking was a matter of organized crime.[14] As a statement from the International Labour Organization to the convention delegates stated: 'In recent years, trafficking in persons, particularly in women and children, has considerably increased and has become a major part of transnational activities and organized crime. Coherent action at the international level is needed to respond to this development more effectively' (ILO 1999). A similar position is reflected in submissions by the High Commissioner for Human Rights (UNHCHR), the United Nations Children's Fund (UNICEF) and the IOM (UNHCHR, UNICEF and IOM 2000).

While the HRC philosophy distinguished between the law enforcement approach and the human rights approach, it is not true that the human rights approach rejects the idea of criminal prosecutions altogether. Rather, the two are seen as essential elements of policy against trafficking. Successful prosecutions of traffickers, according to this philosophy, are only possible if the human rights of trafficked persons are respected. In a letter to conference delegates, the HRC expressed this thus: 'Governments need to make a commitment to protect the rights of trafficked persons, particularly if they want victims and their advocates to cooperate with them in prosecutions' (HRC, Letter to Delegates, October 2000). The HRC position was supported by the UNHCHR, UNICEF and the IOM, who argued that protections for trafficked persons in the Protocol were 'unnecessarily restrictive and not in accordance with international human rights laws' (UNHCHR, UNICEF and IOM 2000).

The two sides of the Trafficking Protocol

The original drafts of the Protocol, submitted by the US and Argentina, refer to trafficking in women and children and explicitly link trafficking to prostitution. Before examining the location of the 'victim' and the 'threat' in the language of the Protocol, it is essential to realize that the subject being constructed as a victim or as a threat is both female and a prostitute. The subject remained such throughout the negotiations, despite the best efforts of the HRC and several state delegations to craft a 'neutral' Protocol, that is, one that did not mention the gender of the subject, or the purpose for which they were trafficked (this is examined in Chapter 5).

The Trafficking Protocol lists, as one of its primary purposes, the need to protect the trafficked person. The title of the Protocol includes protection as one of three key terms: 'prevent, protect and punish'. Provisions concerning protections of trafficking victims are detailed in articles 6, 7 and 8. These protections are comprehensive in scope: indeed, most of the protections advocated by the HRC, the UNHCHR, the ILO, the IOM and UNICEF are covered. The main article covering human rights protections is article 6, which contains provisions regarding the protection of the privacy of victims; housing, counselling, and medical and material assistance; employment; and compensation. The article also calls upon states to take the age and gender of victims into account, with particular regard for the 'special needs' of children. Article 7 concerns the victim's right to remain in the destination country, and article 8 deals with the victim's rights in instances of repatriation.

However, while the list of protections is comprehensive, it is also discretionary. Phrases such as 'in appropriate cases and to the extent possible, state parties shall' (article 6:1); 'Each state party shall consider implementing measures' (article 6:2); and 'each party shall consider adopting' (8:1) leave enactment of these provisions entirely at the discretion of the state. In contrast, the provisions dealing with co-operation between law enforcement and immigration officials (article 10), border control (article 11) and the production and control of passports (articles 12 and 13) contain mandatory language such as, 'Each State Party shall adopt' (article 11:2) and 'Each State Party shall take the necessary measures'.[15]

TREATING VICTIMS LIKE CRIMINALS — PROTECTING THE STATE FROM THE PROSTITUTE

When lobbying delegates, the HRC found that many felt that a too-heavy emphasis on human rights protections in the Protocol would detract from its efficacy as a law enforcement document. That states refused to back strong protections reveals the extent to which they viewed prostitutes not just as women and children vulnerable to organized crime, but as themselves threats to the state, accomplices in the webs of organized crime threatening state order. In order to understand this reaction, we can look in more detail at what happened in the negotiations; in particular, how states responded to the HRC demand for strong protections.

The HRC argued that state delegations were confusing trafficking with smuggling. As mentioned previously, negotiations concerning a separate, additional protocol on the smuggling of migrants were also being conducted within the Crimes Commission. This protocol was concerned with illegal border crossing facilitated by 'organized crime'. When possible, members of the HRC also attended discussions of the Smuggling Protocol. Members of the HRC found that many delegates were using the word 'trafficking' when discussing the Smuggling Protocol. When speaking to delegates, it became apparent that many of them were confused about the difference between 'trafficking' and 'smuggling'. It was very important for the aims of the HRC that this difference was clearly understood, as the core of the human rights approach is that trafficked persons were not criminally responsible for their situation.

To delegates, HRC members pointed out that the Trafficking Protocol was in danger of treating the trafficked person (implicitly a prostitute) as an undocumented migrant, rather than the victim of human rights violations. HRC members argued that the articles concerning border controls appeared to deal with the prevention of undocumented migration and thus belonged in the Smuggling Protocol. The crime of trafficking, they pointed out, necessarily involved deception, coercion or debt bondage. Furthermore, the HRC argued that although the Trafficking Protocol recognized that trafficked persons were victims of crimes, it did nothing to ensure that law enforcement officials would treat them as victims rather than criminals. A particularly telling example of the 'fear of the victim' was the use of the term 'rehabilitation' in an early draft of the Protocol, to describe how states should treat 'trafficking victims'.[16] The High Commissioner for Human Rights captures the duality perfectly in her submission to the Crimes Commission: 'the High Commissioner notes that the term "rehabilitation" as used in international legal texts is generally reserved for offenders. The terms ... victim "restitution", "compensation" and "assistance" would be much more appropriate in this context' (UNHCHR 1999, para. 4).

The degree to which the differences between trafficking and smuggling were understood varied between delegates. Just when it seemed that everyone had agreed to use 'smuggling' during discussions of the Smuggling Protocol and had found a way to express the concept in French and Spanish as well as in English, suddenly delegates started using the phrase 'illegal trafficking' again. While the two protocols use different terminology, confusion regarding criminal culpability persists. In an introduction to its work, the International Centre for Crime Prevention – under whose aegis the Trafficking Protocol was negotiated – continues to show a confusion between the terms:

Globalization has provided the environment for a growing internationalization of criminal activities. Multinational criminal syndicates have significantly broadened the range of their operations from drug and arms trafficking to money laundering. Traffickers move as many as 4 million illegal migrants each year generating gross earnings of between 5 and 7 billion US dollars. (www.uncjin.org)

The confusion between trafficking and smuggling is more than linguistic. It indicates the importance of the ideas of who deserves protection and who deserves punishment. The states that were most open to strong protections for trafficked persons included those that were most vociferous in arguing that the Protocol should treat all prostitution as violence against women (or, as the HRC stated it, those who fought to turn the Protocol from 'an anti-trafficking into an anti-prostitution document') (HRC, *Delete the term 'sexual exploitation* June 1999). This apparently contradictory position is explicable if we recall that decades earlier a key factor in deciding just who should be treated as a white slave was the 'innocence', or not, of the victim. The contradiction put HRC lobbyists on a similarly contradictory footing with these state delegations. Belgium and France were two of the states that were strongest in support of human rights protection, but that were most implacable in demanding that the Protocol strongly condemn all prostitution as 'sexual exploitation'.

States' domestic policies on trafficking reveal the practical impact of the rather innocuous-sounding phrases in articles 11, 12 and 13, giving them a familiar, worrying ring to the HRC lobbyists. The provision in article 11 on border controls is particularly ominous: 'States Parties shall strengthen, to the extent possible, such border controls as may be necessary to prevent and detect trafficking in persons' (article 11:1). The UK, for example, was against strong protections for trafficking victims. As observed in the HRC recommendations, the UK reported that it had a border control policy of identifying certain migrant women as 'possible prostitutes' and a deportation policy targeting sex workers for the purpose of preventing trafficking in women (HRC, *Recommendations and Commentary*, December 1999).

During the white slavery era, restricting immigration was seen as a solution to the problem. Today's policies differ little in form or intent. The potential for discrimination in anti-trafficking policies was recognized by the High Commissioner for Human Rights in her note to the Crimes Commission: 'The High Commissioner draws attention to the fact that national anti-trafficking measures have been used in some situations to discriminate against women and other groups in a manner that amounts to a denial of their basic right to leave a country and to migrate legally' (UNHCHR 1999 para. 25). As with white slavery, anti-trafficking measures to protect 'innocent' women are being used to counter the supposed threat to society posed by 'bad' women. Repressive immigration measures enacted to stop 'trafficking' include limiting the number of visas issued to women from 'origin' countries, increased policing of borders, and high penalties for illegal migrants and those who facilitate their entry or stay (Wijers 1998; Pearson 2002).

THE WEST VERSUS THE REST?

The Campaign Against Trafficking in Women (CATW) claims that Western countries, along with the HRC, were pitted against developing countries on the side of CATW (Raymond 1999). It was not, however, as straightforward as that. In terms of the protection provisions, the HRC found strong allies in both 'developing' and 'developed' countries, including Italy and Thailand. In general, however, the richest countries were most resistant to HRC lobbying for obligatory language concerning aid, assistance and protection in the form of residence permits to trafficked persons. They were resistant for two reasons – first, because of the perceived cost of providing aid, but also, more important, because of their fear of encouraging (illegal) migration to their countries. This was most apparent in rich states' reactions around the issue of residence permits, or victims' right to remain in the country to which they were trafficked (article 8).

A conversation with a delegate from a European country provides an example of how the fear of illegal migration and the reluctance to promote strong rights protections were linked. They also show the less-than-ideal nature of some of the HRC lobbying strategies, as well as the connections between consent and protection that will be elaborated on in the next chapter. At the point in the negotiations when this conversation occurred (June 1999), the draft definition of trafficking linked prostitution to trafficking. The HRC was trying to convince delegates that a definition of trafficking that included voluntary prostitution would mean that they would have to spend precious resources on, and give at least temporary residence to, all migrant prostitutes in a country. The delegate was very receptive to this argument.

Here we can see the unsavoury nature of the lobby trade-off. For rich countries, the desire to limit the definition of trafficking to situations of force came, not because their own legal systems treated prostitution as work (except in the cases of the Netherlands, Germany and Australia), but because of the fear of making things 'too attractive' for migrants. The HRC continued to exploit this fear throughout the negotiations. For example, a letter to delegates during the last, most acrimonious round of discussions stated:

> Scarce resources will be diverted from real trafficking cases in order to 'rescue' and enforce 'rehabilitation' of non-coerced migrant sex workers who do not want to be 'rescued' or 'rehabilitated, States will have to pay hundreds of millions of dollars to 'help' voluntary migrant sex workers who do not ask for nor want help or assistance. This will divert funds away from trafficking victims. Voluntary, non-coerced migrant sex workers would be redefined as 'victims' who may be eligible

to receive benefits, such as, appropriate housing information about legal rights, medical, psychological, economic assistance, employment, education, and training opportunities. (HRC, *Letter to Delegates*, October 2000)

A number of developing countries were also reluctant to back mandatory provisions for assistance to trafficked persons. Many developing countries are considered both 'countries of origin' and 'countries of destination' when it comes to trafficking. While countries such as Brazil were, in principle, in favour of strong protections for trafficking victims, they were worried about the cost of providing adequate protection for their own returning nationals, as well as protections for persons trafficked to their countries. An African delegate revealed that he was worried that funds would be inappropriately used because people would lie about being trafficking victims. The HRC was aware of this concern and took it into account when lobbying these countries:

> The other important issue we should all be keeping in focus is the fact that many countries will try to water down protections and give themselves discretion on whether or not to provide protections. We need to keep arguing for the use of mandatory language, with the phrase 'within available means' or 'to the extent possible' inserted in sections where there is a monetary cost to providing the protections. (HRC email-list, 23 May 2000)

Moral panics and boundary crisis

A more detailed examination of the negotiating positions of two countries with whom the HRC had extensive contact, one 'developing' and one 'developed', is helpful in examining how perceptions of the trafficking victim as an undocumented migrant prostitute influenced the negotiations. These countries are the Philippines and the United States. When the negotiations started, a person who had worked very closely with members of the HRC was appointed as a junior member of the Philippines delegation. Though junior, her arguments held a lot of sway within the delegation, as the more senior members were not experts in the field. Accordingly, the Philippines in the first year of negotiations consistently supported strong human rights protections, and seemed willing to go along with a definition of trafficking that did not include prostitution as 'sexual exploitation'.

This all changed when CATW stepped up their lobby efforts near the end of the first year of negotiations (December 1999). CATW has a very strong presence in the Philippines, and one of its leading members was appointed to the delegation, outranking the HRC contact. She swiftly set about reversing the Philippines' position. Whereas the delegates were previously strong on human rights protections, in the second year of negotiations they said little. The main concern of the Philippines delegation had become the reputation of the Philippines. This was the result of a rumour spread in the Philippines legislature and media that the HRC delegate had said that the Philippines wanted prostitution to be legalized. The HRC delegate was denounced in the Philippine Parliament and thrown off the delegation. The Philippines, and other countries that are perceived to have large numbers of women 'trafficked' from them, are intensely worried about their reputations as the suppliers of the brothels of the world (Tyner 1996).[17] Internally, they have responded by making emigration and even travel for their female citizens more difficult.

SEXUAL DANGER

Restriction of women's mobility also occurred during the white slavery era. As shown in Chapters 2 and 3, while the discourse on white slavery ostensibly was about the protection of women from (male) violence, to a large extent the welfare of the 'white slaves' was actually peripheral to the discourse. A supposed threat to women's safety served as a marker of and metaphor for other fears, among them fear of women's growing independence, the breakdown of the family, and loss of national identity through the influx of immigrants.

Grittner, in his analysis of the American myth of white slavery, describes it in terms of a 'moral panic' as defined by the philosopher Stanley Cohen:

> Societies appear to be subject, every now and then, to periods of moral panic. A condition, episode, person or group of persons emerges to become defined as a threat to societal values and interests; its nature is presented in a stylised and stereotypical fashion by the mass media; the moral barricades are manned by editors, bishops, politicians and other right-thinking people; socially accredited experts pronounce their diagnosis and solutions; ways of coping are evolved or (more often) reverted to ... sometimes the panic is passed over and is forgotten, except in folklore and collective memory; at other times it has more serious and long-lasting repercussions and might produce such changes as those in legal and social policy or even in the way society conceives itself. (Cohen 1973: 64)

During the white slavery era, the moral panic was in part provoked by the desire of women for increased independence. As shown in Chapters 2 and 3, accounts of white slavery served as 'cautionary tales' for women and girls (Guy 1991: 6), with a message that sexual peril is the inevitable fate of women who leave the protection of the family. As Guy observes, 'Fears of white slavery in Buenos Aires were directly linked to European disapproval of female migration. Racism, nationalism, and religious bigotry fuelled anxieties. Men could safely travel abroad, but unescorted women faced sexual danger' (1991: 7). The disapproval was linked to insecurities about urbanization and the appeal of city life to single women seeking independence, and the perceived disintegration of family life, exacerbated by rapid processes of industrialization (Bristow 1982; Grittner 1990). During the white slavery panic, leaflets and posters at railway stations were produced to warn girls off venturing abroad or to the city (Coote 1910). Today's efforts are similar. Article 9 of the Trafficking Protocol, concerning the prevention of trafficking, requires states to undertake campaigns to warn potential victims of the dangers of trafficking. As the example of the IOM poster in Chapter 2 shows, these campaigns focus on warning women of the sexual dangers of life away from home and hearth. Videos and pamphlets directed at 'vulnerable' young women portray in graphic detail the likely fate of those who dare to migrate.[18]

The perceptions of sexual danger both to, and of, female migrants permeated the negotiations. The Protocol was not only gendered, but also sexualized. This becomes especially evident when contrasted with the Smuggling Protocol. Both protocols were intended to address the movement of people across borders by international organized crime networks. However, the migrants addressed in the Smuggling Protocol are seen as complicit in the criminal activities covered by the protocol. The subject of the Smuggling Protocol is an undocumented migrant, knowingly engaging the services of smugglers to cross borders illegally. The language of this protocol is gender-neutral, but this very neutrality indicates that the subject of the protocol is implicitly male (see also Ditmore 2002). By contrast, the language of the Trafficking Protocol is gendered, as reflected in its title 'especially women and children'. The subject of the Trafficking Protocol is female.[19] During negotiations around the Trafficking Protocol, delegates continually spoke of 'women and children' being trafficked. On the surface, the genderization of the protocols seems to reflect a simple binary in ideas of agency: trafficked women are assumed to be duped victims, while smuggled men are assumed to be knowing agents in their own movement.

The gender division of the two protocols can then be seen as 'smuggled men' and 'trafficked women'. However, this reading fails to account for the ways in which both men and women can be seen as victims of, or as complicit in, crime. On the one hand, it is true that men are more likely to be narratively inscribed as resourceful and brave for migrating. However, men are also written as 'victims' – though markedly less often. As both Stenvoll (2002) and Chapkis (2003) note, it is not only within discourses of trafficking for prostitution that divisions are made between 'guilty' and 'innocent'. The divisions are made in debates around migrant smuggling, with 'genuine asylum seekers' pitted against 'bogus asylum seekers' or 'economic migrants'.

On the other hand, it is by no means all migrant women who are imagined to possess the characteristics of the victim. As shown in Chapter 2, the myth of white slavery was never 'closed'; as I observed, if innocence was a constantly recurring theme in narratives about white slavery, this was complicated by the continued presence (or the marked absence) of the image of the prostitute as chaos bringer. The female subject of the Trafficking Protocol was not simply considered as only passive or victimized. Here we can see the remanifestation of the ghost of the white slave, in all her ambiguity. As Chapter 2 demonstrated, debates around white slavery were preoccupied with determining who was to be considered a 'real' victim: women who consented to prostitution were certainly deemed capable of agency (as we now understand the term), and condemned for it. Similarly, the inclination to include controlling and possibly repressive measures, such as those examined above, in the Trafficking Protocol, a document ostensibly crafted to protect an innocent, non-culpable victim, reveals an awareness of the possibility of female (criminal) agency. The HRC, backed by IGOs, lobbied that these provisions were misplaced: that any illegal but voluntary migration or border crossing must be considered smuggling and thus dealt with in the appropriate convention. Yet delegates, while on the one hand fully replicating the white slavery victim image in their interventions, on the other remained motivated by her shadow, the whore. Weighted down with the baggage of myth, the sexualized, female subject of the trafficking protocol could not cross over (migrate?) into the 'neutral' space of the Smuggling Protocol.

FEMALE HONOUR, STATE DISHONOUR

If the 'innocent victim' is one of the defining elements of the trafficking myth, what of the women who are not so easily defined as 'innocent'? Next to the young virgin is her counterpart and mirror image, the hardened prostitute. This, too, is familiar from white slavery stories, as I discussed in Chapter 2. Grittner usefully analyses the 'moral panic' around white slavery in terms of the sociologist Kai Ericson's notion of a 'boundary crisis': in times of cultural stress, a community 'draws a "symbolic set of parenthesis" around certain human behaviour, limiting the range of acceptable action' (Erikson 1969 cited in Grittner 1990: 7). According to Grittner, white slavery was part of a larger boundary crisis in America involving 'women, sexuality, and the family' (1990: 8).

The notion of a boundary crisis is particularly pertinent when looking at women and migration. Drawing on her earlier work, Nira Yuval-Davis (1997) analyses the intersections between discourses of nation and gender at five levels: women as biological reproducers of the nation; women's role in the cultural construction of nations; gender relations; citizenship and difference; and the gendered character of the military and of wars. It is at the second level, that of women's role in the cultural construction of nations, that a link can be made between Grittner's (1990) use of the concept of a boundary crisis and constructions of gender–state relations in discourses of white slavery and trafficking in women. According to Yuval-Davis:

> Women especially are often required to carry this 'burden of representation', as they are constructed as the symbolic bearers of collectivities' identity and honour, both personally and collectively … Women, in their 'proper' behaviour, their 'proper' clothing, embody the line which signifies the collectivities' boundaries. (1997: 45–6)

Donna Guy (1991), drawing on the earlier configuration of gender–state relations in Anthias and Yuval-Davis (1989), signals this link as well:

> The central issue that united anti-white slavery campaigns in Europe and Argentina was the way unacceptable female sexual conduct defined the behaviour of the family, the good citizen, and ultimately national or religious honor… Rather than reflecting a completely verifiable reality, white slavery was the construction of a set of discourses about family reform, the role of women's work in modernizing societies, and the gendered construction of politics (1991: 35).

CATW TARGETS CLINTON

What was the situation with the United States? The US was one of the main instigators of the Protocol, submitting the first draft (concurrently with Argentina, who submitted a separate draft) to the Crimes Commission. This draft referred to 'trafficking in women and children' and also listed prostitution as a type of 'sexual exploitation'. Despite this, the US was very receptive to the arguments made by the Human Rights Caucus, in terms both of human rights protections, and of the need for the Protocol to focus on trafficking of all types of labour. Again, as with the Philippines, this changed in the second year. The temperature rose in December 1999, when CATW mounted an aggressive campaign in the US, accusing the Clinton administration of supporting 'legalized prostitution' at the UN. According to Concerned Women for America (a conservative women's organization that supported CATW's lobby efforts):

> Even more discouraging (after the idea of giving out free condoms in Africa since abstinence is the answer to the African AIDS crisis, not condoms) is a new push coming from the White House. The President's Interagency Council on Women, co-chaired by Hillary Clinton, is calling for the adoption of a definition that would make 'voluntary' prostitution a legitimate form of labor. They base this call on the 'need' for women to have control over their own bodies. This immoral policy would not help women. It would only increase the spread of HIV/AIDS, among other problems. Prostitution is degrading. (CWA 2000)

This was also the point at which the US abstinence approach to AIDS-related foreign policy and to trafficking met, examined below.

In coalition with conservative religious groups, CATW was able to put severe pressure on the US delegation. CATW enlisted the notoriously conservative Senator Jesse Helms in the campaign to discredit the US negotiators and to force them to take an anti-prostitution position at the negotiations.[20] The Clinton administration, in particular the President's Interagency Council on Women, took the attack seriously. They responded by issuing a document kit to relevant parties, including the media, NGOs and legislators, clarifying the US position in Vienna.[21] The kit contained a document entitled (interestingly for this BOOK) 'UN Trafficking Treaty: Myths/Facts', which opened by reaffirming the US anti-prostitution position:

> MYTH: The Protocol will legalize prostitution.
> FACT: The Administration opposes prostitution in all its forms. The United States has perhaps the most far-reaching prostitution laws in the world. There are international human rights and humanitarian laws that fight exploitation and prostitution. We will not agree to a treaty that weakens existing prostitution laws here or around the world. (President's Interagency Council on Women 2000)

The prostitution laws in the United States are overwhelmingly prohibitionist – that is, they target the prostitute as well as, or instead of, supposed 'pimps' and 'procurers'. Many of these laws are a direct legacy of the white slavery campaigns. The anti-prostitution position, which was less prevalent in the US delegation when it began negotiating, gradually became more influential.[22] In December 1999, the US delegation to the

Protocol negotiations introduced a recommendation on preventing prostitution and the need to address the 'demand' for prostitutes. But the real significance of the US position, and the feminist campaign to influence it, would not be felt at the negotiations themselves. Its true impact was as the focal point around which coalitions formed that would influence policy making under the Bush administration. These policies cut foreign aid to countries that appeared to 'support' prostitution and refuse HIV/AIDS funding to NGOs and governments that do not take an explicitly anti-prostitution position (see pages 141–3).

ABOLITIONIST FEMINISM AND THE BOON OF TERRORISM

Under the Clinton administration, abolitionist feminists had limited success in their attempts to influence the position of the US delegation (examined in Chapter 5) and, relatedly, the US Trafficking Bill. However, their influence on US policy grew under the Bush administration as they allied themselves with conservative religious groups; these alliances had been formed during the Trafficking Protocol negotiations. Donna Hughes, former director of CATW, used her regular contributions to the far-right *National Review* to denounce sex worker organizations and activists, including the Network of Sex Work Projects (NSWP). The abolitionist feminist campaign against trafficking was given a boost by the 'war on terror'. Hughes's comments on Bush's Iraq speech to the UN (24 September 2003) show support for the linking of trafficking to terrorism:

> At the United Nations, before key world leaders and an international body that symbolizes human rights, President Bush put the fight against the global sex trade on par with the campaign for democracy in Iraq and the war on terrorism. And as he has done with terrorism, he challenged governments around the world on their complacency: If they tolerate the sex trade, they 'are tolerating a form of slavery.' This is the kind of clarity of thinking and leadership the movement against trafficking and sexual exploitation has been waiting for ... All the activists I've heard from were thrilled and inspired by President Bush's speech ... The president's stated commitment to opposing the global sex trade places the US on the forefront of a new movement for human freedom, rights, and dignity. It was fitting that he made this statement alongside a call for democracy building in Iraq and opposition to terrorism. (Hughes 2003)

In a series of 'nimble juxtapositions' (Haag 1999), organized crime is equated to terrorism; is equated to trafficking. This is a particularly good example of what Laclau (1990) calls 'chains of equivalences', a key part of how ideology works. As summarized by Žižek (1994) this is, 'that meaning does not inhere in elements of an ideology as such – these elements, rather, function as "free-floating signifiers" whose meaning is fixed by the mode of their hegemonic articulation' (p. 12). In 'chains of equivalence' concepts become interchangeable, so when one term is mentioned, the entire sequence is evoked. Laclau uses the example of 'democracy' to explain how chains of equivalence give meanings to terms: 'a signifier like "democracy" is essentially ambiguous by dint of its widespread political circulation: it acquires one possible meaning when articulated with "anti-fascism" and a completely different one when articulated with "anti-communism"' (1990: 28).

The link to terrorism, particularly since the terror attacks of 11 September 2001, makes anti-trafficking an essential element of anti-terrorism. The links to terrorism make the trafficking problem seem even more terrifying and the need for immediate action all the more serious. It makes state intervention seem necessary and right, and justifies curtailment of civil liberties in the name of protection. In this sense, the justifications mesh well with the abolitionist desire to discipline through protective legislation, which is exactly what the following quote from the *Jerusalem Post* illustrates:

> Try telling any man who goes to prostitutes for sexual gratification that in so doing he contributes to global terror, organized crime, slavery, and drug trafficking, and the reaction will be one of incredulity. But according to participants in a Mishkenot Sha'ananim sponsored conference on Slavery 2003: Trafficking in Women, the links between trafficking in women, terror, and organized crime are a grim reality. (17 July 2003)

Suffering bodies, protection and *ressentiment*

In contrast to the HRC, the CATW caucus put very little effort into lobbying states to support strong human rights protections. This is not as illogical as it first seems. As explained in Chapter 1, abolitionism is, in Corbin's (1990) terms 'discreetly prohibitionist'. Historically and today, abolitionists promote the 'law enforcement' approach and call for 'state protection' through police involvement. This is a great irony, as Josephine Butler started her abolitionist campaign as a reaction against the police treatment of prostitutes.

There is a second, related reason that abolitionist feminists are willing to support what appear to be conservative, anti-feminist policies against prostitution. While on the one hand motivated by a desire to help victims, they also actually perceive the sex worker as a threat. The effect of their ideology is to neutralize the sex worker by making her disappear. In the abolitionist analysis, there are no sex workers, nor even any prostitutes, only 'prostituted women'. So men and boys also disappear. One way of 'neutralizing' sex workers is by neutering them – by turning them into presumed sexless children. CATW thus lobbied for the retention of the phrase 'women and children' throughout the Protocol.

This collapse of women and children into one group effectively reduces women to the status of children. Objection to this collapse formed a central element of the Human Rights Caucus position in Vienna. The HRC recommendation paper argued:

> Obviously, by definition, no one consents to abduction or forced labour, but an adult woman is able to consent to engage in an illicit activity (such as prostitution, where this is illegal or illegal for migrants). If no one is forcing her to engage in over one's own life and body. Tsuch an activity, then trafficking does not exist ... Additionally, the historical linkage of 'women and children' has proven problematic in multiple ways. The linkage often encompasses the treatment of women as if they are children and denies women the rights attached to adulthood, such as the right to have control he linkage also serves to emphasize a single role for women as caretakers for children and to deny the changing nature of women's role in society, most notably, women's increasing role as the sole supporter of dependent family members and, consequently, as economic migrants in search of work. Nearly half of the migrants today are women. (HRC, *Recommendations and Commentary*, June 1999: para. 16)

The HRC also argued that the phrase 'women and children' failed to account for types of trafficking involving men, stressing that men as well as women could be 'trafficked'. (This was part of their own sleight-of-hand, making 'the prostitute' disappear, dealt with in Chapter 5.)

WHO'S HURTING NOW?

The 'injured body' of the 'trafficking victim' as used by CATW feminists in their campaign against trafficking, and which informed their lobby position in Vienna, serves as a powerful metaphor for advancing certain feminist interests, which cannot be assumed to be those of sex workers themselves. The term 'injured body' is drawn from Wendy Brown's *States of Injury: Power and Freedom in Late Modernity* (1995). In this work, Brown argues that modern identity politics are based on a feeling of 'injury' caused by exclusion from the presumed 'goods' of the modern liberal state.

Brown suggests that politicized identity's potential for transforming structures of domination is severely limited because of its own investment in a history of 'pain'. The 'pain' or 'injury' at the heart of politicized identity is social subordination and exclusion from universal equality and justice promised by the liberal state. This historical pain becomes the foundation for identity, as well as, paradoxically, that which identity politics strives to bring to an end. In other words, identity based on injury cannot let go of that injury without ceasing to exist. This paradox results in a politics that seeks protection from the state, rather than power and freedom for itself. In seeking protection from the same structures that cause injury, this politics risks reaffirming, rather than subverting, structures of domination, and risks reinscribing injured identity in law and policy through its demands for state protection against injury.

According to Brown, politicized identity, including feminism, displays many of the 'attributes of ... *ressentiment*' (1995: 27): the tendency on the part of the powerless to reproach power with moral arguments rather than to seek out power for themselves. The term *ressentiment* is from Nietzsche, developed in *On the Genealogy of Morals* (1887 [1969]). The turn to Nietzsche accounts for Brown's use of terms such as 'pain' and 'injury' to indicate the effects of marginalization and subordination. Nietzsche postulates that the cause of *ressentiment* is 'suffering': this suffering causes the individual to look for a site of blame for the hurt, as well as to revenge itself upon the 'hurter'. Brown describes the 'politics of *ressentiment*' as follows:

> Developing a righteous critique of power from the perspective of the injured, it [the politics of *ressentiment*] delimits a specific site of blame for suffering by constituting sovereign subjects and events as responsible for the 'injury' of social subordination. It fixes the identity of the injured and the injuring as social positions, and codifies as well the meanings of their actions against all possibilities of indeterminacy, ambiguity, and struggle for resignification or repositioning ... the effort to 'outlaw' social injury powerfully legitimizes law and the state as appropriate protectors against injury and casts injured individuals as needing such protection by such protectors. (1995: 27)

INJURED IDENTITIES AND DISAPPEARING SEX WORKERS

The notion of 'injured identities' offers a provocative way to begin to examine how and why, and where, CATW feminists positioned the 'trafficking victim' in their discourse at the negotiations. Brown's (1995) examination of the historical formation of late modern politicized identities places the problematic of 'logics of pain in the subject formation processes' (p. 55) in a central position. This has immediate resonance: CATW's campaign against trafficking in women constantly reiterates the literal, physical pain undergone by 'third world prostitute' bodies. If 'politicized identity's investment ... in its own history of suffering' (Brown 1995: 55) is a constituent element of late modern subject formation, this may help explain why CATW and Barry rely so heavily on the 'suffering' of Third World trafficking victims in their discourses of women's subjugation.

Brown examines the genealogy of late modern political identity formation in North America in terms of the ways in which identities such as those of gender, race or homosexuality are constructed on the basis of perceived historical 'injuries'. CATW's position on the role of prostitution in women's oppression proceeds along the same 'injury/identity' nexus analysed by Brown. In CATW's analysis, women's subordination is the result of sex. Sex is defined as 'the condition of subordination of women that is both bodied in femaleness and enacted in sexual experience' (Barry 1995: 278). For CATW feminists, sex is power: male power over women.

Though CATW's aim is to protect and fight for 'prostituted women', the presence, the existence, of actual sex workers presents difficulties for them. On the one hand, 'prostituted women' who agree with the feminist abolitionist analysis of their situation are accepted and supported. For example, the group WHISPER (Women Hurt in Systems of Prostitution Engaged in Revolt), composed of former prostitutes who campaign for the eradication of prostitution, has a good working relationship with CATW. On the other, there are the vocal and often politically active sex workers around the world who campaign for acceptance of sex work as legitimate work. These present a conundrum for CATW.[23] Convinced that no one could ever choose to work in prostitution, abolitionist feminists are bewildered by self-identified 'sex workers'. The inability to comprehend a self-chosen sex worker identity means that CATW feminists perceive sex worker rights advocates as being in league with 'pimps' and 'traffickers'. At the negotiations a rumour was spread that the Human Rights Caucus was a front for 'the international prostitution mafia'.[24] In a statement quoted in a newspaper article about the Trafficking Protocol, CATW co-director Dorchen Leidthold called the International Human Rights Law Group (one of the organizations that spearheaded the HRC) 'and other organizations that advocate for legalized prostitution "protection rackets for the sex industry"' (Soriano 2000). As NSWP member and HRC lobbyist Melissa Ditmore recounts, several HRC members were referred to in a CATW newsletter as 'pro-prostitution' advocates. Ditmore responded to this by writing: 'This language is akin to the use of the term "pro-abortion" rather than "pro-choice" by activists who seek to ban abortion' (Ditmore 2002: 58).

POWER AND PROSTITUTION

In claiming the 'injured prostitute' as the ontological and epistemological basis of feminist truth, abolitionist feminists foreclose the possibility of political confrontation with sex workers who claim a different experience. It is this move – the insistence that there is one 'truth' about sex workers' experience, and that this truth must be the basis of feminist political action – that reveals abolitionist ideology's investment in *ressentiment*. This moralism serves to obscure the operations of power in CATW's constructions of prostitute experience.

In abolitionist ideology, the subject of the prostitute is constructed partially through the lens of orientalism. Liddle and Rai argue that orientalist power is exercised when 'the author denies the subject the opportunity for self-representation' (1998: 512). While pitied for having to 'actively incorporate dehumanization into [their] identity' (Barry 1995: 70), First World sex worker activists are at the same time held responsible for women's oppression: 'to "embrace" prostitution sex as one's self-chosen identity is to be actively engaged in promoting women's oppression in behalf of oneself' (Barry 1995: 71). Third World sex workers, however, are not even credited with knowing what sex worker rights are all about. Referring to Third World sex workers, CATW founder Kathleen Barry writes: '"Sex work" language has been adopted out of despair, not because these women promote prostitution but because it seems impossible to conceive of any other way to treat prostitute women with dignity and respect than through normalizing their exploitation' (Barry 1995: 296).

However, it is not only Western feminists who treat Third World sex workers as childlike and unable to speak for themselves. Third World anti-trafficking activists can also take a 'matronizing' stance towards sex workers. This was illustrated at the October 2000 meetings, when a spoken intervention by a member of the Philippines delegation who was also a director of CATW 'seemed intended to define prostitutes as children' (Ditmore 2002: 9). The 'suffering body' is not a one-dimensional image whose sole function is to reassure Western feminists of their moral rightness and superiority. She figures in non-Western feminist (and other) discourses as a metaphor for a number of fears, anxieties and relations of domination (Tyner 1996; Cabezas 1998; Pike 1999; Doezema 2000). For example, the figure of the 'suffering Third World prostitute' serves to symbolize the excesses of the global march of capital, and its negative effects on women. To view the campaign against trafficking in women as an example of imposed 'Western feminism' ignores the national/cultural context in which these campaigns are formed. Writing on Nepal, for example, Pike (1999) demonstrates how deeply current anti-trafficking campaigns are embedded in culture and national history. Of course, many Third World feminists reject the image of 'the Third World women as helpless victims of either patriarchy or a crude, undifferentiated capitalism' (Sangera 1998: 1). A number of Third World feminists and sex workers are at the forefront of political efforts to resignify the place of the prostitute in feminist politics (Kapur 2005; Kempadoo and Doezema 1998; Kempadoo 2005; APNSW 2009).

Third World sex workers' organizations reject the abolitionist portrayal of them as deluded and despairing (see Kempadoo and Doezema 1998). Neither is 'sex work language', as Barry implies, a Western concept picked up by ignorant Third World sex workers who are incapable of understanding its ramifications. While the term 'sex work' was coined by Carol Leigh, a Western sex worker (Leigh 1998), its rapid and widespread adoption by sex workers the world over reflects a shared political vision. As Kempadoo (1998a) documents, sex workers in the Third World have a centuries-old history of organizing to demand an end to discriminatory laws and practices. Building on this history, sex worker rights organizations are today flourishing all over the Third World: 'Sex workers' struggles are thus neither a creation of a western prostitutes' rights movement or the privilege of the past three decades' (Kempadoo 1998a: 21).

Third World sex workers have seen through the matronizing attitude of those who would save them for their own good. It is worth quoting at length from the *Sex Workers' Manifesto* (DMSC 1997), produced at the First National Conference of Sex Workers in Calcutta (attended by over 3,000 sex workers):

> Like many other occupations, sex work is also an occupation ... we systematically find ourselves to be targets of moralizing impulses of dominant social groups, through missions of cleansing and sanitizing, both materially and symbolically. If and when we figure in political or developmental agendas, we are enmeshed in discursive practices and practical projects which aim to rescue, rehabilitate, improve, discipline, control or police us. Charity organizations are prone to rescue us and put us in 'safe' homes, developmental organizations are likely to 'rehabilitate' us through meagre income generation activities, and the police seem bent upon to regularly raid our quarters in the name of controlling 'immoral' trafficking. Even when we are inscribed less negatively or even sympathetically within dominant discourses we are not exempt from stigmatization or social exclusion. As powerless, abused victims with no resources, we are seen as objects of pity. (DMSC 1997: 2–3)

MISSING SEX WORKERS

This denial of the legitimacy of the identity of 'sex worker' is the direct and necessary result of CATW's epistemology of sex work. CATW advocates claim to base their analysis on the 'true' experiences of prostitutes. According to Kathleen Barry, sex in prostitution 'reduces women to a body' and is therefore necessarily harmful, whether there is consent or not (1995). Consequently, prostitutes' 'true' stories of pain and injury serve both to demonstrate the rightness of her theory and are claimed as the empirical basis for that theory. The testimonies of prostitutes thus assume the status of absolute truth. However, only certain versions of prostitutes' experience are considered 'true'. Barry constructs the 'injury' of sex in prostitution in a circular manner. Prostitution is considered always injurious because the sex in it is dehumanizing. However, the sex takes on this dehumanizing character because it takes place within prostitution. In this neat, sealed construction, there is no place for the experiences of sex workers who claim their work is not harmful or alienating. For Barry and CATW, the notion of a prostitute who is unharmed by her experience is an ontological impossibility: that which cannot be. This is the ultimate exercise of power: to deny sex workers their very existence, to insist that they cannot be.

In claiming the 'injured prostitute' as the basis of feminist truth, CATW feminists foreclose the possibility of political confrontation with sex workers who claim a different experience, by denying that we even exist. The metaphysical 'disappearance' of the sex worker was echoed by the physical absence of any prostitutes in CATW's lobby group. According to CATW, there are no sex workers, only 'prostituted women'. If 'sex worker' is a fictional (illegitimate) identity created by the international networks of pimps (and supported by governments in their pay), it follows that those of us who adopt this false identity are either deluded or frauds. Prostitution is dehumanizing, and self-identified sex workers, according to CATW, embrace our dehumanization: we thus collude in our own disappearance. There is a hole where the prostitute should stand: a member of CATW recently characterized prostitutes as 'empty holes surrounded by flesh, waiting for a masculine deposit of sperm'.[25] Hoigard and Finstad (1992), whose work is held up by Barry as exemplary, refer to sex workers' vaginas as 'garbage can[s] for hordes of anonymous men's ejaculations' (quoted in Chapkis 1997: 51). Barry herself says that prostitutes become 'interchangeable' with plastic blow-up sex dolls 'complete with orifices for penetration and ejaculation' (Barry 1995: 35) More than the most rampant version of patriarchy they could dream up, CATW feminists identify the prostitute with her vagina. This echo within CATW of the patriarchal and especially the pornographic is notable (see Brown 1995). The prostitute thus not only lacks – consent, will, desire – she *is* lack. What CATW feminists most want of sex workers is that they close their holes – shut their mouths, cross their legs – to prevent the taking in and the spilling out of substances and words they find noxious.

The trafficker

Until now, this chapter has looked at the perceived threat to the state from the prostitute. What of her 'partner in crime', the trafficker? As we saw in Chapter 3, the 'rise of the pimp system' (Hobson 1987) was believed to be an integral element of 'the white-slave trade'. In white slavery accounts, this network of foreign pimps and procurers did not limit their activities to enslaving innocent girls: we saw how Turner (1907; 1909) linked organized networks of pimps to political corruption. The growth of the 'sex trade', its increasingly 'industrial' characteristics, the links with other types of crime, and the control of prostitution by 'foreign criminal gangs', were all key themes in the white slavery myth. The 'criminal underworld' is once again foregrounded in trafficking narratives, with the existence of 'criminal net-works' behind trafficking an article of faith, constantly repeated in accounts by feminists, NGOs, police, journalists and politicians.[26]

The picture that emerges is of a shadowy parallel structure, an under-world flourishing in the absence of 'borders': actual state borders, but also of 'law and order', broken down as a result of the anarchy of globalization and the unimpeded march of capital. This is not new either, as we saw in Chapters 2 and 3 in relation to white slavery. Dissatisfaction with the lot of the global proletariat fuelled debate, demonstrations and revolutions. As Marx famously used prostitution as an example of and as a metaphor for capitalism, so too did other forerunners of today's anti-globalization activists. The 'No Logo' of its time, Kauffman's novel *The House of Bondage* (1912) used the motif of white slavery to condemn capitalism. As Haag (1999) notes, Kauffman's novel 'grimly diagnosed capitalist society itself as "a gigantic house of bondage, in which the weak are enslaved by the strong"' (p. 70). Anarchist-feminist Emma Goldman commented favourably on Kauffmann's work in her essay *The White Slave Traffic* (1910). Goldman scorns the movement against white slavery as a 'brightly colored toy for babies', arguing that the real evil of prostitution is nothing new and will remain long after the crusaders against white slavery had made their careers.

According to Goldman, 'the merciless Moloch of capitalism that fattens on underpaid labour' drives 'thousands of women and girls into prostitution … these girls feel, "why waste your life working for a few shillings a week in a scullery, eighteen hours a day?"' (1910: 14)

For these commentators and activists, prostitution and white slavery served to symbolize capitalism and to illustrate its worst excesses – in Haag's phrase, they were the result of the 'deceitful "freedoms" of capitalism' (1999: 89). A newspaper report on the Protocol negotiations covers all the elements that give trafficking its current sense of urgency:

> Trafficking is one segment of the brutal transnational organized crime system that dehumanizes and devalues women and children. It's a system that's part of a sophisticated network which relies on a nation's dysfunctional economic, political and social apparatus. Traffickers are nefarious entrepreneurs who view poverty and depressed economies as a lucrative way to exploit a world without borders and exploit women seeking a way out of misery. These criminals traffic women and children like they traffic weapons and drugs. Often travelling the same routes as trafficked drugs, human commodities rake in huge profits. (White [2000])

Reports like these send states scurrying for more border police and anti-globalization activists for more placards, as 'globalization' inspires contra-dictory and confusing reactions in society.

The terror of trafficking reached truly astonishing levels in President Bush's 24 September 2003 speech to the United Nations, regarding the US position in Iraq and on terrorism. Beginning with a reference to the 11 September 2001 attacks, moving through the occupation of Afghanistan and Iraq, Bush spent the last third of his speech denouncing trafficking as the financial base of terrorism, and gave the fight against trafficking the same urgency as the war on terror. In describing trafficking, Bush uses the same religious symbolic term as when exhorting against terror: 'evil'. The 'civilized world' is portrayed as under threat from the uncivilized forces of 'fundamentalist' Islam. The caricature of the evil Arab threatening decent, civilized – i.e. American – society is recognizable from white slavery stories: Saddam Hussein as the card-board, mustachio-twirling villain with paintings of pneumatic women in his palaces, Uday the sadistic whoremonger. The danger is dark, literally in terms of skin colour, and is made all the more frightening because it is sexualized.

The results of anti-trafficking campaigns

National laws on white slavery ended up rebounding on sex workers them-selves, whether such laws were intended to protect sex workers or to protect the nation (often these two forms of protection were elided: as both sinner and sinned against, the wayward young girl was a threat that needed to be neutralized through 'rescue' and 'protection'). The tendency to turn towards the state for protection, rather than questioning state power to regulate and discipline, is one that Brown sees as especially problematic for feminism. She notes:

> women have particular cause for greeting such politics with caution. Historically, the argument that women require protection by and from men has been critical in legitimating women's exclusion from some spheres of human endeavour and confinement within others. Operating simultaneously to link 'femininity' to privileged races and classes ... protection codes are also markers and vehicles of such divisions among women. Protection codes are thus key technologies in regulating privileged women as well as intensifying the vulnerability and degradation of those on the unprotected side of the constructed divide between light and dark, wives and prostitutes, good girls and bad ones. (1995: 165)

Feminist campaigns against trafficking emphasize the human rights violations committed by 'pimps', 'traffickers' or clients against prostitutes. By contrast, sex worker organizations the world over identify the state, particularly the police, as the prime violators of sex workers' rights. The result of shifting the locus of concern from state repression of sex workers to the individual acts of violent men is that these anti-trafficking campaigns often lack a critical attitude towards the state. Ironically, the lack of recognition of state repression of sex workers means that measures to combat trafficking often strengthen the hand of the state at the expense of sex workers.

In her role as the archetypal, sexually violated female, the prostitute must be seen to be undergoing her violation at the hands of a man. For sex workers, however, the space of greatest violence occurs outside of the intimate sexual encounter: in their contact with the state and its agents. Wherever sex workers gather – at conferences and meetings around the world – violence by the police is at the top of the agenda. At a conference I attended of the National Network of Sex Workers in Kerala, India (3–8 March 2003) – attended by over 500 sex workers – many examples of horrific violence by the police were recounted.

The overwhelming effect of feminist-inspired anti-trafficking policies and programmes has been catastrophic for sex workers, especially those in developing countries. It was the concern around trafficking that gave Swedish feminists the political opportunity to enact legislation that penalizes the customers of sex workers. In the United States, abolitionist feminists worked hand in hand with Christian activists to influence US trafficking policy.[27] As examined above, the Clinton administration was vulnerable to attacks about being soft on prostitution (Soderlund 2005). Thus, as Soderlund explains, when two anti-trafficking bills were presented to Congress, one with a broad understanding of trafficking and one that focused narrowly on sex trafficking with 'a few gestures to other forms of forced labor' (Soderlund 2005), the latter was passed into law in 2000. This Trafficking Victims Protection Act (TVPA), according to Chapkis (2003), narrowly defined a very small group of deserving, 'innocent' victims while implicitly offering justification for the repression of the large group of 'guilty' migrants. Nonetheless, the Clinton administration did not endorse an abolitionist position on trafficking, and continued to distinguish between prostitution and trafficking (Weitzer 2007).

Under the Bush administration, abolitionists expected and got a much more sympathetic ear. Soderlund (2005) and Weitzer (2007) have analysed the degree to which the Bush administration used anti-trafficking to further foreign policy goals unrelated to trafficking. The stage was set for this foreign policy manoeuvring by the TVPA, which established the annual Trafficking in Persons, or TIP, Report, in which other countries are ranked in three tiers according to their anti-trafficking efforts. Countries such as Cuba and North Korea are consistently given the worst rating, of category three. Tier ranking helps determine aid given to that country, and thus it is no wonder that many countries have responded by enacting legislation that is viewed as in line with US anti-prostitution policies. So Cambodia in 2008 enacted an anti-trafficking law that penalizes all involvement in the sex industry. The results are described below.

From 15 January 2003, USAID field missions were informed that they were no longer allowed to fund anti-trafficking projects that were 'advocating prostitution as an employment choice or which advocate or support the legalization of prostitution' (Crago 2003). Trafficking has also been linked with US international HIV/AIDS prevention efforts. In discourses on white slavery and trafficking, syphilis and AIDS are metaphors that capture the dual role of protection: of the young girl herself, and the need for protection of the community. A telling use of the metaphor appeared in an article on the Vienna negotiations: 'One reason trafficking is spreading like the HIV/AIDS disease relates to a lack of national and international laws that deal with the problem as an industry' (White [2000]). Tragically, it is more than a metaphor. Under PEPFAR (the US President's Emergency Plan for

AIDS Relief), enacted under legislation adopted in 2003, all organizations that receive federal money are required to agree to adopt an anti-prostitution pledge. The law states that '"No funds ... may be used to provide assistance to any group or organization that does not have a policy explicitly opposing prostitution and sex trafficking.' A separate requirement restricts the use of federal funds: 'No funds ... may be used to promote or advocate the legalization or practice of prostitution or sex trafficking'" (CHANGE 2008: 1). This was the direct result of the lobby efforts of the abolitionist feminist/religious anti-trafficking lobby (Soderlund 2005; Bernstein 2007; Weitzer 2007).

The Network of Sex Work Projects issued a press release when the Bill was announced. It reads:

> This measure could have potentially devastating effects on sex workers, their families and the wider communities in which they live. Projects working with sex workers throughout the world do not 'promote' sex work as 'lifestyle'. Especially in poor countries, projects work with the twin aims of empowering sex workers to protect themselves from HIV, while at the same time helping sex workers to discover other means of generating income. These projects have a proven track record when it comes to reducing HIV among sex workers. Denying them funding is likely to have serious impact on infection rates among the poorest and most vulnerable. (NSWP 2003)

Recent reports such as those by the Center for Health and Gender Equity (CHANGE 2008) as well as the film 'Taking the Pledge' (2006) by the NSWP shows these predictions to have been sadly accurate. Organizations with effective and innovative programmes involving sex workers, such as Sampeda Maheen Mahila Sanstha (SANGRAM) in India, have refused to sign the pledge claiming it would impossibly compromise their work. This has led to a loss of funding and the contraction of planned services. In Bangladesh, sixteen out of twenty drop-in centres for sex workers have been forced to close as a direct result of the pledge. Agencies seeking local partners are prevented from working with sex worker organizations because they won't sign the pledge. Self-censorship is also a large problem, with organizations preferring to play it safe, and cutting planned activities that they fear might fall foul of the pledge.

The PEPFAR pledge has to date not been reversed under the Obama administration. Early signs of how the administration will deal with trafficking and prostitution indicated initially that there may be little change from the Bush era, despite the reversal of the Global Gag Rule prohibiting recipients of US aid from promoting abortion, and despite a generally more open approach to sexuality. Secretary of State Hillary Clinton's comments on trafficking in her confirmation hearing showed abolitionist tendencies. However, the recent appointment of the moderate Luis de Baca as the head of the State Department's Trafficking in Persons Office gives reason to hope for a change in policy.[28]

At the National Network of Sex Workers conference in Kerala in 2003, the international fight against trafficking was unanimously declared to be the single biggest threat to sex worker rights. Sex workers have become politicized around the issue not only through denial of services, but through increasingly punitive and violent practices undertaken in the name of stopping trafficking. These are the 'raid and rescue' policies that are now the preferred method of anti-trafficking intervention by a number of large NGOs such as the International Justice Mission (IJM) as well as governments.[29] The 'rescue' policies they advocate have been condemned by international human rights organizations as a major cause of violence against sex workers (IHRLG 1999), yet they continue to be supported by abolitionist feminists. Donna Hughes calls 'report and rescue' a 'bold new method'. She describes it as follows: 'under this approach aid workers have a duty to catalyze a rescue. They can do so through the official report, or by notifying a nongovernmental or faith-based group that specializes in rescuing enslaved women and girls' (Hughes n.d.). Hughes goes on to attack the NSWP for its policy on sex worker rights.

In a statement released in response to this article, NSWP member Empower Foundation in Thailand responded that 'Far from being a "bold new method" as is being proclaimed, Empower Chiang Mai has been dealing with the issue of "raids and rescues" of women working in brothels for the past 11 years' (Empower 2003: 1). Empower goes on to record one such 'rescue' that occurred in May 2003:

> Journalists and photographers also accompanied the police and 'rescue team'. Photos of the women were taken without their consent and appeared in the local papers ... Women who were 'rescued' understood they had been arrested. They had their belongings taken from them. They were separated from each other. They were unable to contact friends, family or Empower ... In all 28 women were 'rescued'. Some of the women were not employees of that brothel but were simply visiting friends when they were 'rescued'. Women were transported by Trafcord and the police against their will to a Public Welfare Boys' Home. Nineteen women were locked inside and have remained there for the past 31 days. We have no information on the whereabouts or situation of the other ten women. (Empower 2003: 2)

In Cambodia, the 2008 anti-trafficking law has been the subject of ongoing and vociferous protests from local sex worker organizations (APNSW 2008; Overs 2009). A film produced by the Asia-Pacific Network of Sex Workers shows interviews with a number of sex workers who were arrested and incarcerated as the result of anti-trafficking raids under the new law. Several were physically and sexually abused during their arrest and incarceration.[30]

In New York City, a report by the Sex Workers' Project (2009) found that police raids were ineffective at identifying trafficked persons, were most often carried out in a frightening fashion, led to incarceration and deportation of sex workers and trafficked persons, and facilitated bullying and mistreatment of sex workers and trafficked persons.

Disappearing sex workers?

In this chapter, I have examined how the sex worker disappeared in the CATW lobby through the denial of sex worker as identity. I have demonstrated how the powerful ideas around white slavery continue to influence today's abolitionist feminists, through the figure of the suffering Third World prostitute. Through making consent to prostitution impossible, abolitionist feminists epistemologically reposition the prostitute as a slave, in need of feminist intervention to save her.

However, it is of course not only abolitionist feminists who are concerned with the welfare of prostitutes. We need also to examine the influence of the white slave on the 'liberal' feminists who made up the Human Rights Caucus. As explained in Chapter 1, at the heart of GAATW-influenced 'liberal' feminist analysis of trafficking is the distinction between voluntary and forced prostitution, and the corollary view of freely chosen, adult prostitution as work (see Wijers and Lin 1997; GAATW 1997; Doezema 1998). At first glance, it appears as if the 'sex worker' forms the solid basis for the analysis and activism of this group. But as the performance of the HRC at the negotiations shows, appearances can be deceiving. The prostitute inhabits the 'site of sexual violence' in even the most liberal feminist imaginations.[31] While in some feminist imaginations she may be better equipped to negotiate that violence than in others, she remains defined by it. If sex workers 'disappeared' in CATW's definition through their being transformed into 'sex slaves', this HRC position on trafficking works a similar magic. Paradoxically, the best way of protecting sex workers' rights in the debate on defining trafficking was by making sex workers invisible. These deceptive appearances form the subject of Chapter 5.

5 Now you see her, now you don't: consent, sex workers and the Human Rights Caucus

The presence of sex worker rights activists in the Vienna negotiations was a marked departure from the white slavery debates. However, sex worker involvement in the anti-trafficking debates has been marked by a slow start and a reluctant continuation. Although sex worker rights groups and anti-trafficking organizations had worked together prior to the Trafficking Protocol negotiations, sex worker rights movements were slow to recognize the resurgence of trafficking as an international issue, and even after recognition have been reluctant participants in anti-trafficking activities. Why is this so? I believe this can be explained through the relationship between sex workers' rights and feminism, most particularly in the issue of (sexual) 'violence', which is articulated in feminism through the concept of consent. Conflicts, similarities and differences in perceptions of 'consent' were to mark the 'joint lobby' of sex worker rights activists and anti-trafficking activists in Vienna.

Sex worker advocates from the Network of Sex Work Projects (NSWP) advocated positions jointly with other members of the Human Rights Caucus (HRC), and co-drafted lobby documents. Yet the NSWP is not mentioned in any of the documents produced by the HRC, nor is it an official signatory on any of these documents. In an ironic echo of the CATW lobby, sex workers 'disappeared' from the HRC. What led to this disappearance? The answer to this question is linked to a second 'disappearing move': the HRC strategy of seeking to remove all mention of prostitution from the proposed definition of trafficking. This twofold disappearance of sex workers was paradoxically facilitated by the inclusion of sex worker activists in the HRC lobby, as sex worker activists themselves chose to mask their presence. This is intriguing, as it is often assumed that participation heightens visibility and voice. Sex worker activists have long demanded the right to speak for themselves in reaction to feminists whose activities have been read as a silencing of the sex worker voice (L. Bell 1987; Alexander and Delacoste 1987).

The implications (for the relationship between sex worker rights and feminism) of the disappearance of sex workers from the 'liberal' HRC lobby may be even more profound than the implications of the disappearance of the sex worker in abolitionist discourse. This chapter examines in detail the strategy of delinking prostitution and trafficking that the HRC advanced at the negotiations. In particular, I will examine the 'double disappearance' of sex workers in the HRC lobby. I look at the two levels of discourse, each corresponding with one disappearing move. The first is the level of practice: the actual participation of sex workers in the HRC lobby. The second is the level of the definition of trafficking, the level at which meaning-making took place. These two moves are linked in an intricate shadow play, with deceptive sleights-of-hand obscuring, then revealing, the sex worker. Discernible in these shadows is the ghostly figure of the white slave, the mythical maiden whose presence haunted the negotiations.

Delinking prostitution and trafficking

The HRC urged delegates to opt for a definition of trafficking that would avoid linking 'prostitution' and trafficking together. The HRC supported a definition that focused on coercion, and that did not specify the purpose for which a person was trafficked. The essence of the HRC view on trafficking is contained in the following paragraph, taken from one of the HRC lobby documents:

> The core elements of the act of trafficking are the presence of deception, coercion or debt bondage and the exploitative or abusive purpose for which the deception, coercion or debt bondage is employed. Typically the deception involves the working conditions or the nature of the work to be done. For example, the victim may have agreed to work in the sex industry but not to be held in slavery-like conditions or to work in a factory but not in a brothel. The nature of the labour or services provided as such, including those in the sex industry, are irrelevant to the question of whether or not the victim's human rights are violated. The trafficker's use of deceit, coercion, or debt bondage to force the victim to work in slavery-like or exploitative or abusive conditions deprives the victim of her or his free will and ability to control her or his body, which constitutes serious violation of the fundamental rights of all human beings'. (HRC, *Recommendations and Commentary*, January 1999: para. 6)

The HRC stance was grounded in the commitment to stopping trafficking of all persons, male and female, for all sorts of labour. While it is true that this commitment maintained a gender focus (which sits uneasily with the simultaneous commitment to a genderless subject of anti-trafficking activism, as examined below), the HRC and organizations that supported its efforts had genuinely come to believe that anti-trafficking activity had to widen its scope beyond 'women and children'.[1] In response to the definition contained in a first draft of the Protocol, which linked trafficking to prostitution, the HRC argued that the draft

> focuses unnecessarily on one particular form of labour abuse, that in the sex industry ... the special reference to prostitution ... is a gratuitous response to the current public hysteria surrounding this particular from of trafficking ... *the references to prostitution and 'sexual exploitation' should be deleted* from [the definition]. (HRC *Recommendations and Commentary*, January 1999: para. 4, emphasis added)

The proposal to delink trafficking completely from prostitution was an attempt to break with genealogy. To have an international agreement on trafficking that made no mention at all of prostitution would be truly radical, showing that the genealogy of the myth of white slavery could be beaten: it would amount to an epistemological revision of trafficking. However, the effort to move trafficking beyond 'prostitution' to 'coerced migration for forced labour' was ultimately unsuccessful.

Putting the lobby together

From the very beginning of the HRC, sex worker rights advocates worked together with anti-trafficking activists. This commitment on the part of anti-trafficking activists to involve sex workers went beyond a desire to 'listen' to sex workers or to consult with sex workers. It involved actively searching for funds to enable the participation of sex workers in the lobby during the meetings in Vienna. The HRC attended each of the meetings on the Protocol, and sex worker activists took part every time. All documents used by the HRC during the meetings were drafted with significant input from the NSWP sex worker activists. So, in a number of ways, the HRC can be seen as a partnership, with sex workers participating at all levels.

Nonetheless, for the NSWP advocates, the decision to participate in the lobby presented a dilemma. On the one hand, NSWP advocates recognized that working through a lobby was necessary if they hoped to have any influence on the Trafficking Protocol. On the other, because sex workers questioned the legitimacy of the anti-trafficking framework, they were reluctant to lend support to the creation of an international anti-trafficking agreement. Sex worker activists, given years of personal experience with well-meaning legal changes, were highly sceptical about the possible benefits of any new international legislation on trafficking. As examined in the Introduction, a recurring argument in sex worker rights movements has been the need for 'decriminalization': that all sex-work-specific offences should be removed from criminal law, and no new ones created. Instead, it has been argued that existing laws covering sexual violence and workers' rights should be applied to sex work. This argument recognizes that the main-tenance of prostitutes as a separate category under criminal law reinforces their treatment as 'outsiders', as people to whom the protections afforded to others under the law does not apply. This argument was extended to international level in a report of the human rights organization Anti-Slavery International (Bindman and Doezema 1997). This report examined how a range of human rights abuses in sex work, including those referred to under trafficking, would be covered if existing international law was applied to sex workers.

'WHEN TRAFFICKING IS A TARGET, PROSTITUTES WILL ALSO BECOME A TARGET'

A number of NGOs and individuals working in the field of trafficking in women and human rights began communicating with each other late in 1998 about the proposed new Trafficking Protocol, with the view to influencing the outcome of the negotiations by forming a lobby. This pre-liminary, informal group consisted of anti-trafficking groups who supported the idea that sex work should be viewed as legitimate labour, and was initiated by Ann Jordan of the International Human Rights Law Group, Washington, DC, and Marjan Wijers of the Foundation Against Trafficking in Women (STV) based in the Netherlands. Via email and informal meetings, they contacted other anti-trafficking and sex worker rights activists. Emails aimed at hammering out a strategy for lobbying began in December 1998, using the NSWP email list and informal face-to-face meetings.[2] Out of these initial discussions a 'core group' of individuals and organizations emerged, who were to be actively involved in lobbying in Vienna over the next two years.

The first email discussions, which started about a month before the first meeting of the Ad Hoc Committee, scheduled for January 1999, dealt with the draft for the Trafficking Protocol proposed by the United States (A/AC.254/4/add.3).[3] The first fault line that developed between sex worker rights activists and anti-trafficking activists was on how to react to the proposed Protocol. In this first stage of the lobby, two very different positions emerged. The NSWP favoured lobbying against adoption of the Protocol, while anti-trafficking activists favoured lobbying to improve it.

Two quotations from emails from sex workers to the nascent HRC lobby group show how sceptical NSWP activists were about the possible benefits of the proposed international anti-trafficking legislation:

> you might believe that you are helping 'women and children' by calling for new anti-sex laws or even new laws. However, without clearly defining what laws will be made you will likely hurt the very people you aim to help. Almost always the new laws operate against the sex industry (which world wide is a major source of income for many women who in turn support their children with this money). Additionally men who work in the sex industry will be harmed by new anti-sex laws but often their difficulties are never discussed or they are disguised by the 'women and children' banner. (HRC list, 19 December 1998)

> the anti-trafficking framework is inherently problematic in the way it essentializes and separates certain kinds of abuses in the industry which are connected to protection of national borders. Obviously the stakes become slanted for nations that pretend to help 'women', defined as 'good women who don't want to do prostitution'. Mostly the states just wanted to 1.) control borders 2.) give government workers like cops a chance to use their muscle on prostitutes ... [W]hen trafficking is a target, prostitutes will also become a target. (HRC list, 20 December 1998)

Another issue for NSWP activists was the perceived lack of commitment on the part of anti-trafficking activists to fighting against anti-prostitution initiatives:

> Instead of me criticizing this document [the draft protocol], those from anti-trafficking groups should be using this space to organize a response to the anti-prostitution stance of this document. *This response should be developed now and released the moment this thing passes in a form which equates prostitution with trafficking* ... I come back to the basic question. How far are you all going to go to protest this? (HRC list, 20 December 1998, emphasis in original)

'BE RADICAL'? PROTEST OR ENGAGEMENT

Out of the 'core group' discussions a strategy for lobbying began to emerge. Marjan Wijers and Ann Jordan secured funding for people to attend the Crimes Commission meetings, and they drafted a first critique of the proposed Trafficking Protocol. This draft was circulated on the NSWP list for comments, as well as on the HRC list. NSWP members needed to decide what form their participation in lobbying activities should take: whether they should lobby as a separate group, or together with the anti-trafficking activists. One activist wrote: 'Action needed. I am sending everyone the proposed Protocol on trafficking in women and children ... In brief, it sucks ... the NSWP should lobby in its own way and critique the document' (NSWP list, 19 December 1998). On 21 December, the coordinator of the NSWP called for a specific NSWP response to the draft Protocol with input from all members via the NSWP listserve. At the same time, they decided to continue to engage with the anti-trafficking activists and provide help by commenting on the critique drafted by Marjan Wijers and Ann Jordan.

Once the NSWP decided to write its own critique of the Protocol, the key question became how it should be framed: as a straightforward protest against the adoption of new international legislation on trafficking, or as a critique aimed at improving the Trafficking Protocol. Initially, the NSWP decided to try to find a way to combine both positions in a single critique: to be both reformist and radical. The first draft of the NSWP commentary thus stated: 'The NWSP recommends that delegates vote against the document in its entirety. If the Protocol is to be modified then the NSWP recommends [a number of changes]' (NSWP list, 16 January 1999).

NSWP list exchanges about this draft show that members felt uncomfortable with the duality of the protest/reform position. One mail suggested that the NSWP effort would be less effective if it tried both to suggest improvements and at the same time to urge rejection of the Protocol:

> while I agree wholeheartedly that the main problem with the document is that it exists at all, I wonder if we lose credibility if we argue that delegates should vote against it. That is, if we really want to try and change the document. We could, of course, choose to take a principled stand, and argue absolutely and only against adoption. This may be a strategic option, as other organisations such as the Global Alliance Against Trafficking and Anti-slavery International will be arguing for the sorts of changes that we support – well not exactly support, but the sort of damage limitation we recognise is necessary. We could then go on record as a 'protest' voice. Or we could ... go for both, but I am worried that this weakens both positions. What do others think? (NSWP list,18 January 1999)

Discussion on the list led to a majority of NSWP members agreeing that to express this dualistic position in our public response to the Protocol would be ineffective. The NSWP position paper was redrafted and the recommendations for changing the Protocol were removed, leaving only the recommendation that delegates reject the Protocol in its entirety. The first paragraph of the NSWP statement on the Protocol established the NSWP 'protest' position with regards to an anti-trafficking approach:

> Historically, anti-trafficking measures have been more concerned with protecting women's 'purity' than with ensuring the human rights of those in the sex industry. This approach limits the protection afforded by these instruments to those who can prove that they did not consent to work in the sex industry. It also ignores the abusive conditions within the sex industry, often facilitated by national laws that place (migrant) sex workers outside of the range of rights granted to others as citizens and workers. (NSWP, *Commentary on the Draft Protocol*, January 1999)

Visible protest, invisible influence

While the NSWP decided to take an official position against the adoption of the Trafficking Protocol, they recognized that there was little chance that the delegates to the UN would heed their calls. In order to be able to continue to exercise influence on the debate, the NSWP agreed that they would continue to work with the anti-trafficking lobby group, but as individuals rather than NSWP representatives. The decision to join with the Human Rights Caucus, to commit as sex worker rights activists to a position they could not wholeheartedly support, was not an easy one, and remained difficult throughout the entire two years of the negotiations. The NSWP strategy, though in a number of ways successful (as discussed below), nonetheless caused a great deal of frustration for sex worker activists who took part. One the one hand, they felt that their participation was vital to ensuring the maintenance of a strong sex worker rights perspective within the Human Rights Caucus. As one NSWP member expressed it:

> as a person who works closely with the human rights organizations based in the US ... I have seen them utilize precedents and conventions uncritically on occasion and advocate (by mistake) for things which would very much hurt the sex industry. Please do not consider this a strong criticism of any human rights organization here in the US ... but I think we all are aware how in the zeal to 'protect women from traffickers' some organizations promote actions which are harmful. (NSWP list, 19 January 1999)

On the other, the NSWP activists realized that the best possible outcome of their efforts would nonetheless still be a new international agreement on trafficking, which they felt could only ever harm sex workers, rather than protect them.

So the sex workers' first disappearing move was an attempt to resolve this dilemma, enabling them publicly to reject the trafficking framework and at the same time to use their presence to influence the HRC position. The result of this strategy was the supremely ironic invisible presence of sex workers in the HRC lobby. For many of them, who were used to taking on a highly visible and public role as sex workers and activists, this was a strange position to be in. As they buttonholed delegates between sessions, politely waited to discuss their latest document with a delegate, or earnestly argued the merits of a particular point, the 'secret sex workers' in the Human Rights Caucus were highly visible yet invisible; there but not there.

NOW YOU SEE HER, NOW YOU DON'T

By the time of the first meeting of the Ad Hoc Committee, the NSWP advocates had decided on the strategy of using their influence within the HRC, rather than lobbying separately for delegates to reject the document. As recorded in a report of this first session, sent to the NSWP list:

> We all agreed to give the NSWP recommendations to any delegate we spoke to, and to explain briefly what they were about. Our lobbying strategy was, however, to push for changes in the draft Protocol, according to the HRLG (Human Rights Law Group) recommendations, rather than argue for complete rejection of the draft protocol, as the NSWP paper urged. This was in accordance with the strategy that was agreed in discussions on this list. The NSWP document was a 'protest', that explained why trafficking was the wrong framework to deal with labour and human rights abuses for migration in the sex industry. The HRLG recommendations were 'practical', i.e. they addressed what could be changed in the Draft Protocol to make it least harmful. (NSWP list, 2 January 1999)

In order to ensure that the 'protest voice' went on record, HRC lobbyists handed out copies of the NSWP Commentary as well as the HRC Commentary (drafted with NSWP input).

This made for a rather uneasy balance within the HRC, with the NSWP strategy not clearly understood by anti-trafficking counterparts in the HRC. One anti-trafficking activist in the delegation wrote an email expressing her concern that the NSWP advocates were contradicting each other and confusing the delegates (personal mail, 8 February 1999). In my own lobbying, I explained to delegates that the NSWP document was produced by sex worker rights groups, who had asked us as the Human Rights Caucus to pass on our concerns to the delegates. As mentioned above, it was strange to be unable to 'own' this document, to not let on that I was not one of the sex worker activists.

'APPEARANCE IS EVERYTHING'

Though we worked extremely well together and developed close personal relationships, some tensions between the NSWP members and the other members of the HRC remained. Certain members of the HRC who rejected the trafficking framework were worried that if we were identified with sex worker rights activism, the efficacy of our lobby would be diminished. A highly personal, perhaps symbolic expression of this was the reaction to the way I dressed for lobbying. One of the senior HRC members was worried that it was 'too sexy', and she suggested changes of outfit a number of times. It wasn't said, but I experienced her fear as meaning that I looked too much like a prostitute. While I agree that lobbying in fishnets and mini-skirt would not have been a good idea, my sober grey trousers and long-sleeved top seemed to me to be entirely appropriate lobbying garb. Some caucus members shared this fear about how I dressed, but others felt it was misplaced. We reached a point where we treated the matter jokingly as a group, and I threatened to appear in stilettos and push-up bra.

Nonetheless, I felt a real pressure to change my appearance, which led me to question myself. Had I spent so much time doing political activism as a sex worker that I didn't know how to dress for other political work? Sartorial standards for sex worker rights activism are very specific. The unofficial slogan of the NSWP is 'appearance is everything', and it is only semi-ironic. The fishnets, high heels and other symbols of sex work (which differ according to different national, ethnic and sex worker cultures) are standard apparel for sex worker demonstrations and performances. On a purely strategic level, these accoutrements ensure that sex worker protests are not ignored – they are almost guaranteed to make the papers. On another level, sex workers are celebrating stigmatized sex work cultures by publicly asserting the symbols of a despised identity.

It seemed to me that the pressure on me was an instance of the stigma of sex work reaching into our own lobby group. This was another aspect of the 'invisibility' of sex workers: we could be there, so long as we did not *appear* to be sex workers.[4]

The disappearing prostitute and the definition of trafficking

The hidden presence of sex workers in the Human Rights Caucus mirrored the way the HRC argued around 'sex work' in their lobbying efforts at the International Crimes Commission. I now move to an examination of this second level of discourse, focusing on the process that evolved during the negotiations of defining the crime of trafficking in persons.

The definition of trafficking as contained in the final version of the Protocol reads as follows:

> For the purposes of this Protocol:
> (a) 'Trafficking in persons' shall mean the recruitment, transportation, transfer, harbouring or receipt of persons, by means of the threat or use of force or other forms of coercion, of abduction, of fraud, of deception, of the abuse of power or of a position of vulnerability or of the giving or receiving of payments or benefits to achieve the consent of a person having control over another person, for the purpose of exploitation. Exploitation shall include, at a minimum, the exploitation of the prostitution of others or other forms of sexual exploitation, forced labour or services, slavery or practices similar to slavery, servitude or the removal of organs;
> (b) The consent of a victim of trafficking in persons to the intended exploitation set forth in subparagraph (a) of this article shall be irrelevant where any of the means set forth in subparagraph (a) have been used;
> (c) The recruitment, transportation, transfer, harbouring or receipt of a child for the purpose of exploitation shall be considered 'trafficking in persons' even if this does not involve any of the means set forth in subparagraph (a) of this article;
> (d) 'Child' shall mean any person under eighteen years of age. (A/55/385)

Like much international law, this statement is not notable for its elegance, succinctness or coherence. The ambiguities in the text reflect the uneasy compromise delegates made around principled disagreements as to the purpose and subject of the Protocol. On one side were the delegates who felt that the Protocol should take a firm anti-prostitution position. On the other were delegates who, for a variety of reasons, were reluctant to equate prostitution with trafficking under this agreement. These basic differences found expression in protracted discussions about the meaning of 'consent' and the place it should take in the definition of the text.

A comparison of two guides to the Trafficking Protocol, written after the negotiations were completed, shows radically opposing interpretations of the definition of trafficking in persons, along the lines sketched above. Ann Jordan, of the Human Rights Caucus, writes:

The terms 'exploitation of the prostitution of others' and 'sexual exploitation' are not defined in the Protocol or anywhere else in international law. They are undefined and included in the definition as a means to end an unnecessary yearlong debate over whether or not voluntary adult prostitution should be defined as trafficking. Delegates were unable to reach any agreement on this point and so finally compromised on the last day of the negotiations by leaving the terms undefined ... *Thus, the compromise recognises the difference between forced (or involuntary) and voluntary* adult participation in sex work. (Jordan 2002: 32, emphasis added)

We can compare this statement to Janice Raymond's, of CATW:

From the beginning of the Ad Hoc Committee's deliberations, a small group of NGOs supporting prostitution as work, and voluntary trafficking as migration for sex work, lobbied to limit the definition of trafficking to forced or coerced trafficking, to omit any mention of trafficking for prostitution or sexual exploitation, and to delete the term victims from the text as being too emotive. Along with countries that had legalized/regulated prostitution as labour, they worked to restrict protections for victims by limiting the definition to only those women who could prove they had been forced into trafficking. Fortunately, the majority of countries – many of them from the less wealthy and sending countries for trafficking – wanted a definition that protected all victims of trafficking and that was not limited to force or coercion. (Raymond 2001: 4)

How can we explain these differences? In order to examine how this situation came about, I look at consent and how it operated at the negotiations. The vagaries of consent allowed both 'sides' – lobbyists as well as state delegations – to claim victory in the 'consent' wars.

YOUR DEFINITION OR MINE?

The issue of consent was controversial right from the start of the negotiations. As part of the informal working group of the Crimes Commission, the United States and Argentina had both expressed particular concern about the need for an agreement on trafficking. For Argentina, the issue of trafficking in children was paramount. Both countries took the initiative of preparing a draft for the Trafficking Protocol. Both of these drafts were submitted for discussion during the first session. Through comparing these first two versions of the Protocol, we can see the core differences that were to simmer below the surface during the first year, rising to nearly derail the entire Protocol during the final sessions.

The first thing to note is that both of the proposals explicitly link trafficking to prostitution. In terms of their approach to prostitution, the

Argentinian proposal was abolitionist, while the US proposal was a confused mixture of abolitionism and the limitation of trafficking to situations of force. The two drafts defined trafficking as follows:

[Argentina] Article 3

(b) 'International trafficking in children' shall mean any act carried out or to be carried out for an illicit purpose ...

(c) 'International trafficking in women' shall mean any act carried out or to be carried out for an illicit purpose ...

(d) 'Illicit purpose or aim' shall mean: ...

(iii) The prostitution or other form of sexual exploitation of a woman or child, even with the consent of that person. (A/AC/254/8)

[United States] Article 2

2. For purpose of this Protocol, 'trafficking in persons' means the recruitment, transportation, transfer, harbouring or receipt of persons:

(a) By the threat or use of kidnapping, force, fraud, deception or coercion; or

(b) By the giving or receiving of unlawful payments or benefits to achieve the consent of a person having control over another person, for the purpose of prostitution or other sexual exploitation or forced labour.

3. For purpose of this Protocol, trafficking in persons for the purpose of prostitution includes subjecting to such trafficking a child under the age of consent (in the jurisdiction where the offence occurs), regardless of whether that child has consented. (A/AC.254/4/Add.3)

These definitions differ in three main ways, indicated by three key terms. The first of these differences concerns the gender of the subject of the proposals. Both proposals refer in their title to 'trafficking in women and children'. In the body of the text, however, the differences between the two proposals come out. The Argentinian proposal refers throughout to 'women and children', while the US proposal uses the gender-neutral 'trafficking in persons'. This difference was significant enough to be included in a footnote to the official UN draft when the two proposals were combined for the March 1999 session:

The proposal by Argentina is restricted to trafficking in women and children. The proposal by the United States, while recognizing that women and children are particularly vulnerable to trafficking, applies to trafficking in all persons. Whenever this issue arises in this combined text, both options are given. (A/AC.254/4/Add.3/Rev.1: fn. 1)

The second of the key terms that distinguish the two definitions is to be found in the definition of trafficking, specifically, the purposes for which a woman or child could be trafficked. Here 'prostitution' and 'sexual exploitation' are the key terms. In this usage, there is more similarity between the proposals, as the phrases used are nearly identical: 'prostitution or other form of sexual exploitation' (Argentina); 'prostitution or other sexual exploitation' (US). It is clear from this that the US proposal, which here equates prostitution with sexual exploitation, was never intended to recognize 'voluntary' prostitution (as alleged by the CATW lobby, examined below). The inclusion of the phrase 'forced labour' as a term distinct from prostitution makes it even more obvious that prostitution was not considered as a form of labour in this draft.

The third of the key terms is the one that was to prove most controversial at the negotiations – consent. Both proposals include the term. In the US proposal, it functions to distinguish between what is to be considered trafficking in the case of adults and what is to be considered trafficking in the case of children. Children can be trafficked 'even with their consent', that is, without the use of force or deception. For adults, fraud or coercion is necessary for them to be considered 'trafficked', rather than undocumented migrants. The Argentinian proposal does not distinguish between child and adult on the basis of consent. In this proposal, in the case of both women and children, trafficking for 'sexual exploitation' can occur 'even with the consent of that person'.

If the phrase 'even with the consent of that person' sounds familiar, it is because it is nearly identical to those contained in the agreements on white slavery. This is one obvious, lexical way in which the myth of white slavery shaped the negotiations. The Argentinian proposal echoes the language of the abolitionist 1933 International Convention for the Suppression of the Traffic in Women, which stated that trafficking in women occurred 'even with her consent'. In its Preamble, the Argentinian proposal refers to the abolitionist 1949 Convention (a reference that would come back to haunt the negotiations).

MISSING MEN

After considering the two drafts of the protocol during the first session (January 1999), the delegates decided to combine the drafts at the March 1999 (third) session.[5] However, the Argentinian and the US definitions of trafficking differed so essentially that they could not be combined seamlessly into one document. Thus, the March 1999 version of the draft Protocol contained two options for the definition of trafficking. The US definition became 'Option One', and the Argentinian option became 'Option Two'.

The core differences between these two definitions were to form the background for the most contentious debates both between NGOs and between state delegates at the negotiations.

The combined draft still referred in its title only to 'trafficking in women and children'. The presence of this phrase in the title of the draft Protocol reveals that the concern of the drafters was with prostitution: the 'special vulnerability' of women and children referred to in the Argentinian draft is a sexual vulnerability: '*Bearing in mind* that these two categories of person [women and children] are more vulnerable than men to the risk of being victims of certain types of illicit acts' (UN 1999 A/AC.254/8: Preamble, emphasis in original). The 'illicit acts' referred to are *sexual* acts including prostitution, pornography and 'sex tourism', and are all dealt with in detail in the Argentinian definition of trafficking. The phrase 'illicit acts' seems a strange one in this context, an 'illicit act' carrying heavy moral overtones of sexual wrongdoing, rather than a reference to a violent crime committed by an organized criminal group. It is close to the 'immoral acts' with which the white slavery agreements defined trafficking. Its use in the Argentinian draft reveals the moral underpinnings of the discussions in Vienna.

The Argentinian proposal contained in the 'Option Two' definition was supported by the CATW lobby group. As shown in Chapter 4, one way abolitionist feminists make the prostitute 'disappear' is by removing her sexual adulthood. It can be argued that under liberalist ideology, sexual adulthood for women is achieved through their ability to consent to sex. Viewed in this way, it is not that a predefined adult woman is deemed capable of consenting to sex: rather, the ability to consent to sex is what determines her adulthood. For boys and men, the situation is different. When classified as 'children', males are deemed unable to consent to sex.[6] However, adulthood for men is not determined by the ability to consent to sex, but by no longer being bound by consent. Children can never consent to sex, adult women can sometimes consent to sex, adult men never need to say 'no' to heterosexual sex. Men become adult through sexual desire, women through sexual receptiveness. The consent standard so inscribes the duality of active male and passive female sexuality, it is hard to believe that feminists continue to advocate it with such force. Even more astounding is the centrality of the consent standard for sex worker rights advocates, when active female sexuality is the subject.

The HRC supported a modified version of the US proposal for the definition as contained in Option One. They argued that Option Two (the Argentinian proposal) was:

problematic in that it does not clearly set out the elements of trafficking and contains numerous undefined and problematic terms and concepts ... Women are deemed incapable of consenting to any of the activities described in the definitions [of trafficking in women and children], as are children. Adult women are not children and should not be treated as such. (HRC, *Recommendations and Commentary*, March 1999: para. 7)

The HRC further commented on the definition of 'illicit purpose' in the Argentinian proposal:

These provisions conflict with laws in the states where it is legal to be a prostitute and/or operate a brothel, produce pornography, etc. There are two distinct issues not covered here: one, is the ability of children to work in the sex industry and, two, the right of adults to work in the sex industry. This provision deprives adult women to work in any aspect of the sex industry that someone might consider prostitution or 'sexual exploitation'. Instead of attempting to shut down the sex industry, even in countries where it is legal, the Protocol should distinguish between adults, especially women, and children. It should also avoid adopting a patronizing stance that reduces women to the level of children, in the name of 'protecting' women. Such a stance historically has 'protected' women out of their rights. (HRC, *Recommendations and Commentary*, March 1999: para. 7)

They also argued that only a 'neutral' protocol could give adequate recognition and protection to men who were trafficked, and suggested that delegates delete all language limiting the scope of the Protocol to 'women and children'. They argued that the phrase 'paying particular attention to the protection of women and children' was unnecessarily limiting, as the human rights of all trafficked persons needed to be protected:

The Protocol should not imply that the need to recognize and protect the human rights of women and children takes priority over the need to recognize and protect the human rights of men or any other vulnerable group or minority. (HRC, *Recommendations and Commentary*, March 1999: para. 2)

'VICTIM' OR PERSON?

In accordance with their position on the limiting effects of the phrase 'women and children', the HRC argued that the term 'trafficking victim', which was used throughout the combined (March) draft Protocol, should be replaced with 'trafficked persons'. 'Trafficking victim', they argued, carried heavily genderized notions of powerlessness. Their point was underscored by comparison with the concurrent negotiations around the protocol on migrant smuggling, whose language was gender-neutral and whose subject was implicitly male, as examined in Chapter 4. Support for the HRC position of changing 'victim' to 'person' was particularly strong among IGOs such as the ILO, and in the case of the Special Rapporteur on Violence Against Women.

The convoluted 'trafficking in persons, especially women and children' in the title of the final version of the Protocol was agreed upon by the fourth session (June 1999) without much debate. Delegates agreed that the Protocol should focus on more than just trafficking in women and children, but also agreed that the 'special vulnerability' of 'women and children' needed to be recognized. This is illustrated in the joint written submission of Australia and Canada to the Ad Hoc Committee for the third session (March 1999), which stated: 'we have an open mind as to the expansion of the protocol beyond women and children provided that emphasis is maintained in respect of the special circumstances of both women and children' (A/AC.254/5/Add.3).

'Specially vulnerable'

The attempt to shift the focus from the 'vulnerable subject' of 'women and children' to the 'rights-bearing' neutral subject had limited success. The majority of delegates wanted, or at least did not object to, the Protocol addressing trafficking in men as well as 'women and children'. Yet the HRC received little delegate support for the idea of a genderless protocol. The delegates decided to emphasize the special plight of 'women and children' throughout the document. And once the HRC had 'lost' the effort to remove a focus on women and children, they had lost the effort to remove any mention of prostitution from the definition, as these two concepts were completely interdependent.

The exclusion of men from the Argentinian proposal, and the fact that it even had to be discussed at all, is very revealing. The Argentinian proposal, with its abolitionist ideology, would have made it *definitionally impossible* for men to be trafficked. The linking of prostitution and gender is also revealed in the 'special circumstances' referred to in the submission by Canada and Australia. These circumstances are those that women and children arrive into through their 'special vulnerabilities', that is, through their sexual vulnerability. 'Women and children' meant prostitution – for the delegates, a gender-neutral subject of the protocol would not be ending up in prostitution, because the trafficking victim in this document is a prostitute and is female. As sexual vulnerability is gendered, so the prostitute is female.

This is another way in which the white slave myth influences perceptions of the trafficking victim. Here ideology expresses its hegemonic longings, as the absence of men is not due to any analysis of 'evidence'. Men – not 'children' – do work as sex workers, and their presence is consistently disregarded and downplayed by many feminists as a minor phenomenon. Yet the immense body of work on male sex workers – most of it from the HIV/AIDS field – indicates that there are very many male sex workers – and that many of them migrate.[7] It would have been definitionally impossible for men to be trafficked, because men are excluded from that space of 'special vulnerability' that makes it possible for 'women and children' to be trafficked. As I have argued throughout this book, this space is structured by consent.

It is not only CATW's ideology that had missing men. The 'liberal' feminist ideology of the HRC struggled between making the gendered subject 'disappear' and retaining the female object of feminist concern (without women, where's feminism?). This is of course one example of the problem of liberalism faced by and challenged by 'identity politics'. It reflects the classic feminist dilemma within liberalism – whether to argue for inclusion in 'universal' rights or to recognize this 'neutral' conception of rights as the basis of 'women's oppression' (Pateman 1988).

What's wrong with sexual exploitation?

The term 'sexual exploitation' kept delegates busy during the first year. By the third session, it seemed as though the HRC had made some headway with their strategy to make 'prostitution' disappear. When the US and Argentina combined their versions of the protocol into one document, the US dropped the reference to prostitution in their definition (Option One). Thus, the definition proposed by the United States changed from 'for the purpose of prostitution or other sexual exploitation or forced labour' to 'for the purpose of sexual exploitation or forced labour' (A/AC/.254/4/Add.3/Rev 1).

This was a qualified lobby success for the HRC. On the 'success' side, 'prostitution' was removed from one of the definitions being considered by delegates. This was at least partially due to the efforts of the HRC. They spent a lot of time talking to the US delegation, and had done their homework in terms of what the US position was and what arguments were likely to carry weight with the US delegation. As stated above, the US did not want to appear in any way to be condoning or endorsing prostitution. At the same time, as co-initiators of the Protocol, they were determined to advocate a position most likely to achieve consensus. They were receptive to the HRC argument that including prostitution as a form of sexual exploitation would potentially block consensus, as states that permitted 'voluntary' prostitution would not be able to sign. This was confirmed when the Netherlands and Germany indicated that they would never agree to a document that defined prostitution as sexual exploitation.

However, the change to the US proposal was only a partial success, because the ambiguous phrase 'sexual exploitation', still contained in the definition, snuck the whore in by the back door. The term 'sexual exploitation' is a catch-all phrase with an abolitionist genealogy. NSWP members voiced objection to use of the term:

> The basic complaint about the use of the term is as follows. The term 'sexual exploitation' is ambiguous and is open to divergent interpretations, depending upon whether one views sex work as immoral or exploitative per se or as a form of labor. Frequently the phrase is used to define the position of all people involved in the sex industry, even those who work voluntarily under non-abusive or exploitative conditions. (NSWP list, 12 April 1999)

The HRC urged delegates to reject the phrase, and were supported in this by the Special Rapporteur on Violence Against Women, who commented that 'the explicit reference to sexual exploitation diverts attention from the essence of the abuses targeted by this Protocol, namely the forced and exploitative conditions under which a woman works' (*Position paper on the draft Protocol*, A/AC.254/CRP.13).

The majority of delegations, however, sought to retain the term, and the US was asked to provide a definition of 'sexual exploitation'. The US submitted their definition for the fifth session (October 1999).[8] Sexual exploitation was defined as: 'Of an adult, [forced] prostitution, sexual servitude or participation in the production of pornographic materials ... for which the person does not offer herself or himself voluntarily' (A/AC.254/L.54). The US definition of sexual exploitation was in line with their position on the Trafficking Protocol, which, as we have seen, was that it should only address cases of force in respect to trafficking.

At this point in the negotiations, the US delegation had not yet felt the full strength of the religious and abolitionist feminist offensive against their negotiating position (as described in Chapter 4). The US definition of 'sexual exploitation' became one of the mobilizing factors for the CATW offensive. CATW responded to the US definition, claiming that:

> In general, the pro-sex work lobby and some governmental delegations are trying to edit the terms 'trafficking for prostitution' and 'sexual exploitation' from the

entire text. With the exception of the definition of trafficking being debated in Article 2, Option 2, the word 'prostitution' is not mentioned in any other article of the Trafficking in Persons Protocol. The Coalition Against Trafficking in Women and its partner organizations have responded that since most trafficking is for sexual exploitation, a trafficking Convention should name and specify the major purpose for which trafficking occurs. (CATW, *Prostitutes work, but do they consent?*, December 1999)

Delegates at the session were unable to agree on whether or not all prostitution, or only 'forced' prostitution, should be included in the definition of sexual exploitation, and thus the term was left in brackets, meaning that discussion and finalization was deferred to a subsequent session. The only support the HRC received for the complete removal of the term 'sexual exploitation' was from the Netherlands, with whom the HRC worked closely. At the sixth session, the Netherlands submitted a definition of trafficking that made no reference to prostitution or to sexual exploitation, to which the HRC gave their full support (they had drafted it). The Netherlands had recently set its already tolerant attitude towards prostitution on a firm legal foundation.[9] The Netherlands also considered itself to be a world leader on trafficking, as one of the first countries to adopt a trafficking law that allowed a form of temporary residence for 'trafficking victims'.[10]

The Netherlands, however, stood alone in this position. State delegations were very committed to keeping sex somewhere in the Trafficking Protocol. This is again an example of the way in which trafficking *meant* prostitution for most of the assembled delegates. During the seventh session (January 2000), the Netherlands succumbed in the interest of consensus. They joined with the US and Italy and produced an amalgamated proposal in which the term 'sexual exploitation' reappeared.

The seventh session took place after CATW's political coalition-building and media disinformation campaigns in the US and the Philippines, and the ideological temperature in Vienna had risen markedly. Due to the success of the CATW lobby in the United States, the US delegation was put under pressure from the US government to portray the US as strongly anti-prostitution. As a result of this pressure, the US delegation's opening intervention at the seventh session consisted of a statement declaring the US to be totally opposed to all forms of prostitution. At the same time, the US delegation members themselves were aware that there was unlikely to be consensus around this position. The US delegation was anxious to achieve consensus, and thus wanted to preserve a distinction between trafficking and 'prostitution' in the Protocol.

Accordingly, the US along with the Netherlands and Italy drafted and submitted another, perhaps even more ambiguous definition during this session.[11] In this definition, prostitution was not mentioned. 'Sexual exploitation' was included but not defined, although positioned in the text as a form of slavery, servitude or forced labour. As in the case of initiatives by other delegations who opposed an anti-prostitution document, this proposal was less a case of ideological conviction than a pragmatic realization that an anti-prostitution document would likely fail to achieve consensus. Yet another definition was submitted by a group led by the Philippines delegation (now strongly CATW-influenced as explained in Chapter 4), supported by Germany and France.[12] This definition also left sexual exploitation undefined, but it differentiated between sexual exploitation and forced labour and slavery, leaving the way open for states to define prostitution as sexual exploitation.

This meant that delegates and lobbyists faced three separate definitions of trafficking to attempt to deal with during the ninth session, in June 2000. The old Option One from the second and third sessions remained as Option One, and included the US definition of sexual exploitation as (forced) prostitution. Option Two from the second and third sessions (the Argentinian definition) was to a certain extent reflected in the US definition of sexual exploitation included in Option One. Crucially, however, the genealogically laden reference to 'even with that person's consent' – the major difference between the original two definitions – did not appear in *any* of the new definitions. The new Option Two for the ninth session consisted of the US-led informal working group proposal from the seventh session, in which 'sexual exploitation' was left undefined, and prostitution was not mentioned. Option Three consisted of the Philippines-led informal working group proposal from the seventh session, in which prostitution was not mentioned and sexual exploitation was undefined, but differentiated from forced labour and debt bondage. Affairs were thus not only ideologically tense, but hideously complicated, particularly for many of the delegates who had no legal background and a poor grasp of the issues.

However, one thing was clear by this point in the negotiations: that the HRC lobby had failed in their efforts to remove 'sexual exploitation' from the definition of trafficking. The term appeared in all versions of the definition to be considered by delegates during the ninth session. Thus, the stage was set for the next important issue – whether voluntary prostitution would be included in the definition of 'sexual exploitation'.[13] Delegates and lobbyists alike were well aware that 'sexual exploitation' 'meant' prostitution, but as long as it was undefined the HRC could argue that there was 'room' for 'voluntary' prostitution to exist outside the preventions, punishments and protections enacted by the Protocol. After the informal sessions, the word 'consent' did not appear at all in the any of the proposed texts. However, in the final two sessions, the issue of 'consent' reappeared.

Consent to trafficking?

At the meeting in June 2000, after some initial debate, it was clear that no progress at all would be made unless the three definitions were combined into one. The chair asked a small group of state delegations (headed by Brazil), to meet separately and merge all existing proposals into a new draft that could form the basis for consensus.[14] This 'informal' working group returned with the following proposed definition:

> (a) 'Trafficking in persons' shall mean the recruitment, transportation, transfer, harbouring or receipt of persons, by the threat or use of force, by abduction, fraud, deception, [inducement], coercion or the abuse of power, or by the giving or receiving of payments or benefits to achieve the consent of a person having control over another person, for the purpose of exploitation, [irrespective of the consent of the person]; exploitation shall include, at a minimum, [use in prostitution or other forms of] sexual exploitation, forced labour or services, slavery or practices similar to slavery [or servitude]. (A/AC.254/l.205)

The terms in brackets indicate language that still needed to be decided – on which no consensus had yet been achieved. These terms 'inducement', 'irrespective of the consent of the person' and 'use in prostitution or other forms of' sexual exploitation were shorthand for the bitter and intense ideological differences on display in Vienna.[15] The differences concerned the extent to which trafficking should be defined as the result of 'force' – thereby admitting the possibility of consensual prostitution – or whether all prostitution should be defined as violence. While the terms 'inducement' and 'use in prostitution' were resolved without too much difficulty, the phrase 'irrespective of the consent' of the person dominated both the June and October negotiations, with states for and states against retention of the phrase equally determined that they should prevail.

'CONSENT IS THE WEDGE'

In their lobby efforts, CATW linked the issue of consent to that of obtaining criminal convictions, in the process sounding not only insensitive about rape victims, but also stoking law enforcement fears about failing to gain convictions. They argued that an effective definition of sex trafficking must include 'with or without the consent of the victim' (CATW, *Key cases, the problem of consent*, June 2000: 1). If trafficking included coercion, they warned that:

> A narrow definition focused on such conditions allows traffickers to argue, in their own defence, that their victims were not forced into prostitution but 'consented' to migrate for 'sex work'. *Consent is the wedge that allows the sex industry to redefine alleged voluntary trafficking for prostitution as 'facilitated migration' or 'migration for sex work'.* (CATW, *Key cases, the problem of consent*, June 2000: 1, emphasis added)

Through the trope of rape, abolitionists superimpose consent to a sexual encounter on to the commercial framework of trafficking in women:

> our concern remains ... that the definition of trafficking ... if it is limited to a framework of force, will exclude victims of trafficking from protections they need and will shield traffickers from prosecution through the 'consent' defence, *a familiar defence in the prosecutions of all sexual violence.* (Equality Now, *Letter to NGOs*, 20 June 2000, emphasis added)

Very many states found this argument about 'evidence' very persuasive, and made reference to it in their session interventions. The CATW caucus had rightly judged that in a document that was intended first and foremost as a law enforcement tool, arguments that looked likely to increase convictions would be very powerful. The Thai delegation, for example, who had been very receptive to the HRC arguments up to this point, reversed its position on consent when it was linked to prosecutions.[16]

In addition to the arguments linking consent to prosecutions, the CATW lobby group had success in referring delegates to earlier international agreements. The group urged delegates to adopt a definition that would be in line with the 1949 Convention and, most damagingly for the HRC, with the Convention on the Elimination of All Forms of Discrimination Against Women (CEDAW). Many states argued that the Trafficking Protocol needed to follow the precedent set by earlier international law. These states were convinced of the need to restate a link between trafficking and prostitution in the Protocol, and also to condemn prostitution. As the delegate from the Holy See put it:[17] 'The definition must state unequivocally what the crimes are. These should be use in prostitution, especially in prostitution. We know from NGO statistics that trafficking in women and children is most often due to prostitution.' She then went on to refer to the 1949 Convention and CEDAW, using these to argue that 'clearly, the international community wishes states to fight the exploitation of prostitution'. An Egyptian delegate went even further back in time, referring to the Conventions of 1910, 1921, 1933 and 1949 in his intervention.

The HRC lobby efforts switched from arguing that prostitution should 'disappear' from the definition to lobbying for the recognition that it is possible to consent to prostitution:

> Obviously, by definition, no one consents to abduction or forced labour, but an adult woman is able to consent to engage in an illicit activity (such as prostitution, where this is illegal or illegal for migrants). *If no one is forcing her to engage in such an activity, then trafficking does not exist.* (HRC, *Recommendations and Commentary*, June 1999: para. 5, emphasis added)

The HRC had a degree of success with this argument, as a nearly as large and equally implacable group of states were opposed to using the Protocol to make a moral statement about prostitution. Or, as the delegate from the UK termed it, the Commission needed to have 'a legal debate about moral issues' rather than a 'moral debate about legal issues'. These states argued that as force and coercion had already been agreed as the key elements of trafficking, a statement on consent would be redundant. As the Spanish delegate expressed it, drawing on arguments given him by the HRC, 'by definition, no one can consent to abuse or coercion'. Furthermore, he argued that including the phrase 'irrespective of the consent of the person' in the definition could falsely give the impression that someone might be able to consent to force or deception.

Delegates left the June session with the issue of consent no closer to being resolved than it was at the beginning of the session. The final session, in October, saw nearly all of the same arguments aired by the same players. Only the very real possibility that the entire Protocol would have to be dropped allowed states to adopt the compromise definition given at the beginning of this section, in which 'consent' is so placed that all states could agree with it. In the end, the Protocol's definition was a compromise: the use of force or coercion is included as an essential element of trafficking. The definition links trafficking to prostitution in an ambiguous and confusing manner. While 'the threat or use of violence or other types of coercion' to submit someone to 'exploitation' constitutes the crime of trafficking under the Protocol, the document also includes a statement on 'consent': 'The consent of a victim of trafficking in persons to the intended exploitation set forth in subparagraph (a) of this article shall be irrelevant where any of the means set forth in subparagraph (a) have been used' (A/55/383: 5). It is clear from a footnote to the Protocol that this should not be interpreted to mean that states are required to adopt legislation that makes prostitution illegal.[18]

In one sense, the Protocol definition is an advance, confirming the trend towards an implicit international recognition of the distinction between 'force' and 'voluntary' prostitution. If states are left free to respond to prostitution within their countries as they wish, then this allows states that recognize prostitution as labour to join the international consensus on trafficking. However, the Protocol also says nothing about those states whose treatment of prostitutes contravenes international standards of human rights (see Bindman and Doezema 1997). The definition of trafficking thus leaves 'room' for sex workers to exist only outside of the protected space carved out for trafficking victims. However, within the trafficking discourse itself, there is no 'room' for the sex worker. The sex worker is banished to the margins of the text, left to a precarious existence without the cover of international law. In distinguishing between 'trafficking' and 'voluntary prostitution' through the qualifier of 'consent', the Trafficking Protocol offers nothing to sex workers whose human rights are abused, but who fall outside the narrowly constructed category of 'trafficking victim'.

The disappearing subject of trafficking (lose the myth, and who's left?)

As this book has shown, the genealogy of trafficking is grounded in that of prostitution. The HRC came into the negotiations working from a draft Protocol that was framed in terms drawn from earlier international law, and which already defined trafficking in terms of prostitution. The anti-trafficking organizations gathered in the Human Rights Caucus truly believed that trafficking policy could be done 'right', that trafficking could be wrested free from its historical antecedents and turned into a liberatory discourse. The sex workers in the caucus were more sceptical and, in the end, were proved right. As a direct descendant of white slavery, trafficking in women cannot so easily shake off its inherited shape. In international law, in national law and in popular discourse, trafficking in women has meant prostitution. As events showed, it is not easy to displace this genealogy, to make trafficking mean something new.

Though the anti-trafficking organizations in the HRC wanted to rid the Protocol of the prostitute, one of the reasons they didn't succeed (and one of the reasons the myth of white slavery/trafficking remains so powerful) was the lack of recognition of their own investment in the myth: the continued importance for liberal feminism of sexuality as a 'site of violence' and thus the continued importance of the suffering, violated body of the sex worker even for 'consensual prostitution' supporting feminists. Without this body, the subject of liberal feminist concern 'disappears'. What could take her place? The possibilities for finding a new 'subject' are looked at in the conclusion.

6 Towards a reinscription of myth

> Abolish the prostitutes and the passions will overthrow the world; give them the rank of honest women and infamy and dishonor will blacken the universe. – Saint Augustine (Augustine 2007: 2.4.12)

This book began by looking at the difficulties posed by attempting to define 'trafficking in women'. These difficulties, as have been shown, are not primarily caused by differences in empirical evidence; rather, they are the result of divergent ideological positions regarding women's sexuality and the gendered meaning of 'consent'. This book has shown present-day accounts of trafficking to be present-day manifestations of white slavery narratives. Today's alarmist political arguments about the dangers of trafficking have been shown to have their roots in the myth of white slavery. Reviewing feminist and sex worker positions on the matter of prostitution, the book has demonstrated how the notion of consent is central to a perspective on prostitution as a legitimate employment choice, and how these ideas of consent are articulated in political practice and come to inform policy making.

Trafficking in women, myth and consent

In this book, trafficking in women has been analysed as a myth – the resurrection of the myth of white slavery. Looking at trafficking as myth enables us to explain the persistence, appeal and believability of trafficking discourses. Analysis of the trafficking negotiations shows the white slave as an awesome poltergeist, a ghost with the power to move. The power of the trafficking discourse derives from a number of mythical functions: its *appearance* as a description of reality (including through a reification of consent); its function as a surface on which social demands are inscribed; its ability to accommodate differing ideologies; and its function as a metaphor for key social dislocations. The myth of trafficking has been shown to be not a matter of factual truth or falsehood; it is because of this that trafficking is so hard to bring into question.

Awareness of 'trafficking in women' as myth shows us how it enacts its performative power through appearing to be a description of reality. This awareness allows us to shed light on key dilemmas around defining trafficking in women posed at the beginning of this book. One of the ways that myth works is through naturalizing symbolic worlds. This occurred at the trafficking negotiations as the symbolic figure of the 'trafficking victim' was reified through the mechanism of consent. Attempts to define trafficking in Vienna, to decide which situations constituted 'real' trafficking, moved round the fulcrum of consent – just as for anti-white slavery campaigners, consent was the dividing line that distinguished between 'real' and 'unreal' white slavery. Either all migration for prostitution was to be considered trafficking, because choice to engage in sex work was considered impossible; or trafficking was deemed to occur only in those cases in which possible consent was seen as absent: whether consent was deemed possible or impossible, present or absent, it was the standard by which the actual situations of migrating sex workers (and others) came to be determined.

Why trafficking? Why now?

In the twenty years since trafficking has gone from being a concern of a few feminist NGOs to a global issue, representations of trafficking have multiplied immensely. The global myth of trafficking in women takes many discursive forms. Newspaper reports, NGO reports, laws, films and books both fictional and non-fictional – all these go into the corpus of the myth of 'trafficking in women', along with non-recorded vocal expressions, debates and discussions. The global myth of trafficking, then, is the entire sum of the expressions of concern, documentation and fictionalization of trafficking in women, as well as the activities carried out in their production. A newspaper article, for example, that reports on the SAARC declaration on trafficking may give only a dry rendition of the events and a summary of the speeches. This is every bit as mythical as the 'lifestyle' piece that stretches tales of woe over 2,000 heart-rending words (with pictures). I have shown how forms of the myth of trafficking like these were used in the political arena of the trafficking negotiations, as surfaces of inscription for competing ideologies. I have also shown that the actions of actors competing to determine meanings of trafficking are in themselves mythical.

How might a view of trafficking in women as myth permit us to make sense of why this particular feminist concern is so high on the international agenda? As we have seen, white slavery also went from a feminist concern to a state and international concern, inscribed in international documents. It is astounding that of all the issues raised by feminists, in the white slavery era and over the past two decades, 'trafficking in women' has been the one that governments – even those notoriously hostile to feminist arguments – have shown themselves willing to 'jump into bed' with feminists over (under the seductive blandishment of 'consent'). Laclau's handling of myth shows myth as 'incomplete', constantly 'reconstituted and displaced' (1990: 63). Myths are thus able to accommodate a wide variety of ideologies. White slavery appealed to purity reformers, feminists, anti-trust activists, conservative and progressive social groups; all found in the myth of white slavery a way to express their concerns about changes in society. This book has shown how today's trafficking discourses appeal to a similarly wide and disparate collection of social groups. If myth is indeed, as Sorel proposes, 'identical with the convictions of a group' (1908 [1999]: 53), then the myth of 'trafficking in women' is powerful because it expresses the convictions of many different, and even opposed, social groups.

This wide range of concerns brings us to another essential element of myth examined in this book: the function of myth as metaphor. The examination of myth as metaphor has shown how concerns about social change, historical and contemporary, are encoded in the myth of white slavery/trafficking. This approach enables us to answer questions about why the discourses of white slavery have reappeared in the guise of trafficking in women at this particular time. It points us towards the reappearance of key 'social dislocations' (Laclau 1990). The myth has been seen, during the white slavery era, as incorporating and expressing shifting ideas around sexuality, the role of women, notions of race and citizenship, under the pressures of social changes including mass global migration, the impact of feminism, urbanization and the 'commodification of labour'. It is possible to identify similar seismic shifts in social relations today. At the Vienna negotiations, as we have seen, trafficking in women covered a wide range of state and feminist concerns. These included concerns about increasing migration, about violence against women, and about the effect of processes of global economic change on women. The negotiations showed trafficking operating in a like metaphorical function, as the arena in which shifting ideas around sexuality, the role of women and ideas of labour and citizenship were contested. I have shown that the myths of white slavery and trafficking are not simply reflections of social changes, but a key element also involved in producing and contesting them.

Sex work, myth and reinscriptions

Awareness of trafficking in women as myth can help us understand why feminists remain so invested in discourses of trafficking, even after recognition of its harmful effects for sex workers and migrants. We recall that myth may be a matter of 'renouncing and reviling'; that it can be used to promote injustice. Racism and prejudice flourished under the banner of white slavery, as they do under trafficking today. However, the performativity of myth is not necessarily negative. It can also encode hopes for emancipatory social change. White slavery was used to point to the injustices towards migrants, to exploitative working conditions, and to discrimination against women. So too the myth of trafficking, particularly when employed by feminists, both abolitionist and 'liberal', is used to express concerns about actually existing injustices, including the continued prevalence of violence against women, restrictions on women's mobility, and the inequities between developed and developing countries.

Finally, then, we are brought full circle: the myth of trafficking cannot be 'disproved' because it is not a matter of 'fact': and thus it needs to be 'reinscribed'. Taken with Laclau's arguments about the necessity of myth, this means the search for new myth, or perhaps, ways to reinscribe 'old' myths. In Chapter 1, I said that this research also meant for me a realization of the ways in which I was also invested in myth. A story illustrates how this realization was brought home to me.

During the course of writing this book, I spent some time involved in an HIV prevention project in Andhra Pradesh. While there, a representative of a local sex worker organization told me enthusiastically about the theatre performance their group gave as part of their campaign to increase awareness of the need for safe sex. The plot of their drama had a familiar ring. The sex workers acted out the story of a poor young village girl who is approached by a flashy, handsome city man who promises to marry her. She follows him to the city, where he seduces her then demands that she earn money for him by sleeping with other men. She has no choice but to obey, contracts HIV, and, at the end of their performance, dies.

Whilst I was familiar with the ways in which sex workers use stories of victimization as a strategy towards demanding that their human rights be respected, this was the first time I had heard the white slavery melodrama, as if lifted wholesale from the tabloids, in such a direct form. It made me question what it might mean that sex workers were using it. I was reminded of a comment by Judith Walkowitz (1996), in which she describes melo-drama as a form of political theatre for the working class. This story from Andhra Pradesh shows how powerful the myth of trafficking is. It reveals how myth speaks to experience – not just an imagining of an ideal world. It shows how myths can be 'true', not factually, but 'literally'. The sex worker performance was a dramatization, apart from questions of morality and virtue, of power and powerlessness.

In its use by feminists and by sex workers, the trafficking myth does encapsulate those imbalances of power – gender power, economic power, global power – that are 'real'. That is why it is so tempting, so powerful, and also so believable. However, the use of the story by the Andhra Pradesh sex workers also allows us to see how the myth might be reinscribed to challenge existing power relations. While the form of the narrative used by the Andhra Pradesh sex workers echoes that of white slavery stories, its meaning is different. The sex workers followed the performance of the trafficking story by providing safe sex information to the audience. The story was used in a performance designed to combat the stigma around sex work, in particular the intense blame laid on sex workers as spreaders of HIV. Thus, the moral of the story was transformed. As in the NSWP slogan 'Sex workers: part of the solution', these women subverted the 'trafficking in women' narrative to reposition themselves from pariahs to protectors, from fallen women in need of rescue to community educators: experts on safe sex.

The new subject of myth

As the experience of sex workers at the Vienna negotiations showed, the liberal feminist approach to sex work as 'choice' has 'no choice' but to shuffle the sex worker off the global stage when faced with the radical feminist epistemological challenge of sex work as 'violence'. Like rape, when consent is what makes trafficking 'real', the determination will always involve judging whether or not a woman agreed to have sex (for pleasure, money, etc.), rather than on a set of circumstances that can be more objectively observed and judged. Given the pressures that women have been subjected to in the name of consent, the abolitionist desire to do away with the consent standard is completely understandable. Is the choice between on the one hand getting away from the thorny issues of consent by denying that it is possible at all (in regards to prostitution) or on the other accepting the problematic distinction that comes from using consent as the marker between 'free choice' and 'violence'? I return here to the question I posed at the beginning of this book: is it possible to find a way to look at prostitution that doesn't rely on the consent standard?

The answer to this question forms also the starting point of my efforts to replace old myths with new ones – the starting point for a way to deal with the thorny issues raised by anti-trafficking campaigns in ways that do not oppress or limit freedom. What could replace consent as the yardstick by which prostitution is measured? I find myself at the close of this book thus still struggling with the issue of 'consent'. As a feminist, my own perceptions of sexuality are deeply entwined with notions of consent. As a sex worker activist with a commitment to justice for sex workers, I am deeply invested in ideas of 'sex worker rights', ideas which are similarly tied to 'consent'. Thus, I find it difficult to move beyond 'consent' and beyond the myth of trafficking, as well as to conceive of a concept of sex work that does not depend on 'consent'. Perhaps our notion of consent was as unimaginable to those who saw the 'harms' of sex entirely in moral terms, as consent's replacement is to us. Given the power and prevalence of the myth of trafficking, and the importance of consent to feminist perceptions of sexuality, the task of displacing consent and thus of reinscribing the myth will not be an easy one. It presents great challenges for feminist thought and action, as well as for the thought and action of sex worker rights advocates.

These challenges are encountered in attempts to replace, or reinscribe, the subject of the trafficking myth, the 'suffering body' of the female prostitute; to change the focus of our concern from the *vulnerable* subject (capable of being hurt) needing protection, to the *desiring* subject whose primary requirement is not passively confirmed 'rights' but a political arena conducive to the practice of freedom. This replacement or reinscription will necessarily involve overcoming the 'voluntary/forced' dichotomy, and the concept of consent implicated in it, which the myth of trafficking both depends on and propagates. At the beginning of this book, I observed that abolitionist feminists had already overcome the voluntary/forced dichotomy in their ideology of prostitution as *per se* violence. Because prostitution is defined as violence, questions of consent become irrelevant. The challenge is to find a way similarly to move outside the constraints of consent, but to do so in a way that does not involve positioning prostitutes as victims of violence.

Entering the radical space occupied by anti-prostitution feminists to stake out a place there in which to articulate a positive stance towards sex work presents a challenge to feminist, and liberal, theories. Taking sex work (even the name may have to change!) out of the liberal feminist framework of 'consent' challenges many of the ideas of the sex worker rights movement and of feminism. It may necessitate bringing to the forefront alternative ways of thinking about 'sex work' that have lingered at the margins of the movement, and may enable the incorporation of settings and experiences that are difficult to fit within a 'sex worker rights' framework. These settings and experiences include particularly those elements that have traditionally bedevilled attempts to articulate liberal sex worker politics. They include questions around 'choice' that arise regarding the involvement of third parties, youth prostitution and global power inequities. The move of taking sex work out of the free/forced framework may be able to incorporate the postures which are more familiar to us 'insiders' but have often sat uneasily with the version of politics we argue for to the outside world: the embracing, seeking, enjoinment of 'transgression' versus the 'it's a job like any other' official line, and of the fault line between 'sex work' as work and 'sex work' as identity. It may be a move for sex work politics analogous to the queering of gay rights politics, with similar opportunities and challenges for political action: the chief opportunity being the ability to encompass, articulate and imagine a politics of liberation that moves beyond victimization, and the challenge being to translate these politics into meaningful political action.

At the level of practice, these opportunities and challenges are already being faced. Moving beyond the myth of trafficking and towards the framings of new myths that are based on sex workers' own perceptions, desires and hopes can only come through praxis; through changes at the level of political practice. Some of these are beginning to occur as part of already ongoing political processes. Sex worker organizations such as the NSWP and anti-trafficking organizations such as GAATW are attempting to reposition 'trafficking in women' by situating it within broader social movements. Linkages are being formed with migrant organizations and organizations of workers in the informal economy. It is through these processes of building solidarity, exploring commonalities and initiating joint political action that the spectre of the white slave will finally be laid to rest, and from which the subject of a new, emancipatory myth can emerge.

Notes

Introduction

1 When I have told people – many of whom are not in any way involved in the issue – that the topic of my thesis is trafficking in women, not one person has said 'What is that?' Without exception, the response has been to affirm the horror of the problem, how good it was I was working on it, and often to recount a story such as those in Boxes 1, 2 and 3.

2 This story sparked off a discussion on the NSWP online discussion list (as do many other newspaper accounts). The discussion started around the suggestion that the woman was charging $5 a trick. Members found a price this low difficult to believe – even more so when the person was supposedly a trafficking victim. As one list member put it: 'What do others think of the $5 sex slaves in this article? I find it hard to believe. $5 is just too low for me to conceive that this is a trafficking situation. My sense is that if she had to make money for others, they'd at least try to get more money. Someone involved at some level would have to see this as a business, and therefore want reasonable money' (NSWP list-serve 30 July 2003).

A response to this question refers to the lack of actual 'sex slaves' in the body of the article itself: 'the article doesn't actually talk about trafficking *per se* ... the woman who says she charges $5 doesn't say what for, exactly, but she also doesn't [complain] of being totally controlled by anyone. She's taking a long time to pay off a debt and is bitter about being lied to, but she appears to have leeway in her life. So the headline about sex slaves is typical sensationalism' (NSWP list-serve, 31 July 2003).

3 As Hajer explains regarding the definition of ecological problems: 'The political conflict is hidden in the question of what definition is given to the problem, which aspects of social reality are included and which are left undiscussed ... various actors are likely to hold different perceptions of what the problem "really is"' (Hajer 1995).

4 See also Agustín (2002; 2003).

5 The report was commissioned from the GAATW by the UN Special Rapporteur on Violence Against Women.

6   The IOM (2000), while admirably cautious about using migration as a proxy for trafficking, falls into this trap even as it warns against it.

7   My MA thesis was later published in *Gender Issues* (Doezema 2000).

8   Connelly gives the example of how the report's estimate of a total of 5,000 prostitutes 'at any one time' in the city of Chicago was transformed by one such narrative into 'Each year Chicago alone exacts the ghastly toll of five thousand (see Report of Chicago Vice Commission) of these girls to fill the decaying gaps of our great army of twenty-five thousand lost women' (Connelly 1980: 120).

9   France was the European pioneer of regulationist systems, exhaustively detailed by Corbin (1990). Supported by doctors in other European countries and in the US, regulationists joined the international movement against white slavery in order to advance state regulation of prostitution.

10   Walkowitz (1980) has written the classic feminist text on Butlerite feminism and the Contagious Diseases Acts. This paragraph is based on her work.

11   Feminism is not the only discourse with influence on sex worker rights discourses: gay rights, queer politics, human rights discourses and medical discourses have also been variously influential.

12   Though the four distinctions abolition, prohibition, regulation and dissemination are commonly used when referring to prostitution policy, they are 'ideal types', with most existing state policies showing a combination of approaches (West 2000). West notes that this characterization is ' increasingly inappropriate as a description of current developments. A nation-state's measures with regard to prostitution are far from internally homogeneous and may include elements of more than one regulatory framework. There is movement between each regime, reflecting the political influence of competing discourses and organised interests' (p. 106). West looks in particular at the political influence of sex worker rights discourses in the UK, the Netherlands, Australia and New Zealand. Her analysis shows the ways in which a pure 'decriminalist' position, is, in practice, modified by sex worker organizations. The usefulness of the term 'decriminalization' is also waning because the neo-abolitionist feminists have adopted it to refer to their own policy position; that prostitutes themselves should be decriminalized, but that clients, brothel owners and other third parties should be criminalized.

13   The World Charter for Prostitutes' Rights was adopted at the Second International Whores' Conference, Brussels 1985. See Pheterson (1989) for an account of the conference.

14   The inclusion of clients in the list of those punishable by law was done first by Sweden in 1998. Neo-abolitionist feminists claim that this inclusion marks a radical departure from the old system, doing away with the 'gender bias' of laws that target only the female prostitute, not the male client. This is of course true, but it does so at the expense of the sex worker her- (or him-) self. While a full study of the effects of the law on sex workers has yet to be done, preliminary studies indicate that rather than stopping work, sex

workers have retreated to less visible forms of work. As with any disciplinary measure, it is the most vulnerable and visible sex workers – those working on the street – who are most affected by the loss of clients and loss of income. See Kulick (2002; 2003; 2005), Gould (2001) and Kilvington et al. (2001) for examinations of the feminist campaign around the law and of the law's effects on sex workers.

15 Abolitionist and prohibitionist positions have similar political effects, despite their very different underlying views on the meaning of consent and the role of the state in regulating consent.

16 The history of feminist political activism is entwined with this desire to discipline the unruly young woman. It is astounding, and a cause for deep concern that this is still the case.

17 For details of the '100% Condom Programmes', see the NSWP website at www.nswp.org.

18 'Why did you become a prostitute?' has been a staple question on surveys of prostitutes since the dawn of social science. Indeed, prostitutes were among the first groups to be subjected to this new means of 'bio-power' – see S. Bell 1994. And, since the earliest surveys, the answers have remained remarkably consistent – see Pheterson (1990).

19 The question of whether or not adult men 'choose' to be prostitutes is asked, of course, much less often, as most feminists have always considered male sex workers to be such a minor phenomenon that it in no way affected their view of the sex industries as the prime example of women's oppression by men. This is changing, with recent studies looking at 'female sex tourism'(Sanchez-Taylor 2001; Phillips 1998). Many of these studies, however, victimize male sex workers as the latest casualty of the world's unequal distribution of wealth, without considering how 'adding men' to the analysis might affect their overall view of the issue of consent in the sex industry.

20 In the same work Chapkis (1997) makes an exciting challenge to the neo-abolitionist view of prostitution. After reviewing at length the neo-abolitionist arguments that prostitution destroys the prostitute, Chapkis argues for a reconsideration of the role of emotions in labour and in particular in prostitution, calling for prostitution to be viewed as 'emotional labour'.

1 White slavery and trafficking as political myth

1 Publicity flyer for the documentary *Trafficking Cinderella*, directed by Mira Niagolova, distributed at the Transnational Training Seminar on Trafficking in Women, 20–24 June 2000, Budapest.

2 The other great source of influence on myth studies, that of religion, has had much less influence on theorists of *political* myth (Flood 1996; Doty 2000).

3 According to Laclau: 'The crisis of the notion of "ideology" was linked to two interconnected processes: the decline of social objectivism and the

denial of the possibility of a metalinguistic vantage point which allows the unmasking of ideological distortion' (p. 320). Or, more clearly: 'Categories such as "distortion" and "false representation" [only] made sense as long as something "true" or "undistorted" was considered to be within human reach' (1997: 298). The notion of discourse 'ideologized' ideology, as Laclau notes of Žižek's analysis in *The Sublime Object of Ideology* (1994): 'Here Žižek correctly detects the main source of the progressive abandonment of "ideology" as an analytical category: "this notion somehow grows" too strong, it begins to embrace everything, inclusive of the very neutral, extra-ideological ground supposed to provide the standard by means of which one can measure ideological distortion. That is to say, is it not the ultimate result of discourse analysis that the order of discourse as such is inherently "ideological"?' (Laclau 1997: 298).

4   Althusser uses the example of a police officer hailing someone in the street, not by using their name, simply calling 'Hey, you there!'(1971 [2001]: 118). Even without their name being called, this person will recognize themselves in the call of the official: 'The hailed individual will turn round. By this mere one-hundred-and-eighty-degree physical conversion, he becomes a *subject* ... what thus seems to take place outside ideology (to be precise, in the street), in reality takes place in ideology ... That is why those who are in ideology believe themselves by definition outside ideology: one of the effects of ideology is the practical *denegation* of the ideological character of ideology by ideology: ideology never says, "I am ideological"' (1971 [2001]: 118) (see Felluga 2003).

5   This is highly ironic, given that it is arguably Foucault who is most responsible for the present ubiquity of the term 'discourse', and that the other term that is most connected with his work is 'power'.

6   Though I have focused on the 'epistemological' influence of Eagleton and the 'political struggle' influence of Laclau for this study, both of their work on 'ideology' spans and exceeds each of these traditions.

7   There are a number of problems with the 'myth as metaphor' approach, which are looked at more fully in Chapter 3.

8   The term 'false consciousness' has been used by feminists against politically active sex workers. See Bell (1987).

9   Bank echoes Flood in his criticism of what he sees as L. Thompson's over-concern with proving the factual untruth of apartheid myths: rather than falling 'back upon a positivist notion of myth as false stories that can be tested against the standards of historical truth', he argues that 'the boundaries between political myth and historical reality are more complex' (p. 462). For Tudor (1972) it is not the place of a student of politics to denounce a particular set of beliefs as false: rather, the social scientist should be concerned with establishing how and why people think as they do.

10 'For Althusser, one can speak of descriptions or representations of the world as being either true or false; but ideology is not for him at root a matter of

such descriptions at all, and criteria of truth and falsehood are thus largely irrelevant to it' (Eagleton 1991: 18).

11 Perhaps a clear way to illustrate this mechanism is to take a myth/ideology which has already widely been discredited: that of racial inferiority. Leonard Thompson's (1995) work on the myths of apartheid provides an example of the dangers of slipperiness. While disagreeing with the notion of history as 'objective fact', recognizing the value-laden nature of historical enquiry, Thompson nonetheless argues that myth's 'historical truth' and 'scientific probability' are two criteria by which it should be judged. What are the consequences of this move for Thompson's analysis? Few today would argue that the notions of racial inferiority are a fit subject to be proved or disproved through historical fact-finding or scientific investigation. The statement 'Blacks are less intelligent than whites' appears to be a description of reality and thus appears to be a statement that can be proved or disproved by empirical evidence/scientific enquiry. These sorts of statements are now widely seen as expressions of racism (a racist ideology), or as a prime example of Eagleton's description: 'it is fundamentally a matter of fearing and denouncing, reverencing and reviling, all of which then sometimes gets coded into a discourse which looks as though it is describing the way things actually are' (Eagleton 1991: 19). Thus opponents of racism do not attempt to 'prove' scientifically that blacks are as intelligent as whites, for this would give a spurious sheen of legitimacy to the claim in the first place. The trick is to uncover the ways in which racism gets coded into scientific language. Yet, because Thompson fails to recognize this, he ascribes to science (quite bizarrely) the leading role in conquering 'false myths' about race; describing the demise of 'scientific racism' he says: 'the shift in scientific opinion was not easily translated into non-scientific language, nor was it readily injected into the popular consciousness, where deep-rooted racial prejudices gave ground at a much slower rate ... Time lags always exist between the findings of specialists and their incorporation in the basic knowledge of the general public ... however, with laws, political rhetoric, newspapers, radio and television programs and school and college textbooks abandoning racism, on balance the Western mentality has been moving in the direction pioneered by the scientists' (1985: 16–17).

12 The idea that a non-evaluative study of ideology is relativistic has been called 'Mannheim's paradox' after Karl Mannheim (1936). Mannheim took a historicist approach to ideology, rejecting the idea that there existed timeless, eternally true concepts, instead viewing all thought as historically conditioned. His self-reflexive theory of ideology subjected all thought, including his own, to ideological analysis, and so, according to some commentators, leads to a radical relativism.

13 Others have attempted to judge the 'truth' of ideology in ways that do not engage with epistemic issues. For example, Raymond Guess argues that a body of ideas may be functionally and/or genetically false as well as

epistemically false. A body of ideas may be false because it 'incorporates beliefs which are false, or because it functions in a reprehensible way, or because it has a tainted origin' (quoted in Eagleton 1991: 25). Eagleton is uncritical of these attempts, in keeping with what he sees as a radical commitment to socialist truth. Others, however, have been more critical. For example, Mannheim rejected the idea of what he termed the 'genetic fallacy', 'the deduction of the validity of an idea directly from its origins' (McLellan 1995: 38).

2 The construction of innocence and the spectre of chaos

1   A literary echo of campaigning journalist W. T. Stead's (1885) attempts at literal establishment (through doctor's examination) of the virginity of the 'maidens' that he 'bought' in his undercover investigation of white slavery, discussed later in the chapter.

2   Transnational Training Seminar on Trafficking in Women, 20–24 June 1998, Budapest.

3   While choosing to focus on these two figures was obvious, considering their importance, my decision was also influenced by Walkowitz who, in the *The City of Dreadful Delight* (1992), contrasts Stead's and Butler's narratives on white slavery. The influence of this wonderful book on my own analysis extends beyond the choice of central figures, as the main text of this chapter makes clear. Walkowitz also examines the narrative structures and strategies of Stead's text 'The Maiden Tribute of Modern Babylon' (1885). Walkowitz's main concern is with the production of meanings around sexual danger, and how these meanings 'ordered people's experience and helped to construct a sexual subjectivity for men and women' (1992: 83). As the title indicates, the city as symbol of or metaphor for sexual danger is central to her analysis. The city had enormous symbolic resonance in white slavery narratives in every country, and its symbolic power is also a feature of contemporary trafficking tales. The city as a metaphor of danger and corruption will be looked at in more detail in Chapter 3.

While *The City of Dreadful Delight* is not expressly a look at myth, Walkowitz's rich deconstruction of key narratives of white slavery in Britain is, in effect, the deconstruction of a myth. Walkowitz views 'narrative' fairly narrowly as a particular arrangement of written expression. Her purpose in focusing on narrative, as she explains it, is 'to explore how cultural meanings around sexual danger were produced and disseminated in Victorian society, and what were their cultural and political effects' (p. 83). 'The Maiden Tribute' in Walkowitz's analysis is a paradigmatic example of the production of meanings of sexual danger: Stead's descriptions of the violation of virgins enabling the readers to thrill with pleasurable horror at the same time as they righteously denounced the evil of white slavery.

182

4   Haveman (1998) analyses the case of the Netherlands, where the political fight around white slavery was also a constant tension between the two images.

5   The problem of loss of analytical edge is of course wider than the understanding of the 'madonna/whore' dichotomy, and is a feature of much contemporary social analysis which has domesticated the (revolutionary) implications of 'post' (structuralism, modernism, colonial) theory. Binaries, dichotomies, discourses and 'Others', a litany familiar to students all over (and invoked with as much reverence and as little understanding as church liturgy) are now on the cusp of becoming as quaint as 'false consciousness' and 'the proletariat'.

6   'Narrative' is a term that without careful handling can end up in the litany with 'dichotomy' etc. See note 5.

7   Flood (1996) maintains that not every 'given discourse' in which a political myth plays is necessarily 'predominantly narrative in form or function ... A book can consist of chapters which are largely in the form of argument and description, while the sequencing of some or all of the chapters follow a chronological order giving a narrative dimension to the text' (p. 125).

8   Flood uses this quote from Barthes to illustrate his argument that narrative as such was not a consideration for Barthes. Yet he misses the point that for Barthes, this was precisely because 'any image, object or verbal message' (Flood 1996: 165) had the same semiotic structure when used as myth, making the isolation of the 'narrative' aspect unnecessary.

9   This poster caused much discussion on the NSWP list. The NSWP co-ordinator wrote to the IOM in protest, and NSWP member Empower Bangkok produced a satirical cartoon based on the poster. The IOM responded with a defence of the poster, arguing that its 'shocking' nature was necessary to make people aware of the true nature of trafficking.

10 The notion of 'the body' as an important site of study (other than medical) has been immensely productive in cultural studies, and in queer, feminist and post-colonial theory. For a study of prostitution, of course, 'the body' springs immediately to mind. On the face of it, the concern with prostitution in Europe and the United States marks the break between Victorian 'repression' and the 'modern', open approach to sexuality which Foucault (1976 [1981]) contests. Many historians continue to follow this 'end of repression' approach, showing how the campaign against white slavery, especially women's involvement with it, helped initiate the new era of sexual openness. While I agree with the Foucaultian interpretation, it is nonetheless the case that feminists and social hygienists *themselves* experienced and described their willingness to discuss prostitution in public as breaking of silence and an overcoming of shame (Walkowitz 1980).

11 Bell (1994) observes, like Nead (1988), contradictions in presentations of the prostitute body but reads them through Bakhtin's notions of the carnivalesque. She stresses that the presented body was multidimensional and

contradictory, but she still comes up with (nearly) the same 'master-images' as Nead (on the one hand the profane, on the other the sacred/pleasure aspects of the prostitute): 'One a ruined, destroyed, victimized body; the other a destroying body, a disease that spreads and rots the body politic. These images are inversions of one another' (Bell 1994: 45).

12 Men were not considered victims of the 'white slave trade', though the US Immigration Commission Report of 1909 (US Senate 1909) noted that young men were being imported from Europe for 'unnatural practices'. This was a reference to the supposed European perversion of homosexuality and the threat of its importation to the US (Grittner 1990). In today's discourse on trafficking in women, very little mention is made of men being trafficked. Campaigns that focus specifically on child prostitution, in contrast, often highlight the presence of boys, which may reflect an anti-gay bias.

13 The term 'free-floating signifier' comes from linguistics. Laclau uses the example of 'democracy' to explain his usage of the term: 'a signifier like "democracy" is essentially ambiguous by dint of its widespread political circulation: it acquires one possible meaning when articulated with "anti-fascism" and a completely different one when articulated with "anti-communism"' (1990: 28).

14 Doty (2000) explains the difference between a synchronic and a diachronic approach as follows: 'Attention to a specific text of whatever nature, by whatever method, is synchronic or symtagmatic, whereas genre criticism of a body of texts, or comparative motif criticism, is paradigmatic or diachronic. Any one text that presents a number of actors or situations, however, may need to be analyzed with both dimensions in mind' (p. 281).

15 Doty notes that Strauss's structuralism was predominantly concerned with 'the mythical structures of society rather than with clarification or appreciation of actual narratives themselves ... in terms of their immediate semantic significance within the societies producing the myths or rituals' (2000: 283).

16 Historians attribute the first report of white slavery to Alfred Dyer in 1880, a social purity campaigner whose 'exposure' of the presence of English women in brothels in Belgium led to a Parliamentary enquiry (Roberts 1992).

17 The name 'abolitionist' was adopted by anti-prostitution campaigners from anti-slavery campaigns (Irwin 1996).

18 The relationship between middle-class Butlerite feminists and their working-class victim heroines was a complicated one of, on the one hand, identification with female suffering, and on the other, a desire to police and control less-educated and less-fortunate sisters. Prostitutes who refused to play the role of repentant victim were an anathema to many of these feminists, see Walkowitz 1980, Bland 1992 and Burton 1994.

19 The repressive nature of the social purity campaign was recognized and condemned by some feminists of the time. Theresa Billington-Grieg (1913)

published an article in the *English Review* in 1913 in which she argued that feminist anti-white slavery activists had 'provided arms and ammunition for the enemy of women's emancipation' (p. 446). Billington-Grieg undertook an investigation of the white slavery cases publicized by the purity movement and found them to be unfounded or 'spun' beyond recognition. Josephine Butler publicly condemned the repressive aspects of the social purity movement, but many of her erstwhile followers joined the ranks of the social purists (Walkowitz 1980).

20 The veracity of Stead's tale has been the subject of speculation, not least because Stead himself was put on trial for slavery after this account was published. For an account of the trial, see Walkowitz 1992.

21 The potential for contemporary mirrorings of emancipatory white slavery discourses should be investigated and exploited.

22 Sharp and Jordan have collected Butler's works in their *Diseases of the Body Politic: Josephine Butler and the Prostitution Campaign* (2002).

23 The analysis of Butler's use of melodrama is from Walkowitz 1992.

24 Walkowitz (1992) notes how the young men also sacrificed in the Greek myth disappeared in Stead's replacing of the myth to London.

25 Where there are underground chambers in a narrative, sex is never far behind – even if it is never made explicit. The thrill and horror of Victorian (and contemporary) gothic is at least partially sexual. While I am inclined against a narrowly psycho-sexual interpretation of the gothic, there is no doubt that lonely castles and secret chambers have a Freudian resonance.

26 McGrath and Morrow (1991) write that inversion is the 'basic structural principle' of the gothic: 'Subterranean passages, vaults, dungeons, cellars – these are all staples of the early gothicists. Such chthonic, claustrophobic spaces they were! Each was a vivid analogue of the tomb, and each provided a site of inversion, where terror and unreason subverted consensus and rationality, where passion was transformed into disgust, love turned to hatred and good engendered evil' (p. xiii).

Taking into account Bell's (1994) observation in note 11 regarding inversion and the image of the prostitute (destroyer/destroyed), we can see how the gothic narrative worked so well to tell the white slavery myth. Interestingly, the concept of inversion, along with distortion, is an essential element of Marx's theories of ideology.

27 The individual case history of the prostitute as the site of authentic truth has itself a long history: Nead (1988) describes how investigative journalists and religious social workers in the mid-nineteenth century both used the technique.

28 Walkowitz's observation of the legacy of the political effects of Stead's myth creation are appropriate to this study: 'His narrative was taken up, reworked by different constituencies and social forces. These multiple transformations gave rise to complex political effects, which were not exhausted in the nineteenth century' (1992: 85).

29 Irwin (1996) argues that Stead's narrative was successful in arousing public ire because the victims were portrayed as daughters of the middle class. She is rather alone in this interpretation: Walkowitz (1992) extensively documents Stead's political links to socialism and the working class. My own reading of 'The Maiden Tribute' leads me to agree with Walkowitz's interpretation. Nead (1988) argues that white slavery became a popular cause because the plight of the prostitute was transformed into art consumed by the middle class.

30 According to Bristow, the term 'white slavery' first appeared in 1839, in an anti-semitic context (1982: 34).

31 The term 'suffering others' is from Brown (1995) and is further explored in Chapter 5.

3 Metaphorical innocence: white slavery in America

1 The concerns about the arbitrariness of the connections between metaphor and reality in accounts of white slavery were inspired by Henry Tudor's (1972) observations about the allegorical interpretation of myth. Tudor argues against a hermeneutical interpretation of myth because a given myth could have a number of possible allegorical interpretations. According to Tudor, the questions of *why* messages were encoded in mythical language at all is not answered by a hermeneutical approach.

2 Hobson (1987) shows a recognition of the problems with the metaphorical approach in her critique of Connelly (1980), when she takes him to task for an over-reliance on the psycho-social interpretation of prostitution. She suggests that the concern with prostitution expressed in 'anti-prostitution' and white slavery campaigns actually *was* a concern with prostitution. She does, however, recognize the 'symbolic content' of anti-prostitution, in particular the campaign against white slavery.

3 See Bell (1994) for an application of Bakhtin's notion of the 'carnivalesque' to Western prostitution discourse.

4 Haag (1999) makes the most radical claims about the effect of the white slavery campaigns on changing liberal ideologies, arguing that the Progressive responses to prostitution helped shape the modern notion of personal freedom which encompasses, for example, sexual and reproductive freedoms.

5 Most historians do take this approach, Haag (1999) being a notable exception.

6 The term 'abolitionist' is confusing, as Josephine Butler adopted the term to refer to her work against the Contagious Diseases Acts. Because the term 'abolitionist' is still used in current debates around prostitution to indicate a certain political position (see Introduction), I will use the tautological phrase 'anti-slavery abolitionists' when referring to campaigns against black slavery.

7 This phrase comes from *The Social Evil in Chicago*, the report of the Chicago

Vice Commission of 1911, considered by historians to be one of the most influential anti-white-slavery documents.

8 Though when Haag (1999) deals with other 'tropes of sexual consent and violence', such as interracial marriage and interracial rape, the symbolic power of 'whiteness' in a sexual context is well recognized and provocatively explored.

9 See Grittner (1990).

10 Disturbingly, while decrying the racist elements in white slavery narratives, historians like Hobson (1987), Grittner (1990) and Connelly (1980) themselves all too easily slip into stereotypical thinking where 'non-white slavery' is concerned. While white slavery in its literal meaning is seen by them as an exaggeration of reality, a distortion of truth, with historical and modern sources interrogated heavily, they take accounts of the traffic in non-white women, and the involvement of non-white men in this trade, as literal truth. While it is beyond the scope of my research to investigate the 'facts' as presented by Bristow (1977), the uncritical acceptance of the evidence for this trade is distressing.

11 Haag (1999) bolsters her argument for the relative irrelevance of 'white' in white slavery by tracing its first appearance in radical postbellum thought in the US. Bristow (1977), however, traces the first use of the term to a letter from Victor Hugo in which he used the term in an anti-semitic fashion to refer to prostitution.

12 An exception to this general tendency is Jane Addams (1912), who devotes a few pages to investigating the cause of the high number of 'colored' women involved in 'the social evil'. Her writing shows that mixture of social progressiveness and conservative morality that characterizes her work. On the one hand, including a consideration of black women's work in prostitution in a book on white slavery is highly remarkable. This progressive tendency is also reflected in her targeting of social and economic conditions – slavery and its aftermath – rather than innate tendencies as the cause of black involvement in prostitution. However, while she argues that slavery is to blame for black people's lack of moral restraint, the impression is still one of a group in society whose moral evolution has not reached that of white society: 'The community forces the very people who have confessedly the shortest history of social restraint, into a dangerous proximity with the vice districts of the city. This results, as might easily be predicted, in a very large number of colored girls entering a disreputable life ... it seems all the more unjustifiable that the nation which is responsible for the broken foundations of this family life should carelessly permit the negroes, making their first struggle towards a higher standard of domesticity, to be subjected to the most flagrant temptations which our civilization tolerates' (Addams 1912: 119).

13 White opinion, backed by 'evolutionary' science, was that black fighters, as members of an 'inferior race' were physically and psychologically inferior to whites. While black fighters were widely believed to have harder heads than

whites, this was seen as the result of their smaller brain capacity. Blacks were seen as passive, lacking the will to win, shifty and lazy. This was used to explain white dominance of the sport: when Johnson began to beat white heavyweights, these same inferior characteristics were now used as an explanation of his victories (Roberts 1983).

14 Parkin was a prominent anti-white-slavery campaigner, who contributed several chapters to Bell's *Fighting the Traffic in Young Girls* (1910b). These chapters, however, give little indication of his virulent racism.

15 Grittner (1990) includes a remark to the US legislature by Representative Gordon Russel of Texas, a fervent advocate of the Mann Act: 'Let me tell you gentlemen, no nation can rise higher than the estimate which it places upon the virtue and purity of its womanhood.' After struggling to end the slavery of 'the black man' Congress could do no less than help 'abolish the slavery of white women. This bill is a tribute to every pure and good woman in this land' (p. 83). Grittner observes that, 'Russell's heavy-handed linking of white women and black men was aimed at his fellow Southerners. A vote against the Mann Act could be interpreted back home as a failure to prevent miscegenation and as an incitement to black men. The debate occurred at a significant time in the South, when the Jim Crow laws [legal segregation] were firmly in place and the white communities were still filled with sexual fears about black men' (1990: 95).

16 This was again an anomaly: Grittner (1990) records that sentences under the Mann Act were lighter when the woman was already a prostitute.

17 The Jewish community was very sensitive to accusations of white slavery, and Jewish organizations were at the forefront of anti-white-slavery efforts. See Bristow 1982.

18 Connelly's (1980) reading of the narrative of 'The True Story of Estelle Ramon of Kentucky', included in Bell's *Fighting the Traffic in Young Girls* (1910b), explores the metaphorical resonances of the 'country girl in the city'.

19 Sims (1910a) is very fond of the 'wolf and lamb' metaphor, an example of the fairy-tale influences on the white slave melodrama genre.

20 A notable exception to the narrative equation between beauty and virtue is provided by Ophelia Amigh, Superintendent of the Illinois Training School for Girls (a reformatory). She recounts the story of Nellie, 'a very ordinary looking girl and below the average of intelligence, but as tractable and obedient as she is ingenuous. She is wholly without the charm which would naturally attract the eye of the white slave trader' (1910: 123). Nellie's obedient nature meant she was allowed to leave the so-called Training School for Girls and take up work as a housemaid. From here the story follows familiar paths, and Nellie ends up in a Chicago house of shame: 'How she was found and rescued is a story quite apart from the purpose which has led me to tell of this incident – that of indicating how tightly the slave traders have their nets spread for even the most ordinary and unattrac-

tive prey. They let no girl escape who they dare to approach' (1910: 123).

21 Disease, especially syphilis, was a power metaphor in its own right. The diseased body of the prostitute symbolized the contagion of society (Walkowitz 1980; Bell 1994; Nead 1988).

22 As I indicated when this story was first mentioned above, Sims is carried on the wave of rhetorical enthusiasm to the point of narrative unreliability. As the story is recounted, the 'little Italian peasant girl' is telling her tale to sympathetic listeners, including Assistant US District Attorney Parkin, the prosecutor in the Jack Johnson case who hoped Johnson's conviction would lead to laws against miscegenation. The 'little Italian peasant', arrested in the Chicago brothel raids due to enforcement of the 1907 Immigration Act, at first, 'like most of the others taken in the raids, stoutly maintained that ... she was in a life of shame from choice and not through the criminal act of any person' (Sims 1910b: 54). However, after being interrogated and persuaded of the good intentions of Parkins and company, she 'broke down and with pitiful sobs related her awful narrative. That every word of it was true no one could doubt who saw her as she told it' (ibid.). Descriptions of her beauty from the standpoint of Sims who 'saw her as she told it' provide a fine narrative contrast with her horrible disfigurement later.

23 The term 'psychological clearinghouse' is Connelly's own (1980: 7).

24 This belief in 'the rise of the pimp system' is still extremely prevalent and powerful today. Many sex worker activists oppose the use of the term 'pimp'. Laws aimed to 'stop pimping' have routinely been turned against sex workers, their lovers, business managers and families. Stereotypes about the relationships between pimps and prostitutes perpetuate the passive, damaged image of female sexuality and pathologize sex workers' intimate relationships. Furthermore, the 'pimp' image in the US and in Britain is constructed through racist notions about the brutality and hypersexuality of black men. See Pheterson 1986 and the articles about pimping at the NSWP website, www.nswp.org.

25 See Stange (1998) for analysis of the theme of labour power, commodity exchange and white slavery.

26 The image of 'the vice trust' was an analogy to other, corporate trusts, which were linked to graft and corruption in the city. While Hobson unquestioningly accepts the myth of 'the rise of the pimp system', she does contest the interpretation of it as a 'vice trust'. Rather than 'a highly organized prostitution empire in the hands of few vice moguls', she argues that prostitution was controlled by an 'informal network' of immigrants (1987: 145).

27 Bristow (1982) is an exception: his history of the Jewish experience of 'white slavery' takes a multi-country focus.

4 'Prevent, protect and punish'

1   The states that signed the agreement were France, Germany, Britain, Italy, Russia, Sweden, Denmark, Belgium, Holland, Spain, Portugal, Norway and Switzerland.

2   See Wijers and Lin 1997 and Haveman 1998.

3   The abolitionist position continued to dominate international law until the 1980s, when a number of agreements began to recognize a distinction between 'voluntary' and 'forced' prostitution. See Doezema 1998.

4   Roberts (1992) argues that the League of Nations' concern with white slavery in 1921 was the result of migration routes used by prostitutes, including Jews escaping the pogroms of Eastern Europe.

5   For documentation of the sex worker rights movement, see Alexander and Delacoste, 1987; Pheterson 1989; Chapkis 1997; and Kempadoo and Doezema 1998.

6   While it is fairly clear how 'smuggling of migrants' and 'trafficking in persons' might be addressed in the same convention, the questions of 'weapons' might not be so readily apparent. The link is the connection between all three and the subject of the 'main convention': organized crime. The delegations were unable to reach consensus on the Arms Protocol, and it was abandoned during the final session.

7   From the UN General Assembly Resolution calling for the convention: 'On the recommendation of the Commission on Crime Prevention and Criminal Justice and the Economic and Social Council (Council resolution 1998/14 of 28 July 1998), the General Assembly adopted resolution 53/111 of 9 December 1998, in which it decided to establish an open-ended inter-governmental ad hoc committee for the purpose of elaborating a compre-hensive international convention against transnational organized crime and of discussing the elaboration, as appropriate, of international instruments addressing trafficking in women and children, combating the illicit manu-facturing of and trafficking in firearms, their parts and components and ammunition, and illegal trafficking in and transporting of migrants, including by sea. In its resolution 53/114 of 9 December 1998, the Assembly called upon the Ad Hoc Committee on the Elaboration of a Convention Against Transnational Organized Crime to devote attention to the drafting of the main text of the convention, as well as of the above-mentioned inter-national instruments.'

8   Not all NGOs were involved in lobbying; several chose just to observe the proceedings.

9   Jordan notes that 'Priority areas within the mandate of the UN Crime Commission are: international action to combat national and transnational crime, including organized crime, economic crime and money laundering; promoting the role of criminal law in protecting the environment; crime prevention in urban areas, including juvenile crime and violence; and

improving the efficiency and fairness of criminal justice administration systems' (2002: 2 fn 5).

10 The US Immigration Commission of 1909 felt new measures were needed because the US could expect help from Europe with the 'white slave trade' but not with 'voluntary travel of prostitutes to the United States'. The 1909 Commission Report was, according to Connelly, 'permeated with the contemporary belief in the racial inferiority of the 'new' immigration' (Connelly 1980: 57). What is particularly interesting in this report are the indications of the increase in numbers of women refused entry to the United States and/or deported because they were suspected of being prostitutes.

11 There is an entire mythos of its own around organized crime, from *The Godfather* and *The Sopranos* in the US, to Japanese Yakuza in Manga comics. When this particularly potent body of myths intersects with the sexually charged myths of white slavery/trafficking, the result is a heady brew indeed.

12 The US and Argentina submitted separate drafts for the January 1999 meeting; by the March 1999 meeting these had been combined into one. For more on this see Chapter 5.

13 The Dutch approach to prostitution was not actually reflected in the law until 2000. It was a part of the well-known 'tolerance' approach of the Dutch to contentious social issues, such as prostitution and drug use, which is sadly in decline. For an examination of the 'tolerant' Dutch approach to trafficking with reference to the 2000 change in the law, see Visser (2003). For a comprehensive study of the Dutch response to white slavery and trafficking, see Haveman (1998).

14 The case of IGO submissions is an interesting one. As NGOs such as GAATW have matured, they have widened their sphere of influence: not only through successful lobbying, but also through having former members (also more mature!) in new positions of (relative) power. Within the 'human rights' areas of the UN, for example, the 'GAATW approach' has had more influence than the 'CATW approach'. Radika Coomariswami, former UN Special Rapporteur on Violence Against Women, is very open about her move from being an abolitionist to a GAATW position. The advisor on trafficking to the UNHCHR in Geneva has a GAATW background.

15 See also Jordan 2002.

16 The term 'rehabilitation' is very commonly used when referring to prostitutes, and commonly refers to a situation of forcible detainment in state 'rehabilitation centres' or on NGO premises (Human Rights Watch 1995; Empower 2003). At the Third annual National Sex Workers Network meeting in Trivandrum, Kerala, India (3–8 March 2003) which I attended, an entire session was devoted to discussing the repressive effects of these 'rehabilitation' policies.

17 Thailand has responded by aggressively promoting its mandatory condom use policy for brothels, in which – in an echo of the Contagious Diseases Acts

– the police ensure that brothel workers are taken for STD examinations. See Overs and Longo 2003.

18 Andrijasevic (2007) has written about the representation of women in anti-trafficking campaigns.

19 Or a child; the linking of women and children is examined below in this chapter.

20 For an account of how the feminist/conservative coalition influenced US domestic trafficking legislation, see Chapkis 2003 and Crago 2003.

21 At one point (January 2000), a rumour went round that the US delegation was 'not allowed' to talk to members of the Human Rights Caucus.

22 The US delegates were not pleased with the pressure put on them to denounce prostitution, as they were worried – correctly, as it turned out – that a strong anti-prostitution position would make them appear to be blocking consensus on the Protocol. At the final session, the US took the position of agreeing with all majority positions 'in the name of consensus'. The Philippines blocked consensus up to the last session, with their insistence that all prostitution be listed as sexual exploitation in the definition of trafficking. Other state delegations and the session chair became extremely frustrated by the Philippines' intransigence. This frustration eventually resulted in a complaint to the head of the Philippines delegation concerning the behaviour of the CATW member of that delegation; the complaint was made by the influential Chair of the informal working group on the definition of trafficking.

23 There are many more sex worker organizations that support the view of sex work as labour than there are of those who support the feminist abolitionist position. Globally, WHISPER is the only organization that identifies with this perspective. See Chapkis 1997 for a discussion of WHISPER. Books by Nagle (1997) and Kempadoo and Doezema (1998), as well as articles on the NSWP website (www.nswp.org), demonstrate the strength of the sex worker rights position among sex workers worldwide.

24 See also the account by fellow NSWP member Melissa Ditmore (2002).

25 This statement was made by Evelina Giobbe during the NGO Consultation with UN/IGOs on Trafficking in Persons, Prostitution and the Global Sex Industry: 'Trafficking and the Global Sex Industry: The Need for a Human Rights Framework', 21–22 June 1999, Palais des Nations, Geneva.

26 Newspaper reports on trafficking seldom fail to raise the spectre of a vast international criminal syndicate. The imagery used to describe these gangs is rife with metaphors of inescapability: 'tentacles', 'net', 'ring', as in the following extract from a UK article: 'Cambodia is the hub of a people-trafficking racket with tentacles stretching across South-east Asia and links with several Asian mafias' (*Independent*, 28 August 2003). The language used often switches register from the neutral 'criminal gangs' to the more titillating 'prostitution rings' or 'vice rings': 'Under the new deal, a criminal could be prosecuted in one member state for operating a sex ring in another

member state' (Reuters, 28 September 2001). This hooks into another widespread mythical image, that of the 'pimp'. Both the 'international criminal syndicate' and the 'pimp' of the prostitution ring are images that carry heavy xenophobic and racist baggage. For example, Stenvoll (2002: 8), in an article examining the response of newspapers in Norway to the increase in Russian sex workers in the rural northern area of Finnmark, shows how the focus in the reports on the Russian mafia fits nicely into larger public discourses about the assumed criminalization of Russian society.

27 For analysis of the feminist–Christian coalitions and their impact on US policy, see Chapkis 2003, Soderlund 2005, Bernstein 2007 and Weitzer 2007.

28 See the Columbia University Gender and Sexuality Law Blog at http://blogs.columbia.edu/genderandsexualitylawblog.

29 For an analysis of IJM's activities and connections with US government policy, see Soderlund 2005 and Bernstein 2007.

30 These human rights abuses are further documented in Overs 2009.

31 The phrase 'site of sexual violence' is taken from a comment made by a leading feminist at an anti-trafficking conference in Delhi (6–9 January 2004). She argued for the continued importance for feminism of the idea of sexuality as a 'site of violence'.

5 Now you see her, now you don't: consent, sex workers and the Human Rights Caucus

1 This was a gradual change in focus for GAATW-affiliated anti-trafficking organizations. For example, a 1997 GAATW report on trafficking was entitled *Trafficking in Women for the Purposes of Prostitution, Forced Labour and Marriage* (Wijers and Lin 1997). This report contained a definition of trafficking that still mentioned prostitution, albeit forced prostitution. By the time of the 2001 GAATW Human Rights Standards, however, the phrase 'trafficking in women' had been dropped in favour of 'trafficking in persons'. The Human Rights Standards use gender-neutral language throughout, and suggest a definition of trafficking that does not mention any specific type of occupation or service for which a person might be trafficked. The Standards, do, however, contain sections of gender analysis of trafficking.

2 The emails concerning the Protocol circulated on two lists that I was a member of. The first is the NSWP list, a facilitated list for all those who support the NSWP aims. Membership is through nomination and seconding by existing list members. The other list (or group) was that of the Human Rights Caucus, and consisted of NSWP members, anti-trafficking activists and human rights activists. This group was limited to those who actively participated in strategy and/or lobbying. NSWP-list mails are referred to in the text as 'NSWP list', Human Rights Caucus mails as 'HRC list'.

3   The Argentinian proposal for the draft Protocol (A/AC.254/8), submitted concurrently to the Crimes Commission, came to the attention of the HRC a few weeks later.

4   Gail Pheterson's exploration of this in her book *The Whore Stigma* (1986) has been very influential on my political development.

5   The Trafficking Protocol was not discussed during the second session.

6   Except of course in the amazingly paradoxical situation of a male child being deemed capable of rape, a fine example of the consent conundrum.

7   An excellent place for information on male sex work is the NSWP website (www.nswp.org), as well as publications by the European Network Male Prostitution (ENMP), which does a lot of work on migration issues.

8   The fifth, sixth and seventh sessions were 'informals'. Though supposedly mere drafting exercises, they were actually very influential, as the discussion in this chapter shows.

9   In another of the ironies in which the Crimes Commission debate was so rich, the Netherlands had coupled the recognition of prostitution as labour with a legal provision prohibiting non-Europeans from engaging in sex work in the Netherlands in the name of stopping trafficking. See West 2000 and Visser 2003.

10 'In the Netherlands ... in 1988 a special ruling was inserted in the Alien Code, holding that at the least suspicion of a person being a victim of trafficking that person should be allowed a "reflexion period" of three months' time to consider pressing charges. When the person decides to press charges, she or he is entitled to a temporary staying permit until the criminal process is completed. In case a person cannot return to her or his country she or he is entitled to apply for permanent residence' (HRC, *Recommendations and Commentary*, October 1999: paras 5, 7).

11 Italy also prided itself on being a leader in terms of domestic anti-trafficking efforts. These efforts combine one of the most generous right-to-remain policies for 'trafficking victims' with some of the most zealous and repressive deportation campaigns for illegal prostitutes and other migrants. Italy thus typifies, in its domestic policy, the division between the 'innocent' victim and the foreign threat. See Pearson 2002.

12 That Germany was included in this group was puzzling for the HRC as German domestic regulation of prostitution (to a certain extent) regulates prostitution as labour. In addition the German delegation had until this point been very receptive to HRC arguments. Meetings in Germany with a member of the delegation revealed that key delegation members had been replaced with more conservative members. In addition, the German delegation thought that the definition proposed by the Philippines would allow countries to determine for themselves whether voluntary prostitution was trafficking. Germany did not want an anti-prostitution document, and fought against this trend in later sessions. The participation of France is much more readily explainable, as France is a heavily abolitionist country –

as abolitionist now as they were regulationist at the time of the white slavery debates.

13　Like CATW, the members of the HRC did not confine their lobby efforts to the sessions of the Crimes Commission. In the period between the fifth and the eleventh sessions, they put enormous effort into marshalling support for our position. HRC members wrote op-ed pieces, gave interviews, and organized letter-writing campaigns.

14　The resulting proposal was a combination of Options Two and Three, Option One having been in effect abandoned by all delegates. See footnote 8 of the draft Protocol for the tenth session (A/AC.254/4/Add.3/Rev.7).

15　The lack of consensus around 'servitude' reflected another set of concerns, relating to the status of the term in international law.

16　This elision between rape and prostitution is even more clearly evident in the following newspaper interview with Pam Rajput, Chair of Asia Women's Watch: 'The defining policy question for activists is, "should the definition be centered around a women's consent or the exploitation of women by the trafficking industry?" Rajput says the issue of consent is nothing but "lip service" by those who profit from it. To illustrate her point she recalls a telling court case: "In India there was a woman who was raped by the police officials and the court said, 'Well, she didn't shriek enough to indicate her lack of consent.' So what is this consent? This consent is a very, very, dangerous kind of notion" ' (White [2000]: 3).

17　The Holy See is allowed to negotiate as a state at the UN. The Holy See delegation was well informed and highly resourced.

18　This clarification is now contained in the 'Interpretative notes for the official records (*travaux préparatoires*) of the negotiation of the United Nations Convention Against Transnational Organized Crime and the Protocols thereto' (A/55/383/add.1: 12).

Primary sources

Documents Relating to the Vienna Negotiations around the 2000 Trafficking Protocol

DOCUMENTS FROM THE SESSIONS OF THE AD HOC COMMITTEE ON THE ELABORATION OF A CONVENTION AGAINST TRANSNATIONAL ORGANIZED CRIME (INCLUDING ONLY THOSE SESSIONS IN WHICH THE PROTOCOL WAS DISCUSSED)

First Session, 19–29 January 1999

Draft protocol to combat international trafficking in women and children supplementary to the United Nations convention on transnational organized crime. Proposal submitted by the USA, A/AC.254/4/Add.3.

Consideration of the additional international legal instruments against trafficking in women and children Draft elements for an agreement on the prevention, suppression and punishment of international trafficking in women and children, supplementary to the Convention against Transnational Organized Crime. Submitted by Argentina A/AC.254/8.

Proposals and contributions received from Governments. A/AC.254; A/AC.254/ Add.1; A/AC.254/Add.2.

Third Session, 8–12 March 1999

Revised draft Protocol to Prevent, Suppress and Punish Trafficking in Women and Children, Supplementing the United Nations Convention against Transnational Organized Crime. Proposal submitted by Argentina and the USA /AC.254/ 4/Add.3/Rev.1.

Proposals and contributions received from Governments. A/AC.254/5/Add.3.

Fourth Session, 28 June–9 July 1999

Revised draft Protocol to Prevent, Suppress and Punish Trafficking in Persons, especially Women and Children, Supplementing the United Nations Convention against Transnational Organized Crime. A/AC.254/4/Add.3/Rev.2.

Fifth Session, 4–15 October 1999

Revised draft Protocol to Prevent, Suppress and Punish Trafficking in Persons, especially Women and Children, Supplementing the United Nations Convention against Transnational Organized Crime. A/AC.254/4/Add.3/Rev.3.

Proposals and contributions received from Governments. A/AC.254/5/Add.12, A/AC.254/5/Add.13.

Sixth Session, 6–17 December 1999

Revised draft Protocol to Prevent, Suppress and Punish Trafficking in Persons, especially Women and Children, Supplementing the United Nations Convention against Transnational Organized Crime. A/AC.254/4/Add.3/Rev.4.

Proposals and contributions received from Governments. A/AC.254/5/Add.16.

Seventh Session, 17–28 January 2000

Revised draft Protocol to Prevent, Suppress and Punish Trafficking in Persons, especially Women and Children, supplementing the United Nations Convention against Transnational Organized Crime. A/AC.254/4/Add.3/Rev.5.

Proposals and contributions received from Governments. A/AC.254/5/Add.19.

Ninth Session, 5–16 June 2000

Revised Draft Protocol to Prevent, Suppress and Punish Trafficking in Persons, especially Women and Children, supplementing the United Nations Convention against Transnational Organized Crime. A/AC.254/4/Add.3/Rev.6.

Proposals and contributions received from Governments: A/AC.254/5/Add.25, A/AC.254/l.201, A/AC.254/L.194, A/AC.254/L.196, A/AC.254/L.197.

Recommendations of the informal working group on article 2 bis of the revised draft Protocol (etc.). A/AC.254/L.205.

Amendment to article 6 of the revised draft Protocol (etc.). A/AC.254/L.206.

Eleventh Session, 2–27 October

Revised draft Protocol to Prevent, Suppress and Punish Trafficking in Persons, especially Women and Children, Supplementing the United Nations Convention against Transnational Organized Crime. A/AC.254/4/Add.3/Rev.7.

Revised draft Protocol against the Smuggling of Migrants by Land, Air and Sea, Supplementing the United Nations Convention against Transnational Organized Crime. A/AC.254/4/Add.1/Rev.6.

Proposals and contributions received from Governments: A/AC.254/5/Add.28, A/AC.254/5/Add.29, A/AC.254/5/Add.32, A/AC.254/5/Add.33, A/AC.254/5/Add.36.

Recommendations of the informal working group on article 2 bis of the draft Protocol (etc.). A/AC.254/L.248.

FINAL DOCUMENTS

Protocol to Prevent, Suppress and Punish Trafficking in Persons, especially Women and Children, supplementing the United Nations Convention against Transnational Organized Crime. A/55/383.

Interpretative notes for the official records (travaux préparatoires) of the negotiation of the United Nations Convention against Transnational Organized Crime and the Protocols thereto. A/55/383/Add.1.

DOCUMENTS FROM OTHER UN BODIES

Note by the International Labour Organization on the additional legal instrument against trafficking in women and children. 16 July 1999. Distributed at the fourth session, 28 June–9 July 1999. (No UN number record.)

Comments submitted by the United Nations Children's Fund. Distributed at the fourth session, 28 June–9 July 1999. A/AC.254/CRP.17.

Message from the High Commissioner for Human Rights, Mary Robinson, to the Ad Hoc Committee on the Elaboration of a Convention against Transnational Organised Crime. Presented at the fourth session, 28 June–9 July 1999. A/AC.254/ CRP.17.

Position paper on the draft Protocol to Prevent, Suppress and Punish Trafficking in Women and Children, submitted by the Special Rapporteur on Violence against Women. Distributed at the fourth session, 28 June–9 July 1999. A/AC.254/ CRP.13.

Informal note by the United Nations High Commissioner for Human Rights. Distributed at the fourth session, 28 June–9 July 1999. (No UN number record.)

NGO DOCUMENTS – HUMAN RIGHTS CAUCUS AND MEMBER NGOS

Each session

Recommendations and Commentary on the Draft Protocol to Combat International Trafficking in Women and Children Supplementary to the Draft Convention on Transnational Organized Crime (various drafts and final documents). January 1999, March 1999, June 1999, October 1999, December 1999, January 2000, June 2000, October 2000. Cited in the text as HRC, *Recommendations and Commentary.*

June 1999

Recommendation: Delete the term 'sexual exploitation': Undefined, Controversial, Unnecessary.

Cases from the Field and the Need for Human Rights Standards for the Treatment of Trafficked Persons.

October 1999

Commentary on the United States Proposal (A/AC.254/L.54) to the Draft Protocol (etc.) on 'sexual exploitation'.

Commentary on Proposals Made by States to the Draft Protocol (etc.).

December 1999

The definition of 'trafficking of persons': Art. 2 bis of the Draft Protocol on Trafficking.

Intervention by Asian Women's Human Rights Council.

Intervention by Fundacion Esperanza.

Intervention by the Global Alliance Against Trafficking in Women.

Message to Delegates.

Note on 'Servitude'.

June 2000

Statement of the International Human Rights Law Group, a member of the Human Rights Caucus: The Proposed Definition of Trafficking, 07-06-2000.

Statement of the Human Rights Caucus on the Proposed Definition of Trafficking, 07-06-2000.

Comments by the Human Rights Caucus and Human Rights Watch regarding the 'Informal consultation on Article 2 bis 6, June 2000, Report of the Chairman'.

September 2000
Letter to NGOs, email distribution.
Letter to Madeleine Albright, US Secretary of State, 5 September.

October 2000
The 1949 Convention and the Threat to Consensus.
Letter to delegates.
Letter to delegates, with additional points.

NGO DOCUMENTS — COALITION AGAINST TRAFFICKING IN WOMEN CAUCUS (INTERNATIONAL HUMAN RIGHTS NETWORK) AND MEMBER NGOS

1999
Elements for a new Protocol to Prevent, Suppress and Punish Trafficking in Women and Children, Supplementing the United Nations Convention against Transnational Organized Crime. Distributed at the fourth session, 28 June–9 July 1999.
Recommendations relating to Protocol to Prevent (etc.). June 1999.
'Prostitutes Work, but Do They Consent?' Report on the 6th Session of the Ad Hoc Committee of a Convention against Transnational Organised Crime. June 1999.

2000
Definition of Trafficking–Transnational Crime Convention Trafficking in Persons Protocol. May 2000.
Letter to US Secretary of State Madeleine Albright. Equality Now, 6 May 2000.
Key Cases: The Problem of Consent, June 2000.
Letter to NGOs. Equality Now, 20 June 2000.
Report on the 9th Session of the Ad Hoc Committee of a Convention against Transnational Organized Crime. June 2000.
Recommendations relating to Protocol to Prevent (etc.). October 2000.

NGO DOCUMENTS — NETWORK OF SEX WORK PROJECTS
Commentary on the Draft Protocol to Combat International Trafficking in Women and Children Supplementary to the Draft Convention on Transnational Organized Crime (various drafts and final document). January 1999.
Letter to Madeleine Albright, US Secretary of State. 19 May 2000.

OTHER DOCUMENTS
Statement from ECPAT International on the Draft Protocol (etc.). Distributed October 1999.
Letter to Madeleine Albright, US Secretary of State. Jesse Helms, US Senator. 19 January 2000.
UN Trafficking Treaty: Myths/Facts: US President's Interagency Council on Women. 18 January 2000.

Trafficking in Persons: the USAID Strategy for Response. USAID 2002.

Notes and internal reports taken during UN sessions, after meeting with delegates, and during HRC meetings by myself and other HRC members.

FACILITATED EMAIL LISTS

NSWP list serve. Postings have been made anonymous for the research. All original emails on file.

Stop-traffic list serve. Archives available to the public at www.stop-traffic.org.

PRIVATE EMAILS

Human Rights Caucus email group. Postings have been made anonymous for the research. All original emails on file.

Additional personal emails. Emails have been made anonymous for the research. All original emails on file.

NEWSPAPERS, PERIODICALS AND WIRE SERVICES

English Review (1913)
Guardian (UK)
Independent (UK)
Jerusalem Post
McClure's Magazine (1907, 1905)
Pall Mall Gazette (1885)
Sunday Times of Zambia
Reuters

ELECTRONIC SOURCES

Anti-Slavery International website: www.antislavery.org
APNSW website: www.apnsw.org
CATW website: www.catw.org
GAATW website: www.gaatw.org
International War and Peace Reporting: www.iwpr.net
National review online: www.national-review.com
NSWP website: www.nswp.org
Reproductions online journal: www.hsph.harvard.edu/Organizations/healthnet S.Asia
Salon: www.salon.com
Shewire: www.shewire.org
Stop-traffic archives. www.stop-traffic.org
UN Crimes Commission website: www.uncjin.org
Purdue University: www.purdue.edu
Womenswire: www.womenswire.org

REPORTS

The Social Evil in Chicago. 1911. The Vice Commission of Chicago.

Importing Women for Immoral Purposes. 1909. US Senate, 61st Congress, 2nd Session, doc. 196, pp. 3–61.

Works cited

Addams, Jane. 1912. *A New Conscience and an Ancient Evil*. New York: Macmillan.

Agustín, Laura M. 2002. 'Challenging "Place": Leaving Home for Sex'. *Development* 45 (1): 110–17.

Agustín, Laura M. 2003. 'Sex, Gender and Migrations: Facing up to Ambiguous Realties'. *Soundings* 23: 84–98.

Agustín, Laura M. 2008. *Sex at the Margins: Migration, Labour Markets and the Rescue Industry*. London: Zed Books.

Alexander, Pricilla, and Frédérique Delacoste, eds. 1987. *Sex Work: Writings by Women in the Sex Industry*. Pittsburgh: Cleis Press.

Althusser, Louis. 1971 [2001]. 'Ideology and Ideological State Apparatuses'. In his *Lenin and Philosophy and Other Essays*. New York: Monthly Review Press.

Amigh, Ophelia. 1910. 'Another Warning to Mothers of Innocent Country Girls'. In *Fighting the Traffic in Young Girls or War on the White Slave Trade*, edited by E. A. Bell. City not given: G. S. Ball.

Anarfi, John K. 1998. 'Ghanaian Women and Prostitution in Côte d'Ivoire'. In *Global Sex Workers: Rights, Resistance and Redefinition*, edited by K. Kempadoo and J. Doezema. New York and London: Routledge.

Andrijasevic, Rutvica. 2007. 'The Spectacle of Misery. Gender, Migration and Representation in Anti-Trafficking Campaigns.' *Feminist Review* 86: 24–44.

APNSW. 2008. *Caught Between the Tiger and the Crocodile*. Video, Bangkok: APNSW.

APNSW. 2009. *Asia-Pacific Network of Sex Workers website*, www.apnsw.org.

Augustine, Saint. 2007. *De Ordine*, South Bend: St Augustine Press.

Austin, J. L. 1962. *How to Do Things with Words*. Oxford: Clarendon Press.

Barthes, Roland. 1973. *Mythologies*. Translated by A. Lavers. London: Paladin.

Beer, Janet, and Katherine Joslin. 1999. 'Diseases of the Body Politic: Ehite Slavery in Jane Addams' *A New Conscience and an Ancient Evil* and Selected Short Stories by Charlotte Perkins Gilman'. *Journal of American Studies* 33 (1): 1–18.

Bell, Ernest A. 1910a. 'A White Slave Clearing House. A White Slave's Own Story'. In *Fighting the Traffic in Young Girls or War on the White Slave Trade*, edited by E. A. Bell. City not given: G. S. Ball.

Bell, Ernest A., ed. 1910b. *Fighting the Traffic in Young Girls or War on the White Slave Trade*. City not given: G. S. Ball.

Bell, Laurie, ed. 1987. *Good Girls/Bad Girls: Feminists and Sex Trade Workers Face to Face*. Seattle: Seal Press.

Bell, Shannon. 1994. *Reading, Writing and Rewriting the Prostitute Body*. Bloomington and Indianapolis: Indiana University Press.

Berman, Jacqueline. 2003. '(Un)Popular Strangers and Crises (Un)Bounded: Discourses of Sex-trafficking, the European Political Community and the Panicked State of the Modern State'. *European Journal of International Relations* 9 (1): 37–86.

Bernstein, Elizabeth. 2007. 'The Sexual Politics of the "New Abolitionism"' *Differences*, 18 (5): 128–51.

Billington-Grieg, Theresa. 1913. 'The Truth about White Slavery'. *English Review*, June 1913, 435–46.

Bindman, Jo, and Jo Doezema. 1997. *Redefining Prostitution as Sex Work on the International Agenda*. Anti-Slavery International and the Network of Sex Work Projects. London.

Blanchet, Thérèse. 2002. *Beyond Boundaries: A Critical Look at Women, Labour Migration and the Trafficking Within*. USAID. Dhaka.

Bland, Lucy. 1992. 'Purifying' the Public World: Feminist Vigilantes in Late Victorian England'. *Women's History Review* 1 (3): 397–412.

Blee, Kathleen M. 1992. *Women of the Klan: Racism and Gender in the 1920s*. Berkeley: University of California Press.

Brass, Tom. 2000. *Peasants, Populism and Postmodernism: The Return of the Agrarian Myth*. London: Frank Cass.

Bristow, Edward J. 1977. *Vice and Vigilance: Purity Movements in Britain since 1700*. Dublin: Gill and Macmillan, Rowman and Littlefield.

Bristow, Edward J. 1982. *Prostitution and Prejudice: The Jewish Fight against White Slavery 1870–1939*. Oxford: Clarendon Press.

Brockett, L, and Alison Murray. 1994. 'Thai Sex Workers in Sydney'. In *Sex Work and Sex Workers in Australia*, edited by R. Perkins and G. Prestage. Sydney: University of New South Wales Press.

Brown, Wendy. 1995. *States of Injury: Power and Freedom in Late Modernity*. Princeton University Press.

Brussa, Licia. 1999. *Health, Migration and Sex Work. The Experiences of TAMPEP*. Transnational IDS/STD (Integrated Disease Surveillance, Sexually Transmitted Diseases) Prevention Among Migrant Prostitutes in Europe (TAMPEP). Amsterdam.

Burton, Antoinette. 1994. *Burdens of History: British Feminists, Indian Women and Imperial Culture, 1865–1915*. Chapel Hill: University of North Carolina Press.

Burton, Antoinette. 1998. 'States of Injury: Josephine Butler on Slavery, Citizenship, and the Boer War'. *Social Politics* (Fall 1998): 338–61.

Butler, Judith. 1990. *Gender Trouble: Feminism and the Subversion of Identity*. London: Routledge.

CHANGE. 2008. *Implications of US Policy Restrictions for HIV Programs Aimed at Commercial Sex Workers*. Takoma Park: Center for Health and Gender Equity.

Chapkis, Wendy. 1997. *Live Sex Acts: Women Performing Erotic Labor*. New York: Routledge.

Chapkis, Wendy. 2003. 'Trafficking, Migration and the Law: Protecting Innocents, Punishing Immigrants'. *Gender and Society* 17 (6): 938–57.

COIN. 1994. *La Industria del Sexo por Dentro*. COIN. Santo Domingo.

Connelly, Mark T. 1980. *The Response to Prostitution in the Progressive Era*. Chapel Hill: University of North Carolina Press.

Coote, William A. 1910. *A Vision and Its Fulfilment*. London: National Vigilance Association (NVA).

Corbin, Alain. 1990. *Women for Hire: Prostitution and Sexuality in France after 1850*. Translated by A. Sheridan. Cambridge, MA: Harvard University Press.

Crittenton, Charles Nelson. 1910. 'The Traffic in Girls'. In *Fighting the Traffic in Young Girls or War on the White Slave Trade*, edited by E. A. Bell. City not given: G. S. Ball.

Dedrick, Florence Mabel. 1910. 'Our Sister of the Street'. In *Fighting the Traffic in Young Girls, or War on the White Slave Trade*, edited by E. A. Bell. City not given: G. S. Ball.

Derks, Annuska. 2000. *From White Slaves to Trafficking Survivors: Notes on the Trafficking Debate*. Working Paper Series, Center for Migration and Development, Princeton University. Working Paper No. 00-02m, May 2000.

Derrida, Jacques. 1967 [1977]. *Of Grammatology*. Baltimore: Johns Hopkins University Press.

Ditmore, Melissa. 2002. 'Trafficking and Sex Work: A Problematic Conflation'. PhD Dissertation, Department of Sociology, City University of New York.

DMSC. 1997. *Sex Workers' Manifesto*. Presented at First National Conference of Sex Workers in India, 14–16 November 1997, Calcutta.

Doezema, Jo. 1998. 'Forced to Choose: Beyond the Voluntary v. Forced Prostitution Dichotomy'. In *Global Sex Workers: Rights, Resistance and Redefinition*, edited by K. Kempadoo and J. Doezema. New York and London: Routledge.

Doezema, Jo. 2000. 'Loose Women or Lost Women? The Re-emergence of the Myth of White Slavery in Contemporary Discourses of Trafficking in Women'. *Gender Issues* 18 (1): 23–50.

Doezema, Jo. 2001. 'Ouch! Western Feminists' "Wounded Attachment" to the Third World Prostitute'. *Feminist Review* 67: 16–38.

Doty, William. 2000. *Mythography: The Study of Myths and Rituals* (2nd edn). Tuscaloosa: University of Alabama Press.

Eagleton, Terry. 1991. *Ideology: An Introduction*. London: Verso.

Eagleton, Terry. 2003. *After Theory*. London: Allen Lane/Penguin.

Elshtain, Jean Bethke. 1974. 'Moral Woman and Immoral Man: A Consideration of the Public–Private Split and Its Political Ramifications'. *Politics and Society* (4): 453–73.

Empower. 2003. Email to NSWP listserve, used with permission, on file with author.

Enloe, Cynthia. 1989. *Bananas, Beaches and Bases: Making Feminist Sense of International Politics*. London: Pandora.

Felluga, Dino. 2003. *Modules on Althusser: On Ideology. Introductory Guide to Critical Theory*. Purdue University. www.purdue.edu/guidetotheory/marxism/modules/althusserideology.html. Acccessed May 2004.

Fisher, T. 1997. *Prostitution and the Victorians*. Stroud: Alan Sutton.

Flood, Christopher. 1996. *Political Myth (Theorists of Myth)*. New York: Routledge.

Foucault, Michel. 1975 [1991]. *Discipline and Punish: The Birth of the Prison*. London: Penguin.

Foucault, Michel. 1976 [1981]. *The History of Sexuality: Volume One: An Introduction*. London: Penguin.

GAATW. 1999. *Human Rights Standards for the Treatment of Trafficked Persons*. Global Alliance Against Trafficking in Women, Bangkok.

Geertz, Clifford. 1969 [1973]. 'Ideology as Cultural Practice'. In his *The Interpretation of Cultures: Selected Essays*. New York: Basic Books.

Gibson, Lisa. 2003. 'Innocence and Purity vs. Deviance and Immorality: The Spaces of Prostitution in Nepal and Canada', MA thesis, Institute of Development Studies, University of Sussex, Brighton,

Gibson, Mary. 1986. *Prostitution and the State in Italy, 1860–1915*. New Brunswick: Rutgers University Press.

Gilman, Charlotte Perkins. 1981. 'His Mother'. In *The Charlotte Perkins Gilman Reader*, edited by A. J. Lane. London: Woman's Press.

Gilman, Charlotte Perkins. 1991. 'Is America Too Hospitable?' In *Charlotte Perkins Gilman: A Non-Fiction Reader*, edited by L. Ceplair. New York: Columbia University Press.

Goldman, Emma. 1910. *The White Slave Traffic*. New York: Mother Earth Publishing Association.

Gould, Arthur. 2001. 'The Criminalisation of Buying Sex: The Politics of Prostitution in Sweden'. *Journal of Social Policy* 30 (3): 437–56.

Gramsci, Antonio. 1971. '*Selections from the Prison Notebooks*', edited by Q. Hoare and G. N. Smith. London: Lawrence and Wishart.

Grittner, Fredrick K. 1990. *White Slavery: Myth, Ideology and American Law*. New York and London: Garland.

GSN. 1997. *Crime and Servitude*. Global Survival Network. Washington, DC.

Gülçür, Leyla, and Pinar Ilkkaracan. 2002. 'The "Natasha" Experience: Migrant Sex Workers from the Former Soviet Union and Eastern Europe in Turkey'. *Women's Studies International Forum* 25 (4): 411–21.

Guy, Donna J. 1991. *Sex and Danger in Buenos Aires: Prostitution, Family and Nation in Argentina*. Lincoln, NE and London: University of Nebraska Press.

Haag, Pamela. 1999. *Consent: Sexual Rights and the Transformation of American Liberalism*. Ithaca, NY: Cornell University Press.

Hajer, Maarten. 1995. *The Politics of Environmental Discourse: Ecological Modernization and the Policy Process*. Oxford University Press.

Haveman, Roelof. 1998. *Voorwaarden voor Strafbaarstelling van Vrouwenhandel*, University of Utrecht.

Hobson, Barbara Neil. 1987. *Uneasy Virtue: The Politics of Prostitution and the American Reform Tradition*. New York: Basic Books.

Hodes, Martha. 1997. *White Women, Black Men: Illicit Sex in the Nineteenth-Century South*. New Haven: Yale University Press.

Hoigard, Cecilie, and Liv Finstad. 1992. *Backstreets: Prostitution, Money and Love*. Cambridge: Polity Press.

Hughes, Donna M. 2002. 'The Demand: The Driving Force of Sex Trafficking'. Paper presented at the conference on 'The Human Rights Challenge of Globalization in Asia-Pacific US: The Trafficking in Persons, Especially Women and Children', Globalization Research Center, University of Hawaii at Manoa and the East–West Center, Honolulu, Hawaii, 13–15 November 2002.

Hughes, Donna M. 2003. *A Special Evil: Bush vs. Slavery*. National Review Online. www.national-review.com. Accessed 26 September 2003.

Hughes, Donna M. n.d. *Accommodation or Abolition? Solutions to the Problem of Sexual Trafficking and Slavery* (Online news magazine). National Review Online. www.nationalreview.com. Accessed 1 May 2003.

Human Rights Watch. 1995. *The Human Rights Watch Global Report on Women's Human Rights*. Human Rights Watch. New York.

ICPR. 1985. *World Charter for Prostitutes' Rights*. International Committee for Prostitutes' Rights. Amsterdam.

ILO. 1999. *Note by the International Labour Organization on the Additional Legal Instrument Against Trafficking in Women and Children*. July 1999. On file with author.

IOM. 1995. *Trafficking and Prostitution: The Growing Exploitation of Migrant Women from Central and Eastern Europe.* International Organization for Migration. Geneva.

IOM. 2000. *Migrant Trafficking and Human Smuggling in Europe.* International Organization for Migration. Geneva.

Irwin, Mary Ann. 1996. ' "White Slavery" as Metaphor: Anatomy of a Moral Panic'. *Ex Post Facto: The History Journal* 5: online issue at http://userwww. sfsu.edu/ ~epf/past.html.

Jana, Smarajit, Nandinee Bandyopadhyah, Mrinal Kanti Dutta and Amitrajit Saha. 2002. 'A Tale of Two Cities: Shifting the Paradigm of Anti-Trafficking Programmes'. *Gender and Development* 10 (1): 69–79.

Jeffries, Sheila. 1997. *The Idea of Prostitution.* Melbourne: Spinifex Press.

Jeffries, Sheila. 2008. *The Industrial Vagina.* New York: Routledge.

Kapur, Ratna. 2005. *Erotic Justice: Law and the New Politics of Post-Colonialism.* London: Glass House Press.

Kauffman, Reginald Wright. 1912. *The House of Bondage.* New York: Grosset and Dunlap.

Kempadoo, Kamala. 1998a. 'Introduction: Globalizing Sex Workers' Rights'. In *Global Sex Workers: Rights, Resistance and Redefinition,* edited by K. Kempadoo and J. Doezema. New York and London: Routledge.

Kempadoo, Kamala. 1998b. 'The Migrant Tightrope: Experiences from the Caribbean'. In *Global Sex Workers: Rights, Resistance and Redefinition,* edited by K. Kempadoo and J. Doezema. New York and London: Routledge.

Kempadoo, Kamala, ed. 1999. *Sun, Sex and Gold: Tourism and Sex Work in the Caribbean.* Lanham: Rowman and Littlefield.

Kempadoo, Kamala, ed. 2005. *Trafficking and Prostitution Reconsidered: New Perspectives on Migration, Sex Work and Human Rights.* Boulder and London: Paradigm.

Kempadoo, Kamala, and Jo Doezema, eds. 1998. *Global Sex Workers: Rights, Resistance and Redefinition.* New York and London: Routledge.

Kermode, Frank. 1969 [2000]. *The Sense of an Ending.* Oxford University Press.

Kilvington, Judith, Sophie Day and Helen Ward. 2001. 'Prostitution Policy in Europe: A Time of Change?' *Feminist Review* 67: 78–93.

Kulick, Don. 2002. 'The Criminalization of Clients and the "Politics of Ick" in Sweden'. In *Prostitución,* edited by R. Osbourne. Madrid: UNED (Universidad Nacional de Educación a Distancia). Spanish translation.

Kulick, Don. 2003. 'Sex in the New Europe: The Criminalization of Clients and Swedish Fear of Penetration'. *Anthropological Theory* 3 (2): 199–218.

Kulick, Don. 2005. 'Four Hundred Thousand Swedish Perverts'. *Gay and Lesbian Quarterly* 11 (2): 205–35.

Laclau, Ernesto. 1990. *New Reflections on the Revolution of Our Time.* London and New York: Verso.

Laclau, Ernesto. 1997. 'The Death and Resurrection of the Theory of Ideology'. *Modern Language Notes* 112: 297–321.

Lazaridis, Gabriella. 2001. 'Trafficking and Prostitution: The Growing Exploitation of Migrant Women in Greece'. *European Journal of Women's Studies* 8 (1): 67–102.

Leidthold, Dorchen. 2000. 'Presentation to UN Special Seminar on Trafficking, Prostitution and the Global Sex Industry – Position Paper for CATW'. Presented at the UN Special Seminar on Trafficking, Prostitution and the Global Sex Industry, 17–19 June 2000, Geneva.

Lévi-Strauss, Claude. 1968. *Structural Anthropology*. London: Allen Lane.

Lévi-Strauss, Claude. 1978. *Myth and Meaning*. London: Routledge and Keegan Paul.

Lin, Leam Lim, ed. 1998. *The Sex Sector: The Economic and Social Bases of Prostitution in Southeast Asia*. Geneva: International Labour Organization.

Lyons, Harriet D. 1999. 'The Representation of Trafficking in Persons in Asia: Orientalism and Other Perils'. *Re/productions* 2 (Spring 1999). Online journal: www.hsph.harvard.edu/Organisations/healthnet/S.Asia. Website no longer active. Paper on file with author.

McGrath, Patrick, and Patrick Morrow. 1991. *The New Gothic*. London: Penguin.

MacKinnon, Catherine. 1987. *Feminism Unmodified: Discourses on Life and Law*. Cambridge, MA: Harvard University Press.

MacKinnon, Catherine. 1989. *Toward a Feminist Theory of the State*. Cambridge, MA: Harvard University Press.

McLellan, David. 1995. *Ideology* (2nd edn). Minneapolis: University of Minnesota Press.

Mai, Nicola. 2009. 'Migrant Workers in the UK Sex Industry. Final Policy-relevant Report'. http://wwwlondonmet.ac.uk/research-units/iset/projects/esrc-migrant-workers.cfm.

Mak, Rudolf. 1996. *EUROPAP: European Intervention Projects, AIDS Prevention Projects*. Ghent: Academia Press.

Malvery, Olive, and William N. Willis. 1912. *The White Slave Market*. London: Stanley Paul and Co.

Mannheim, Karl. 1936. *Ideology and Utopia*. London: Routledge and Kegan Paul.

Mirkenson, Judith. 1994. 'Red Light, Green Light: The Global Trafficking of Women'. *Breakthrough* (Journal of the Prairie Fire Organizing Committee).

Mohanty, Chandra. 1988. 'Under Western Eyes: Feminist Scholarship and Colonial Discourse'. *Feminist Review* (30): 3–8.

Moon, Katherine. 1997. *Sex among Allies: Military Prostitution in US–Korea Relations*. New York: Columbia University Press.

Murray, Alison. 1998. 'Slavery and Trafficking: Don't Believe the Hype'. In *Global Sex Workers: Rights, Resistance and Redefinition*. New York: Routledge.

Nagle, Jill, ed. 1997. *Whores and Other Feminists*. New York and London: Routledge.

Nead, Linda. 1988. *Myths of Sexuality*. London: Blackwell.

Nietzsche, Friedrich. 1887 [1969]. *On the Genealogy of Morals*. Translated by W. Kaufmann and R. J. Hollingdale. New York: Vintage Books.

NSWP. 2003. *NSWP Calls on G8 to Support Sex Work Projects*. Network of Sex Work Projects.

O'Connell Davidson, Julie. 1998. *Prostitution, Power and Freedom*. Oxford: Polity Press.

O'Conner, Monica, and Grainne Healy. 2006. *The Links Between Prostitution and Sex Trafficking: A Briefing Handbook*. Downloaded from the CATW website at www.catw.org.

OSCE. 1999. *Trafficking in Human Beings: Implications for the OSCE*. Office for Democratic Institutions and Human Rights. Warsaw.

Outshoorn, Joyce. 1998. 'Sexuality and International Commerce: The Traffic in Women and Prostitution Policy in the Netherlands'. In *Politics of Sexuality: Identity, Gender, Citizenship*, edited by T. Carver and V. Mottier. London: Routledge.

Overs, Cheryl. 1998. 'International Activism: Jo Doezema Interviews NSWP coordinator, Cheryl Overs'. In *Global Sex Workers: Rights, Resistance and Redefinition*, edited by K. Kempadoo and J. Doezema. New York and London: Routledge.

Overs, Cheryl. 2009. *Caught Between the Tiger and the Crocodile: The Campaign to Suppress Human Trafficking and Sexual Exploitation in Cambodia.* Bangkok: APNSW.

Overs, Cheryl, and Paula Longo. 2003. *Making Sex Work Safe.* Rio de Janeiro: NSWP.

Overs, Cheryl, Jo Doezema, and Meena Shivdas. 2002. 'Just Lip Service? Sex Worker Participation in Sexual and Reproductive Health Interventions'. In *Realizing Rights: Transforming Approaches to Sexual and Reproductive Well-Being*, edited by A. Cornwall and A. Welbourne. London: Zed Books.

Pateman, Carole. 1988. *The Sexual Contract.* Cambridge: Polity Press.

Pearson, Elaine. 2002. *Human Traffic Human Rights: Redefining Victim Protection.* Anti-Slavery International. London.

Pheterson, Gail. 1986. *The Whore Stigma: Female Dishonor and Male Unworthiness.* Dutch Ministry of Social Affairs and Employment, Emancipation Policy Coordination. The Hague.

Pheterson, Gail. 1989. *A Vindication of the Rights of Whores.* Seattle: Seal Press.

Pheterson, Gail. 1990. 'The Catagory 'Prostitute' in Scientific Enquiry'. *Journal of Sex Research* 27 (3): 58–65.

Phillips, Joan. 1998. 'Tourism-Oriented Prostitution in Barbados: The Case of the Beach Boy and the White Female Tourist'. In *Sun, Sex and Gold: Tourism and Sex Work in the Caribbean*, edited by K. Kempadoo. Lanham: Rowman and Littlefield.

Pike, Linnet. 1999. 'Innocence, Danger and Desire: Representations of Sex Workers in Nepal'. *Re/productions* 2 (Spring 1999). Online journal: www.hsph.harvard.edu/Organisations/healthnet/S.Asia

Poe, Edgar Allan. 1839 [1984]. 'The Fall of the House of Usher'. In *Complete Stories and Poems of Edgar Allan Poe.* New York: Doubleday.

Propp, Vladimir I. 1928 [1968]. *Morphology of the Folktale.* Translated by L. Scott. Austin: University of Texas Press.

Radu, Paul Cristian. 2003. *Freedom at Midnight: Human Trafficking in Romania.* Balkan Crisis Report 403. Part 2. International War and Peace Reporting (IWPR). www.iwpr.net. Accessed 5 August 2003.

Raymond, Janice. 1999. 'Report on the 6th Session of the Ad Hoc Committee on the Elaboration of a Convention against Transnational Organized Crime'. On file with author.

Raymond, Janice. 2004. 'Prostitution on Demand: Legalising the Buyers as Sexual Consumers'. *Violence Against Women* 10 (10): 1156–86.

Roberts, Nicky. 1992. *Whores in History: Prostitution in Western Society.* London: HarperCollins.

Roberts, Randy. 1983. *Papa Jack: Jack Johnson and the Era of White Hopes.* New York: Free Press.

Roe, Clifford. 1910. 'The Auctioneer of Souls'. In *Fighting the Traffic in Young Girls or War on the White Slave Trade*, edited by E. A. Bell. City not given: G. S. Ball.

Rosen, Ruth. 1982. *The Lost Sisterhood: Prostitution in America, 1900–1918.* Baltimore and London: Johns Hopkins University Press.

Said, Edward. 1976. *Orientalism.* Harmondsworth: Penguin.

Sanchez-Taylor, Jacqueline. 2001. 'Dollars Are a Girl's Best Friend? Female Tourists' Sexual Behaviour in the Caribbean'. *Sociology* 35 (3): 749–64.

Sassen, Saskia. 2002. 'Countergeographies of Globalisation'. Paper presented at the conference on 'Gender Budgets, Financial Markets, Financing for Development', 19–20 February 2002, Berlin.

Saussure, Ferdinand de. 1959 [1974]. *Course in General Linguistics*. Translated by W. Baskin. London: Fontana/Collins.

Sex Workers' Project. 2009. *Kicking Down the Door: The Use of Raids to Fight Trafficking in Persons*. New York: Sex Workers' Project.

Sharp, Ingrid, and Jane Jordan, eds. 2002. *Diseases of the Body Politic: Josephine Butler and the Prostitution Campaign*. New York and London: Routledge.

Sims, Edwin W. 1910a. 'Introduction'. In *Fighting the Traffic in Young Girls or War on the White Slave Trade*, edited by E. A. Bell. City not given: G. S. Ball.

Sims, Edwin W. 1910b. 'The Menace of the White Slave Trade'. In *Fighting the Traffic in Young Girls or War on the White Slave Trade*, edited by E. A. Bell. City not given: G. S. Ball.

Sims, Edwin W. 1910c. 'The White Slave Trade of Today'. In *Fighting the Traffic in Young Girls or War on the White Slave Trade*. City not given: G. S. Ball.

Skrobanek, Siroporn, ed. 1997. *The Traffic in Women: Human Realities of the International Sex Trade*. London: Zed Books.

Slotkin, Richard. 1985. *The Fatal Environment: The Myth of the Frontier in the Age of Industrialisation, 1800–1890*. New York: Atheneum.

Smith-Rosenberg, Carroll. 1985. *Disorderly Conduct: Visions of Gender in Victorian America*. New York and Oxford: Oxford University Press.

Soderlund, Gretchen. 2005. 'Running from the Rescuers: New US Crusades Against Sex Trafficking and the Rhetoric of Abolition'. *National Women's Studies Association Journal* 17 (3): 64–87.

Sorel, Georges. 1908 [1999]. *Reflections on Violence*. Cambridge University Press.

Soriano, Jennifer. 2000. 'Trafficking in Sex' (1 February 2000). www.shewire.com. Accessed 4 February 2000.

Spivak, Gyatri. 1988. 'Can the Subaltern Speak?' In *Marxism and the Interpretation of Culture*, edited by C. Nelson and L. Grossberg. Chicago: University of Illinois Press.

Sprinker, Michael. 1987. *Imaginary Relations: Aesthetics and Ideology in the Theory of Historical Materialism*. London: Verso/NLB.

Stange, Margit. 1998. *Personal Property: Wives, White Slaves and the Market in Women*. Baltimore: Johns Hopkins University Press.

Stead, William T. 1885. 'The Maiden Tribute of Modern Babylon'. *Pall Mall Gazette*, Part 1: 6 July 1885; Part 2: 7 July 1885; Part 3: 8 July 1885; Part 4: 10 July 1885.

Stenvoll, Dag. 2002. 'From Russia with Love? Newspaper Coverage of Cross-Border Prostitution in Northern Norway, 1990–2001'. *European Journal of Women's Studies* 9 (2): 143–62.

Sturdevant, Saundra Pollack, and Brenda Stoltzfus. 1992. *Let the Good Times Roll: Prostitution and the US Military in Asia*. New York: New Press.

Sullivan, Barbara. 2000. *Rethinking Prostitution and 'Consent'*. Presented at Australian Political Studies Association Conference, 3–6 October 2000, Canberra.

TAMPEP. 1999. *TAMPEP Report 4*. TAMPEP. Amsterdam.

Thompson, John B. 1984. *Studies in the Theory of Ideology*. Cambridge: Polity Press.

Thompson, Leonard M. 1995. *History of South Africa*. New Haven: Yale University Press.

Torfing, Jacob. 1999. *New Theories of Discourse: Laclau, Mouffe and Žižek*. Oxford: Blackwell.

Troung, Thanh-Dam. 1990. *Sex, Money and Morality*. London: Zed Books.

Tudor, Henry. 1972. *Political Myth*. London: Pall Mall.

Turner, Denys. 1983. *Marxism and Christianity*. Oxford University Press.

Turner, George Kibbe. 1907. 'The City of Chicago: A Study of the Great Immoralities'. *McClure's Magazine* 28: 575–92.

Turner, George Kibbe. 1909. 'Daughters of the Poor: a Plain Story of the Development of New York City as a Leading Center of the White Slave Trade of the world, under Tammany Hall'. *McClure's Magazine* 34: 45–61.

Tyner, James A. 1996. 'Constructions of Filipina Migrant Entertainers'. *Gender, Place and Culture* 3 (1): 77–93.

UNHCHR. 1999. *Informal Note by the United Nations High Commissioner for Human Rights*. *A/AC.254/16*. 01-06-99. On file with author.

UNHCHR, UNICEF and IOM. 2000. *Note by the Office of the United Nations High Commissioner for Human Rights, the United Nations Children's Fund and the International Organization for Migration on the draft protocols concerning migrant smuggling and trafficking in persons*. *A/AC.254/27*. 8 February 2000. On file with author.

US Senate. 1909. *Importing Women for Immoral Purposes: A Partial Report from the Immigration Commission on the Importation and Harboring of Women for Immoral Purposes*. 61st Congress, 2nd Session, 1909, doc. 196, pp. 3–61.

Vice Commission of Chicago. 1911. *The Social Evil in Chicago*. Chicago: Vice Commission of the City of Chicago.

Visser, Jan. 2003. 'Dutch Prostitution Policy in a European Context'. Paper presented at the Seminar on Prostitution Control and Globalization, 5 September 2003, Oslo.

Walkowitz, Judith. 1980. *Prostitution and Victorian Society: Women, Class and the State*. Cambridge University Press.

Walkowitz, Judith. 1992. *The City of Dreadful Delight: Narratives of Sexual Danger in Late-Victorian London*. London: Virago.

Watenabe, Satoko. 1998. 'From Thailand to Japan: Migrant Sex Workers as Autonomous Subjects'. In *Global Sex Workers: Rights, Resistance and Redefinition*, edited by K. Kempadoo and J. Doezema. New York and London: Routledge.

Weitzer, Ronald. 2007. 'The Social Construction of Sex Trafficking: Ideology and Institutionalization of a Moral Crusade'. *Politics and Society* 35 (3): 447–75.

West, Jackie. 2000. 'Prostitution: Collectives and the Politics of Regulation'. *Gender, Work and Organization* 7 (2): 106–18.

West, Jackie, and Terry Austrin. 2002. 'From Work as Sex to Sex as Work: Networks, "Others" and Occupations in the Analysis of Work'. *Gender, Work and Occupation* 9 (5): 482–501.

White, Lisa. [2000]. *The U.N. Takes on Trafficking*, www.womenswire.org. Accessed 4 August 2000.

Wijers, Marjan. 1998. 'Keep Your Women Home: European Policies on Trafficking in Women'. Unpublished manuscript on file with author.

Wijers, Marjan, and Lin Lap-Chew. 1997. *Trafficking in Women, Forced Labour and Slavery-Like Practices in Marriage, Domestic Labour and Prostitution*. Utrecht and Bangkok: Foundation Against Trafficking in Women (STV)/Global Alliance Against Trafficking in Women (GAATW).

Yuval-Davis, Nira. 1997. *Gender and Nation*. London: Sage.

Žižek, Slavoj. 1994. *The Sublime Object of Ideology*. London: Verso.

Index